THE
EMPOWERED
WOMAN'S
GUIDE TO DIVORCE

Jill Murray

THE
EMPOWERED
WOMAN'S
GUIDE TO DIVORCE

A Therapist and a Lawyer Guide You
Through Your Divorce Journey

Jill A. Murray, Psy.D.
Adam R. Dodge, J.D.

THE EMPOWERED WOMAN'S GUIDE TO DIVORCE: A THERAPIST AND A LAWYER GUIDE YOU THROUGH YOUR DIVORCE JOURNEY

iUniverse books may be ordered through booksellers or by contacting:

iUniverse
1663 Liberty Drive
Bloomington, IN 47403
www.iuniverse.com
1-800-Authors (1-800-288-4677)

Because of the dynamic nature of the Internet, any web addresses or links contained in this book may have changed since publication and may no longer be valid. The views expressed in this work are solely those of the authors and do not necessarily reflect the views of the publisher, and the publisher hereby disclaims any responsibility for them.

Any people depicted in stock imagery provided by Thinkstock are models, and such images are being used for illustrative purposes only. Certain stock imagery © Thinkstock.

ISBN: 978-1-5320-2609-6 (sc)
ISBN: 978-1-5320-2608-9 (e)

Library of Congress Control Number: 2017911537

Print information available on the last page.

Contents

PART THREE: LEGAL ISSUES DURING DIVORCE

PART FOUR: EMOTIONAL ISSUES DURING DIVORCE

PART FIVE: AFTER DIVORCE

Acknowledgments

Jill Murray:

Writing a book doesn't happen in a vacuum. Many lovely people helped me, inspired me, and supported me through the writing of this book. First and always of these is my husband, Frank Murray, III, who is my love, my life partner, best friend, and biggest cheerleader. I never dared imagine him and then one day, he appeared.

I would also like to thank and acknowledge:

My children, Jennifer and Michael, who inspire me to be the person I hope to one day become.

My grandsons, Dominic and Louis, who are so precious and perfect it would defy even the most skilled wordsmith to express what they mean to me.

My daughter-in-law, Katharine, and son-in-law, Tony, who treat my children with the love and respect that I always hoped they would find in their spouses.

My long time editor, Stephanie Gunning, who helped us see the big picture and expertly guided us from start to finish.

The clients and staff at Laura's House Domestic Violence organization: You are the epitome of bravery and commitment.

Psychologist Paul Fick, Ph.D., my mentor and friend, who is one of the best men I will ever know.

My writing partner and friend, attorney Adam Dodge, who helped to make this book a reality. His sensitivity to women in pain and his compassion for the human spirit have made collaborating on this book a wonderful journey. I hope there are other books in our future together.

My amazing female friends who support and encourage me: I can't imagine where I would be without you.

And, to every woman reading this book looking for answers, guidance, and clarity during a most grueling time of your life, I thank you for the honor of helping to clear a path.

Adam Dodge:

Writing this book was one of the most challenging and rewarding experiences of my life. I could not have done it without the support and guidance of the amazing people in my life. I would like to express my gratitude to:

My mom and dad, who blessed me with the tools, support, and love throughout my life to reach for my goals. You were there to catch me when I struggled.

My big sisters, Michele and Lolly, for all your love and support despite me being the most annoying little brother ever.

My nephews and nieces, Nick, Sophia, Jack, Joe, Chloe and Caroline. I love you all so much.

Peter, Marisa, Oliver, and Macy, my other family, who love me like one of their own.

Margaret Bayston, my mentor and friend, who always helps me see the big picture and has pushed me to realize my potential.

Maggie Diaz, my colleague and friend, who inspires me and shows me what is possible when two driven people work together to help others.

My go-to support person, Shellee, for always being there and providing the just the right advice and perspective.

And to my co-author and mentor, Dr. Jill, who has so enriched my life as both a colleague and friend, I would have never done this without you, thank you so much.

My friends and family enrich my life. I cannot believe how lucky I am to have you all.

Introduction

DR. JILL AND ADAM

"I made a vow and I need to stick it out."

  "He told me he'll take the kids and the house if we get a divorce."

  "We need to stay together for the kids. They need a father."

  "I can stand whatever he does to me as long as he's a good dad."

  "Everyone's got baggage. Maybe I should just stick with the 'baggage' I know."

  "I stayed with him after the first affair and now there's another one. Can I leave?"

  "He looks like such a great guy to everyone else."

  "I cry myself to sleep every night and he really does not care at all."

  "I feel like I dated one person and he turned into this other person once we married."

  "I feel so alone in my marriage."

"I wouldn't be able to take care of myself financially if I divorced him."

"It's like I don't even exist or matter in this marriage."

"My single friends tell me that dating is horrible. Could it be worse than this?"

"If I could wave a magic wand and have it over, I would. But a divorce . . . ?"

"If I stay, at least I can have my kids all the time. Not seeing them for a week?"

"He doesn't know how to do anything. How can I let me kids be with him?"

"I know he doesn't love me, but is that really so important after eighteen years?"

"He's told me no one else would want me and maybe he's right."

Dr. Jill:

There is a reason why you're reading this book at this time in your life and in your marriage. You may have been thinking about the possibility of divorce for a while or maybe you've reached your limit recently, but the alternative to marriage still seems too scary to pursue. Perhaps your husband has told you that he's considering divorce and that idea hasn't even been on your radar screen. Could it be that you've been suffering in silence for so long that you just want to get it over with now? Or do you want to give it one more shot?

Perhaps you are further along in your decision making. Maybe you have already left your husband or kicked him out of the house, and now, before you confront the task of dividing your assets, you would like to know more about your legal rights. Maybe you're feeling anxious about going to court or want to try mediation or a do-it-yourself option to save money. Perhaps recent conversations with your ex regarding the division of assets or the custody of your children have become acrimonious and you want to feel more empowered when you speak with him.

Whatever your reasons for picking up this book, my coauthor, attorney Adam Dodge, and I welcome you to this safe place. The idea of this book was hatched in my brain at least a decade ago when I found, as a therapist, that although many of my counseling patients were considering divorce some were afraid to consider divorce even though their marriages were beyond repair or had so emotionally devastated them that they could barely function. They didn't know how to think about their situation, as it was so emotionally overwhelming. I found, too, that many of these women asked me for legal advice, which I am neither schooled nor ethically able to dispense. It was common for me to hear them make remarks such as "He told me that if we divorce he won't have to pay me a dime," "He told me that he'll take the kids from me," "I'll have to sell our home and live in a dinky apartment," "He'll decide how much alimony he's going to give me," and on and on. These women were paralyzed with fear and afraid to act because until then their husbands had dispensed all the legal advice in their households and they took what these men were telling them as gospel.

When I spoke with attorney friends of mine, they related that they experienced an opposite phenomenon. Their divorce clients were emotionally drained, frightened, and often used them as therapists, when all the lawyers wanted to do—and were professionally trained to do—was to help these women legally as best they could.

I thought, *If I could find a wonderful, brilliant, and compassionate attorney who understood the ins and outs of what women go through on the legal side the way I do on the emotional side, I would love to write a self-help book for women contemplating divorce, going through a divorce, and navigating their post-divorce lives.*

Then, I met Adam. What a perfect fit!

Adam:

When Dr. Jill told me she wanted to write a book with an attorney to provide dual perspectives to women going through divorce, the idea instantly resonated with me. Her idea made so much sense and fit perfectly with my experience helping self-represented women! In divorce, emotional health and the legal process are woven together. The roles of the therapist and attorney quickly become blurred. As Dr. Jill mentioned, attorneys often feel like they are taking on the role of a therapist. I have certainly felt that way. Therapists I work with field legal questions about divorce all the time, and yet they are not able to answer them. Meeting with a therapist and an attorney simultaneously isn't a viable solution, but we believe this book is the next best thing.

This is the book I wanted to write when I stopped representing women in their divorce proceedings and started helping them represent themselves. When I made that change, it forced me to look at divorce in an entirely new way. That's when the light bulb went on. Almost immediately, patterns emerged. I began to see mistakes and missteps that many self-represented women make over and over, and identified ways to prevent them. I saw ways women could improve their effectiveness and understanding of the divorce process from start to finish, and develop skillsets to put them in the position to succeed. It was exciting.

For the last five years, I've been cataloguing and developing effective and realistic strategies, tips, explanations, hacks, and concepts to help self-represented women navigate divorce. These are now laid out in this book. My goal is to empower you to make informed decisions, set realistic expectations, think critically, and avoid common mistakes—thus empowering you at the end of your marriage. These concepts are applicable before, during, and after divorce, so you will not need to learn something new at each stage of the divorce process.

I work in California, but the information in this book is applicable in any state. You'll find that the concepts covered, which range from how to go about researching divorce to navigating the courtroom to life after divorce, are universal to anyone representing herself.

Both of Us:

Our book is not intended to sway you one way or another about divorce. We'd like to present all the options to you and let you know what to expect from both a therapeutic and a legal perspective. There is a lot to consider and we'd like to answer questions you didn't even know to ask. We have tried to anticipate your feelings and your questions, and what you may go through in the divorce process at different stages before, during, and after.

Never forget that in reading this book you have a team behind you, helping you make strategic decisions. You have a therapist, a lawyer, and most importantly, you have you. You yourself are smarter and more capable than you may be giving yourself credit for being.

That said, this book is not intended to substitute for the individualized legal advice you would get from an attorney or the individual counseling or couples counseling you would get from a psychologist or marriage and family therapist. Think of the book instead as a playbook to empower you to avoid common mistakes and navigate the divorce process successfully both legally and emotionally. It's a guide to empower you to find the answers the right way so that you can make informed decisions and set realistic expectations about the journey ahead. Fortunately, there are plenty of resources to obtain legal advice specific to your scenario or situation, and this book provides a roadmap of how to get to those resources if you desire.

This is not a one-size-fits-all book. Given your situation and geographic location, there are bound to be some things in this book that don't apply to you. We think that's probably true with any other self-help book you would run across in the marketplace. We don't profess to know the procedures at every courthouse in United States. We doubt anyone knows that. So, it's possible some of the tips and strategies provided in our book may not be applicable to your courthouse or state—but many of them will be and they will be extremely valuable to you. Adam, the attorney on our team, has made an effort to be comprehensive and detailed in each section of the book that discusses legal issues in recognition of this possibility.

Some of the topics covered in different chapters of this book may not be on point for you, but our hope is that we have provided enough options so that at least many will be.

In this book, you will see that each of us has written the chapters related to our own expertise. So that you can distinguish which of us is having a conversation with you at any point, the author is always identified at the beginning of the chapter.

We hope that this book offers you the understanding, peace, and clarity you need to confront the difficult decision and process you're contemplating.

Take good care.

PART ONE

Emotional Issues Before Divorce

"Divorce. *I don't even think I can say the word. It's ugly. It sounds wrong on my tongue and doesn't sound like my voice when it comes out of my mouth. Is it actually me saying that word?"* —Janet, age thirty-seven, married nine years

"*I can't believe I'm even thinking about divorcing my husband. How did this happen? Where did things go so wrong?* —Belinda, age forty-one, married fourteen years

"*I'm embarrassed really. I feel like a loser, a complete failure."* —Robin, age thirty-one, married three years

"*What am I supposed to tell my children if I divorce their daddy? Mommy couldn't stick it out? I couldn't cut it? Not even for you? That's a real great mom. I didn't have them so they could come from a broken family. Wouldn't it be selfish of me to put my own feelings ahead of a six- and an eight-year-old? Children are better off with two parents in the same house, right?"* —Mimi, age forty-four, married eleven years

"*I haven't been able to look at my husband for almost twenty years now. Just the thought of touching him makes me sick. Yet, here I am, at the age of sixty-four, still with him. I used to have an excuse: the kids. Well, those kids are grown, married, and have kids of their own, so what's my excuse now? What am I going to do at my age as a single woman? Sail around the world? Take up skydiving? My husband's not a bad guy. He doesn't drink too much. He doesn't hit me. He doesn't spend money on hookers. I just don't love him and I haven't for a long time. But I don't know if that's a good enough reason to divorce him."* —Linda, age sixty-four, married forty-three years

"*This is my second marriage. Well, third, to be honest. But the first one happened when I was nineteen and only lasted less than two years, so I make believe it doesn't count. The second one was to an alcoholic that I was married to for nine years and had a son with. This one has been sixteen years and we have two children together: a boy and a girl. He drinks too. A lot. But not every day. He binge drinks. He goes on benders for several days every month or so. When he's not drinking, we get along reasonably well and have a nice family. But we never know when it's going to start or why. He's a different person when he drinks, vicious and out of control. He's scary to the kids and gets in pushing and shoving matches with my oldest son when he tries to intervene. That scares the younger ones. He says mean things to all of us and breaks things. He tells us he hates us and that we're a waste of his time and money.*

"*My oldest son has threatened to move out, but is afraid to because he takes up the protector role of me and the younger kids when my husband drinks. My husband is like Jekyll and Hyde. We've pleaded for him to get help, but he refuses. I've gone to Al-Anon and therapy. I talk to my girlfriends and my mother. My mother says that*

3

the devil I know is better than the devil I don't. She tells me I should just take the kids on a little vacation when he drinks and when I come home, he'll be fine. My friends tell me I should hit the road and take him for everything he has for what he's put me and the kids through. Al-Anon and my therapist tell me I can't be defined by his decision to drink and that I must live my own life.

"I have no idea what's the right thing to do. I just know that I'm miserable and my kids are miserable and I'm keeping them in this environment and he won't stop drinking or even get therapy. It's good when he doesn't drink. Why can't he see that? I wish I could just wake up and the decision would be made for me." —Greta, age fifty, married sixteen years

No woman gets married with the idea that she may divorce. You got married because you loved your man and it was the right decision at the time. Whether you've been married two years or forty-two years, whether you have children, whether you work full-time outside the home or you are a full-time homemaker, whether you took religious vows or had a civil ceremony, thinking about divorce is frightening, destabilizing, and demoralizing. Contemplating the choice to divorce may cause you to lose faith in yourself and your decision-making abilities.

You are thinking of turning your entire world upside down, of making the second biggest decision of your life—the first being *to marry*. Divorce is a step not to be taken lightly or without a lot of thought. It's not a quick decision or an easy one. No one knows your experience like you do and no one has to live with that decision except you and your children, if you have kids. No one can tell you what's right for you. That's A LOT of pressure. From both personal and professional experience, I can tell you that this type of decision is excruciating. Anyone who tells you the choice is black or white is either lying to you or has never been in the position you are in now.

There are many reasons why making a decision to divorce is so difficult. In Part One, "Emotional Issues Before Divorce," you and I will talk over some of these reasons so that you can start to understand if a divorce is the right decision for you and your family. Yes, it's an emotional decision, but I'd also like to see you make a logical decision first and foremost.

There is no urgency to make this decision. Maybe it seems like you need to decide right this minute, but I'm here to tell you that you have all the time in the world. This is big. This affects more than just you. You have the luxury of time and space to read this book and think about whether this is the right choice and the right time. Maybe it's one or the other, but not both. Maybe it's both, but you just can't push yourself to do it yet. Please believe me when I say that whatever you decide to do right now—and later—is alright. You have the right to think everything through and make the right decision for you.

If you're ready, let's get started.

CHAPTER 1

Six Concepts That Will Change Your Life

DR. JILL

"My husband has cheated on me three times that I know of. There might be more, but three is bad enough, right? Three is enough reason to divorce someone, isn't it? I'm asking because I'm not sure if it is or isn't. I know that sounds stupid, but my dad cheated on my mom and she stuck it out for us kids, and now they're older they seem happy. My husband also calls me names. He tells me I'm stupid or says, 'Why don't you understand this? You have a college education. Anyone would understand this.' Or he tells me I'm lazy or ungrateful. I didn't think I was, but he says it so often maybe he's right.

"He has this look that he gives me when he's displeased. It just paralyzes me. Sometimes, he'll be in a mood and criticizes everything about me: I use the wrong fork, I eat ketchup with my scrambled eggs, I like deep-dish pizza instead of thin crust, I have bags under my eyes, I put on two pounds. He mocks my voice. I'm either too flat chested or why am I wearing a push-up bra. My dress is too short or too frumpy. I don't ever know what he wants from me. But here's the thing: I have a pretty good life. We don't live paycheck to paycheck. He's a good provider. My daughters and I have whatever we need. But lately, both of my girls have asked me why I stay with their father. They'll say, 'He's so mean to you,' 'Why do you put up with that?' or 'Dad's a jerk.' I wouldn't want them to be with a man who treated them the way their father treats me. It would kill me. But I'm afraid—terrified actually. I can't leave and I can't stay. I'm really stuck and can't seem to move off this spot."—Rebecca, age fifty-eight, married twenty-one years

7

"What if I'm wrong? What if I divorce him and he does all this changing and marries someone else and is the best husband to her? Then, I've put up with all this crap for nothing and someone else gets the benefit of all the changes he says he'll make. Can he really change? Should I stick around and see if he's going to make those changes? He's told me that a dozen times and he changes for a few weeks and then goes back to being who he is. But what if this time he really does change and I divorce him, and then I'll never know if we could have made it work?" —Allison, age thirty-seven, married seven years

Divorce—been there, done that. Twenty years ago, I divorced the father of my children, a man I met when we were seventeen-year-old high school kids. The person I grew up with and went through every major and minor decision in my life for two decades. That guy.

The period when I was going through the process of deciding to split up and then actually going on to divorce my first husband was the most grueling time in my life. I really believe I went a little bit—okay, a lot—crazy. When I look back on the woman I was at that point, it doesn't feel like it was me, as I am today. The person I was during those months and years—yes, it took me *years* to make the decision to divorce—never imagined that I would become the woman I am today.

Back then, I never imagined that I would ever feel happy. I never imagined that I would feel confident. I never imagined that I would be able to make my own money and survive on it. I never imagined that I would be able to adequately mother my children. I never imagined that I would be professionally successful and have an impact on other people's lives. I never imagined that I would have true friends I could trust and find comfort with. And I never, ever imagined that I would find love, contentment, acceptance, and joy in another partner again. *But I did all of that!*

The fear of every day and every decision that I lived with for so many years was debilitating. Being told by my *wusband*—as in, the man who *was* my husband—that I wasn't loved or good enough was soul crushing. Questioning everything about myself destroyed every fiber of my being. I don't know if I appeared confident to others, but inside I was completely empty. Although I don't consider my marriage to have been abusive, I can tell you for sure that it was not psychologically healthy for me and probably wasn't for him either.

Marriages unravel a little at a time: one comment, one decision, one careless suggestion, one thoughtless action accumulates along with the next. If your spouse has not supported you or has criticized you, you may find yourself constantly questioning your worth or wondering if life would really be any different than it currently is if you left your husband, and you may be trying to figure out if you are strong enough to make this decision. *You are not a bad person for thinking these thoughts.* They are a response to pain and dissatisfaction. No one marries with the idea that she may divorce. No one has children with the idea of breaking apart the world she knows. The desire to end a marriage arises once you're already in a marriage.

When I question whether I should make a decision that involves taking a risk to change, I deliberately recall the words of the well-known psychologist Virginia Satir: *"Most people prefer the certainty of misery to the misery of uncertainty."* They help me to do what's necessary to improve my situation. Perhaps they'll help you as well.

You may have been miserable for a long time, but at least it's your misery. You know what it looks like and what to do to survive it. You understand the routine you put yourself through to get through each day or each insult. In comparison to your established lifestyle, the thought of divorce may be like the thought of jumping off a cliff and not knowing if you'll land safely, without catastrophic injury. What if your post-divorce life is worse?

Before you decide if or when you will divorce, I'd like you to think about six concepts I think are life changing and will help you as you read through this book.

Truth #1: Love Is a Behavior

When you were a little girl, were you told to listen to your heart? I was as well. Let me tell you why that is possibly the worst advice anyone can give you. Your heart is a pump. Its job is to pump blood through your body, not to make decisions for your life. Let your heart do its job and listen to your brain, because your brain's job is to make decisions.

When you listen to your heart, your emotions can tell you anything you want to hear. *I feeeel like he loves me. I feeeel like he didn't mean the hurtful things he just said. I feeeel sorry for him because he had a tough childhood so he doesn't understand how to treat a woman. I feeeel like he will change.* You get the idea.

If you stop for a moment and don't attach feelings to your husband's behavior, what does it look like to you? What would it look like to a stranger?

Here is where the idea that love is a behavior comes in. When we begin looking at *behaviors* rather than *feelings*, what you are feeling becomes easier to understand. Strange, isn't it? When you look at a person's behavior—rather than listening to your feelings—everything becomes clear.

Love—and I'm not just talking about the romantic love you've had for your husband, but also the love you have for your children, friends, family, and *yourself*—is all about the behavior that people exhibit to you on a daily basis and the love you show others as well.

I'd like you to try a simple experiment: For the next four days, look solely at the behavior those significant in your life show you. Behavior only. I think you may be shocked, amazed, and perhaps a little disappointed.

Truth #2: You Have a Right to Be Happy and Free of Fear

This seems basic, doesn't it? Of course, you have a right to be happy. Therefore, I would ask you: When was the last time you were truly happy in your marriage? When was the last time you were happy with yourself in your marriage? When did you last feel like a good and worthwhile person? An equal partner? Confident? Contented? Valuable? When was the last time you weren't living in fear? Perhaps you aren't afraid that your husband is going to be physically violent. That's a bonus. But when was the last time you weren't afraid of saying the *wrong* thing? Acting in the *wrong* way? Afraid of making the *wrong* decision? Not being the wife he wants? Afraid that you're a bad mother or worse daughter or friend because he told you so? Afraid of your thoughts? Afraid that you're *wrong* as a person?

You have a right to be happy and free of fear just because you were born. It's that simple. You have that right because that is what your higher power wants for you. You have that right because, why wouldn't you? *Why don't you?*

Would you tell your children they don't have those rights? Would you tell anyone you care about that they don't have those rights? Then you do as well. It's that simple.

You may think that you don't have a right to get a divorce because it may not make you happier. You may also think you don't have a right to be happy "at your children's expense" or because it means you are "being selfish." Those are all incorrect assumptions that keep you stuck.

Ask yourself this: If you were living fearlessly, how would you be living your life today? What decisions would you make? Would you be happier and have a sense of pride about yourself?

Truth #3: You Only Have Control of Three Things in Your Life

Stop the presses! You only have control of three things in your life? You thought you had control of all you survey? How can this possibly make sense, and more importantly, how does this knowledge make you feel, better or worse? Let me explain and then you will see how easy your life becomes. You have complete control of:

- **Your own thoughts.** If you're anything like the rest of womankind, you lie awake at 2 AM for no particular reason except that you are thinking, worrying, wondering, asking "What if?" and beating yourself up for something you did the previous day, week, or year, making plans, and generally feeling like a crazed loon. You feel like your mind has a mind of its own.

  But what are you going to accomplish at 2 AM? You're awake because you haven't taken control of your thoughts. You've given up control to the alien in your brain known as anxiety. I am here to tell you that when you take control of your thoughts as if they were unruly children, you feel more powerful. You—and only you—get to decide how you think about anything. Your husband doesn't control your thoughts. He may have injected unhealthy and untrue thoughts into your head, but it is your choice if you choose to believe them.

- **Your own actions.** Here's an idea I know for certain: No one makes another person do anything. We all have complete control and responsibility for our own actions. If another person has been unkind to you, it was a plan for a payoff they were receiving by hurting you. Everyone has control over every single thing they do to and for themselves and others. Therefore, your actions are a choice.

- **Your own reactions.** While you don't have control over the way another person treats you, you *do* have complete control over the way in which you choose to respond to every situation and interaction. This means that although you cannot control if others will like decisions you make—that is within their own thought control—you can choose your response if they don't like your choice.

  We all have days when a friend or coworker is snippy with us. This usually upsets us and we get anxious and spend time wondering what we did or said that was wrong or "caused" that person to treat us in that way. What would happen if, instead of making their behavior your fault, you gave the responsibility back to them? If you told yourself, *That person may have had a fight with his (her) partner or child this morning and isn't feeling good about himself (herself) right now. I trust that if I've done something to upset him (her), he (she) will let me know how so I can apologize if it's necessary.* See how much better you feel already? We can all choose how we respond to any situation that presents itself to us and that choice is a powerful one.

The idea to understand here is that while you have complete control over your own thoughts, actions, and reactions, so does everyone else in your universe. We spend a lot of time in our relationships trying to control the way others think, act, and react. When we give up that idea and take perfect control of our own three things, each of us instantly become Queen of the Universe! Our own universe, that is.

You may have already spent an inordinate amount of time in your marriage trying to help your husband understand what you need, who you are, what you don't like, or how sad and alone you feel. Yet, you are still contemplating divorce. That is because he has control over the way he thinks about what you've told him, how he acts toward you, and how he chooses to react in any situation related to you. You cannot change that fact. Your time and energy is far better spent taking control of *your* life, because you have the power to change that.

Truth #4: You Have Free Will

Now that you know you have complete control over how you think, act, and react, you will have to admit that you have free will. No one makes you do anything. You take charge of your brain and decide how to lead it. The good news is you can decide differently at any time. You have the opportunity to take a different path. No one *makes* you do anything. You—and you alone—get to decide how your life will look.

Truth #5: You Have a Right to Change Your Mind

Do you believe that if you decided something many years ago—perhaps without all the information to make a better choice—you have to stick with it for the rest of your life? I'm talking, of course, about the decision to make wedding vows. Perhaps your life looks different now than when you married. Maybe you are a different person or maybe your husband is different. Or maybe your husband is the same person he always was, except you failed to recognize who he was sooner because you were afraid or naive. Maybe you've grown in separate directions or you now understand that you don't have to tolerate unkind behaviors.

We take wedding vows for many reasons and we say them with all good intentions. Perhaps you've held up your end of the bargain as best you can under the circumstances, but now you understand that your husband has not *loved, honored, or respected you* the way he promised. You've tried and tried to alter either your behavior or his behavior, or both of your behaviors, with little or no success.

You now have a right to change your mind.

Truth #6: You Cannot Change Your Partner

Do you remember the three things you have control over: your *own* thoughts, your *own* actions, your *own* reactions? And you recall that your husband has control over the same three things? This means that the things he's doing and saying to you or about you are completely within his control. He is making a conscious choice to do and say them, and you are making a conscious choice to stick with it despite his choices. You've talked to him, you've begged him, you've cried to him, you've read books, and perhaps gone to therapy, and he's still doing the things that destroy you.

Or maybe there are 368 things about him that annoy you even though he's not truly a bad guy. That's okay. You don't need to make him a bad guy to seek a divorce. Neither of you must be a bad person. Maybe you just aren't your best selves with each other.

It's alright to release yourself and your husband from this marriage because he has shown you who he is and the person or the way he is doesn't serve your highest self. It's alright to wave the white flag and admit this didn't work.

This decision is not giving up. It's acceptance. And acceptance is a beautiful thing. It means you can stop trying to change something that will not change no matter what you do.

I believe that when people show you who they are, you should believe them. You don't need to make excuses for them and you don't need to change them. You just have to accept that they have shown you in the only way they can powerful knowledge about who they are. Believe them. Thank yourself for seeing the truth and accepting those people's honesty. You are, in fact, the person who is being dishonest if you choose to disregard what is in front of you and what another—including your husband—has so generously and easily shown you.

Don't try to change your husband any longer. Just take control over how you think about the truth, act in light of understanding it, and react from now on. *You are the real and true change agent in your life, not your husband.*

How Have the Six Basic Truths Affected Your Life?
A Self-Reflection Exercise

I would like for you to take the rest of this day or week to contemplate the six truths and the ways in which your refusal to accept them has impacted your life. The purpose of this exercise is to help you use this powerful new knowledge to move forward with a decision about divorce and your future happiness.

On a piece of paper, make a list of non-loving behaviors you've accepted during your marriage. Every single one you can recall. Save room below each item on your list for additional reflections.

Once that's done, next to each item on your list, write down how you chose to think about it, how you acted, and the ways in which your reactions affected your well-being.

Next, write down your answers to these questions.

Why do you believe that you don't have a right to be happy? Who was the first person who implied that? A long-suffering mother? Does it come from a religious belief in self-sacrifice?

What has caused you to be afraid and doubt yourself?

Do you believe you have free will? In what areas of your life have you relinquished your will, your choice, and your opinion? Why did you do that?

What vows did you take on your wedding day? How have you attempted to live up to those promises? Where have you fallen short?

Has your husband failed to keep his promises? How?

In what ways have you tried to express your feelings of dissatisfaction to your husband? Have you attempted to talk to him? What have been his reactions?

Has your husband changed in response to a request you made? If so, for how long and in what ways? Have any changes been meaningful or long term?

What has your husband done when you've cried or you've told him how alone or desperate you've felt?

How has your husband responded to suggestions of ways to help your marriage?

Take as much time as you need to direct yourself through this activity. It can be an intense process, so take breaks and return to it as needed. When you feel complete, like you have nothing more to add, look back over what you've written. If you're like other women who have done this exercise, you will see many patterns of behavior and thoughts in what you've written—patterns of ideas and behaviors you've done over and over without any difference. Or you may now realize that there are steps you could take to improve your marriage that you have not yet taken and would like to try before giving up on it.

Does this information make you feel helpless or hopeless? My hope is that you will be empowered to take the detailed knowledge that is now in front of you in black and white and turn it into *hopeful* action.

You are now in charge of your life, my friend. You are in the driver's seat and can decide how the rest of your life will continue. Take that power and make whatever changes you have the control to make. That may mean staying in your marriage and making decisions about how you will cope. That may mean terminating your marriage and making decisions about how you will cope. Whatever that decision will be, you are now in charge!

CHAPTER 2

Breaking Up Is Hard to Do

DR. JILL

"I work part time and don't make much money on my own. Not enough to take care of myself, much less our kids. I can't just pick up and leave. I don't see a way to stay and I don't see a way to go." —April, age forty, married nineteen years.

If anyone tells you that making the decision to end a marriage is simple, they're lying. Straight up lying. If friends or family members tell you, "Just leave the bum," it's because they don't understand how difficult it is.

Women are relationship oriented. Our whole lives revolve around relationships. Think of the conversations you've had with your female friends over the years. I can guarantee you that they've been about relationships: your relationship with your partner and your children, with your siblings, parents, and other family members, and with your friends and coworkers, your children's teachers, and even your pets. Sure, we women care a lot about global warming and the situation in the Middle East, but what we talk about the most is relationships. If our relationships are going well, life is swell. Conversely, the rest of our lives can be fantastic, but if any of our relationships is stressful, nothing else really matters. It stands to reason that ending a marriage is possibly the most gut-wrenching decision we women make.

It's alright to take as much time as you need to make the decision to divorce or stay married. The only exception to this guideline would be if you or your children were being abused, and we will discuss that shortly. In my many years as a psychotherapist, I've found that there are many reasons why making the decision to divorce is difficult. For example, how many of these issues are you struggling with right now?

- Feelings of personal failure
- Family expectations and fear of being ostracized by family members
- Fear of disobeying God
- Religious expectations and fear of being ostracized at your house of worship and losing your religious community
- Societal pressures and becoming a social science "statistic," such as that the partners in half of all couples will be divorced more than once in their lives. (No one wants to be in that half!)
- Fear of losing friends
- Financial fears: of losing your home, income, lifestyle
- Responsibility for "breaking up the family"
- Fear that your children will blame/hate you or will be maladjusted (believing "My children deserve to have an intact family")
- Believing "It's all my fault"
- Fears of loneliness and "going it alone"
- Fear of new custody arrangements (wondering "What will happen to the children if I'm not there?")
- Fear of the "divorcee" or "single mom" label
- Fear of not being loved again
- Fear of being "damaged goods"
- Not wanting to give up the fantasy/illusion of your ideal marriage
- Wondering "What if he changes?"

These are all valid fears and concerns. Not one is trivial and any one is enough to make you pull the covers over your head and forget the whole thing. But before you do that, let's look at what each of these fears and concerns really means.

Feelings of Personal Failure

"I feel like a big loser. Like I lost at the biggest thing in my life." —Beth, age forty-two, married sixteen years.

Feeling like a failure is the most common reaction women have when deciding to divorce. We not only take relationships seriously, we are the emotional centers of our marriages. What I'd like you to think about is who *you* are. Yes, you are a wife, and you may be a mother as well. You are also a daughter, and perhaps a sister, a friend, and a child of God. You may also be a working-outside-the-home person, a yoga enthusiast, a hiker, and a scrapbooker. You might be a person who likes salted caramel ice cream, the color turquoise, and yellow roses. You may be a woman who enjoys Earl Grey tea with lemon and extra-crispy bacon.

The point is: You are a lot of things. Your identity as a wife and mother may be the most important descriptions of you, but these aspects of you don't define you entirely. You are a whole and complete person with or without the title of *wife*.

Family Expectations and Fear of Being Ostracized by Family Members

"Everyone in my family loves my husband. I think they like him more than they like me, to tell you the truth. I've kept my mouth shut about the ugliness in my marriage because my husband insists that what goes on in our home stays in our home. They don't know the names he's called me. My parents rely on him for little things, and he and my brother are pals, so they all think he's a great guy." —Brittanie, age thirty-two, married five years

Living up to family expectations is never easy, especially when you have a high-achieving family. That might mean that your siblings and parents are successful with their careers, finances, educations, or relationships. Trying to accommodate the expectations of your family is difficult, especially when you are thinking of divorce. Believing that you will disappoint your family or they won't understand or accept your reasons is crushing. Still worse is the expectation that they will choose your husband over you.

This does happen in families. I will tell you candidly that it happened to me when I divorced my children's father, and that experience was at least as horrible as the divorce itself. I lost my mother and brothers in the process and it was very lonely. I came to understand—as you will as well, should this happen to you—that the way they treated me was consistent with how I was treated previously. This was something I had never really looked at until then.

Ideally, your family—especially your parents—want you to be happy and content. But it's up to you, not them, to decide what makes you happy. If you stay in your marriage to please anyone but yourself, you will never be content with being married. Your family either loves you and will support your decision—even if they dislike it—or they won't. Either way, it's your life and marriage, and no one can ever know what it feels like to be in your relationship and life except you. Looking for approval from everyone else in your life is a fruitless, pointless pursuit. At the end of the day, only you have to be content with your decisions.

Religious Expectations and Fear of Disobeying God or of Being Ostracized at Your House of Worship and Losing Your Religious Community

"I made a vow before God to stay with my husband for better or worse. A lot of my life takes place in my church. My children go to school there. I belong to a women's study group. I've gone to that church since I was a child and now it's a great source of comfort and support, not only to me, but to my children as well. People don't get divorced in my church. It just isn't done. I would lose everything." —Nancy, age thirty-nine, married fourteen years

If your relationship with your higher power is involved in your decision to divorce, I understand that you may believe that your standing for eternity must be considered, as well your happiness and the needs of your children. I also empathize if you are connected to your house of worship and its support systems at many connection points: social life, counsel, education, and more.

You may be worrying that if you divorce your relationship with your clergy will be affected. Perhaps you believe that if you divorce you will not be a good _____ (insert your religious affiliation: Jew, Christian, Muslim, and so on), and that having once made a vow before God "for better or for worse," you are pledged to stick with your marriage no matter what. You may feel sure that you will be judged by God, your clergy, and other parishioners if you break up with your husband. And you may be correct.

Here is what I know for certain: Our higher power wants us to be happy. We are God's children and God loves and forgives us. Our happiness and service to God and others is of paramount importance. I also know that most the people of most faiths look upon abandonment as an acceptable reason for divorce. I would ask you to consider whether your husband has abandoned the promises he made to you before God: to honor and respect you and keep himself only to you. If he has abandoned you emotionally, physically, or spiritually, there is cause for divorce.

I have spoken at numerous clergy conferences and houses of worship throughout the years and what I have found is that when clergy members are educated about unhealthy relationships, they reconsider their stance on divorce. Not that they encourage divorce, but they understand the reasons why a woman might have difficulty retaining her place in her religious community after deciding to make that decision. They appreciate that the woman needs nonjudgmental support and guidance. The woman needs to be held up by her religious community and guided in an unbiased manner, knowing that her higher power will continue to love her.

If you decide to divorce, I would encourage you to talk honestly with your spiritual advisors and the people in your worship community. You needn't give details—even though you may be asked for them. Just let them know that you have been struggling for a long time and you would like to ask for their support no matter what decision you make. Tell them that you are asking not only for yourself, but also for your children's sake. If they turn away from you, understand that they are not exhibiting the traits of compassion and charity that their higher power expects of them.

Societal Pressures and Becoming a "Statistic"

"I never thought I'd be among the fifty-one percent of married couples who get a divorce. I'm smart and capable. I'm a hard worker and a good person. People like me don't get divorced. We get help. We work through rough patches and don't give up. I really thought I was different." —Grace, age thirty-one, married three years

"When are you getting married?" Isn't that the first thing others ask you after you've been dating a guy for several months? It's an expectation: You're getting married. Why not? Aren't we all supposed to get married? Everyone has that one special someone waiting for them in whose presence our lives supposedly will be complete. The inference is that you are not a whole person on your own, that you need a man to complete you.

Do you remember the line in the movie *Jerry McGuire:* "You complete me"? It's the big, romantic moment that many women gush over. Frankly, it made me a little ill.

Why can't a woman be whole on her own? Because, the expectation in our society is that we will find the man who completes us and then we will know true happiness. Every fairytale we grew up on cemented that plan.

What happens now that you have learned that this expectation was a hoax? The man you married not only didn't complete you, he depleted you. He diminished your feelings of confidence, well-being, and trust in yourself and the world. You may be feeling disappointed and confused, as well as a host of other emotions.

How will you fit into society now, when all the recipes in your cookbooks serve two, when yin balances yang, when there is Heckle and Jeckle, tea for two? How will you fit into your group of friends when all or most of them are married? What will you do with the bare space on your left ring finger, and how long will it take before the white circle where you ring used to sit doesn't stand out to the world, shouting, "I used to be married, but that didn't work out so now I don't feel like I fit in anywhere."

If you spend your life trying to fit an ideal that you didn't design, you won't get an opportunity to learn new things about yourself to see where you more naturally fit or fit now. You're allowed to leave your job and find a new one—perhaps one that's a better fit for your skills and interests. You're allowed to change your mind. You're allowed to start over. You're allowed to say, "The decisions I made for myself at twenty-six (or whatever age you married) are not the same decisions I would make for myself today." You can do that.

Fear of Losing Friends

"My friends envy us and call us Barbie and Ken. They think we have a perfect marriage. I can't even imagine how they would react if I told them we were divorcing. I'm sure I would lose most of them and they would gossip behind my back."—Gail, age forty-four, married fourteen years

Fear of losing friends in a divorce is the real deal. I can tell you from personal experience, having lost all my friends but one. It's debilitating and confusing, and just doesn't make any sense. When you are going through the most difficult time in your life, you would expect your friends to be there for you, right? After all, you've always been there for them. These were the girlfriends you shared everything with. Well, maybe not everything . . .

While some of us tell our friends that our kids are driving us crazy or we are upset with a teacher or coach, many of us won't say word one about disappointment in our marriage. Part of it is embarrassment or shame, feeling like the marriage is our responsibility and we aren't doing well enough. We are the reason for the failure. To admit something so personal as the truth about our marriage means that 1) we must own it, and 2) we must confront our denial.

Maybe you aren't ready to do either of those things yet. What I can tell you is this: When you divorce, you eliminate a toxic relationship from your life, which is both crushing and freeing. How many times have you told your children after a disappointment, "If your friend treats you that way, maybe he's not such a good friend after all." Well, the same sage advice applies to you. If you lose a friend because you are divorcing—which has nothing directly to do with her—then I guess she wasn't truly a friend after all. That's hard to hear and harder to experience. When you divorce, you have the opportunity to rid yourself of every toxic relationship in your life . . . and maybe those "friends" fit into that category.

Financial Fears: Of Losing Your Home, Income, or Lifestyle

"Some years ago, when I told my husband I was going to see an attorney, he became ice cold and said, 'Fine, you do that. You'll learn that you're going to lose this house and have to go back to work full time. Good luck living in a two-bedroom condo and working fifty hours a week. And, oh by the way, I'll have the kids fifty percent of the time.' This panicked me to my soul so I cancelled the appointment. I hadn't worked since my oldest child was born. That was the way my husband wanted it and I admit that I was thrilled. I wanted to be the kind of stay-at-home mom who did carpool, baked cookies, and took care of our home. Jeff worked long hours, but I appreciated how hard he worked and that I had this opportunity because of it. In the meantime, technology and the working world passed me by.

"After what he said, I stayed with him and he acted like he had the upper hand and could do whatever he wanted because I wouldn't leave. Now, my eldest child is going off to college and I feel less afraid. Recently I've been taking computer classes without my husband knowing and going on job interviews. I've also consulted a lawyer who laid out what I can expect to get in the divorce, and it turns out that all these years my husband was wrong." —Bonnie, age fifty-three, married twenty-five years

Fear of losing everything you have in a divorce can greatly influence your decision making. Being afraid that your income or lifestyle may be greatly impacted doesn't make you petty or superficial. Whether you are a working in a company or CEO of your family, loss of what you've had that makes you comfortable is scary. Bonnie's situation is all too common in a potential divorce situation. But like Bonnie, once you consult with an attorney you may find that your fears are diluted. Just because your husband tells you what the "law" is doesn't make it so.

Concern of Bearing Responsibility for "Breaking Up the Family"

"My son adores his father. They are best buddies. I really thought that the relationship they share would be enough to keep our marriage together. But I can't deal with the criticism about every little thing. I can't handle him calling me 'stupid' or 'lazy' or 'crazy' anymore. I don't know what's going on with our finances and he makes all those decisions without my having a voice. He treats me like a second-class citizen in my own home. But there's my son and if I divorce his dad, it will be my doing. I will be taking his

daddy away from him. When he's older, I'm sure he'll tell me that I destroyed his family. I just don't think I can do that to him." —Hailey, age thirty-four, married five years

Let's talk for a moment about YOU breaking up your family. Why is the state of your marriage 100 percent your responsibility? It may be a good idea for you to make a list of the challenges in your marriage and why you are considering divorce at this time. Next to each item, list whether that is your issue, his issue, or a joint problem. For instance, if we look at Hailey's examples, whose responsibility is it that her husband calls her names or makes all the financial decisions? I would say that these are her husband's poor decisions. It's important for you to look at what is yours and what is your husband's, and take full responsibility for actions that are solely yours. One person doesn't break up a family unit.

Fears that the Children Will Blame/ Hate You or Will Be Maladjusted

"I can't remember how long I hated my mom for divorcing my dad. It was a long, long time. My dad seemed like such a great guy. He took us on vacations and gave us gifts for no reason. He came to my piano recitals and my brother's soccer games. I never saw him being cruel to my mom. She, on the other hand, was a strict disciplinarian who made us toe the line. She was on us to load the dishwasher and make our beds, and obsessively checked our homework. She always needed to know where we were and knew when we were lying. I don't know how she knew, but she did. We used to call her the CIA, for Caroline Intelligence Agency. When she divorced my dad, I was stunned and hurt and knew that it had to be her fault. Now that I'm thinking about divorce myself, I worry that my daughter will feel the same way." —Angie, age forty-one, married nine years

Children may know more than you think about what's going on in their household. But they don't know everything. The dad that looks like a great guy because he's charismatic and fun might be degrading to Mom behind closed doors. The dad who makes funny jokes might be making those jokes at Mom's expense. Conversely, the mom who does the "dirty work" every day may be the more caring, responsible parent.

I can't tell you how your children will react if you decide to divorce. Some are relieved and most are very sad. I can't tell you if they will grow up to be maladjusted young adults. There are too many factors that go into that: their peer group, what they watch on TV, music they listen to, technology, and so on. While I can't deny that the best equation for children is to grow up in a two-parent family in which Mom and Dad love each other and treat each other with the utmost respect and devotion, if this isn't true in your relationship, it is more important for children to grow up with two parents who are individually happy and modeling the behavior they would like their children to exhibit, even if this takes place in separate households.

Believing "It's all my fault"

"I'm doing this. I'm getting the divorce, not him. I couldn't make it work. He doesn't want this, I do. Can I live with this guilt?" —Audra, age thirty-two, married four years

I don't know the reasons why you are contemplating divorce, but I'm sure there are several. No one gets a divorce for the fun of the experience. But as you go through this book, your thoughts will crystallize and the right decision for you will become apparent to you. Let me just say this to you now: Be very clear about shame and responsibility. Don't allow his shame to become your shame. It takes two people to make a marriage work and it takes two people to dissolve a marriage as well.

Fears of Loneliness and "Going It Alone"

"I've never been alone since the day I was born. I went from my parents' house to having a roommate in college. Then, I had a roommate in my first place after I graduated. Three years later, my boyfriend and I moved in together. Two years after that, we got married. Just thinking of living alone is painful. How do I learn how to do that? How do I learn how to be independent and do things by myself?" —Sarah, age forty-nine, married twenty-two years

Perhaps you understand how Sarah feels. When you've been married—whether you have children—there is a certain reliable rhythm and routine to your life. You know what to expect day in and day out: the items he

26

would like from the market, certain dinners that are met with approval, TV shows you watch in the evening, errands or chauffeuring kids on the weekends. Although you may not be satisfied in your marriage, there is a comfort in the routine that you know.

There is a difference between being alone and being lonely. You may need to look at your marriage and decide if, even though you've been with your husband for several years, you've felt alone. I can assure you that feeling alone when you are married is the loneliest place in the world.

Fear of New Custody Arrangements

"He's never made a peanut butter and jelly sandwich. He doesn't know the way each one of the kids needs to do homework. He doesn't know their schedules or who their friends' parents are. He's never fixed my daughter's hair or helped my son pick out clothes for school. He doesn't even know all the work that goes into getting them out of the door for school. I can't even imagine what could happen to them safety wise, not to mention their schoolwork, if we share custody." —Hannah, age forty-one, married eleven years

Yes, it will be different for your kids if you divorce. You may feel worried about what will happen to your children when you're not around. But unless there is a compelling reason why their father shouldn't have any custody and is mandated to supervised visitation, they will be in his sole care sometimes. Perhaps that will be after school, at a dinner during the week, overnight, or for a weekend. He may be awarded an entire week of vacation. You won't be there. This may or may not be fair to the children.

I'll leave it to Adam to share his thoughts on the legal issues related to this subject because he is the legal expert. But I will tell you this: There is a learning curve to being a parent and just because you knew instinctively how to parent your children, or you do it better than your husband, care more, or just have always done more, doesn't mean that he can't learn how to parent them well now. Not only are children resilient, they are also remarkably good teachers. The way their dad will parent them in your absence may not be the same way you parent them, but it may be good enough.

Remember, you won't be out of the picture after divorce; you just may not be with your kids as much as you are now. Your responsibility is to make sure they are not in harm's way when they are with their dad. Homework, bathing, and so on, are things for you to teach them to do independently or for them to take up with their father. Giving him access to information, such as friends' phone numbers, other parents' names, online school information, and an activity schedule, of course, is a way to help make your children's lives easier. So, while I understand that it won't be the same as you, it may be a close enough approximation that your children will still be happy. Children generally don't expect dads to be moms.

Fear of the "Divorcee" or "Single Mom" Label

"When I think about being divorced, the first thing that comes into my mind is the word divorcee. *I'm a divorcee. A single woman. I'm checking 'divorced' or 'unmarried' in the box. Taking off my wedding ring. Seeing a bare finger on my left hand. Maybe it would sound like stupid stuff to most people, but it's really hard for me to handle."* —Karen, *age thirty-six, married six years*

As women, we are defined in many ways and with many titles: *wife, spouse, married* are just a few—and a significant few. Literally divorce is life changing. If we take away those identities, who are we? Oftentimes, we wrap ourselves up in labels and don't look deeper. The real question is: Who are *you?*

Throughout this book, I will invite you to look into yourself for your identity and what feels right for you in this stage of your life and going forward, whatever your marriage decision may be. Are you still "someone" if you aren't a wife? Do you still exist if you aren't someone's spouse? I would encourage you to hold off on attaching any new labels to your "self." Labeling disinhibits your personal growth and discovery.

Fears of Not Being Loved Again and Feeling Like "Damaged Goods"

"I am afraid that I will never find love again in my life and never feel love for anyone else. I don't know if I can feel anything anymore. I've felt numb for so long. I don't

honestly believe that anyone else would want me, but I also don't think I want anyone either. Maybe I was just too damaged by my marriage." —Maggie, age fifty-six, married twenty-five years

Perhaps you've been in a marriage in which your husband tells you that you are unworthy of love; that you are unlovable; that no one else will ever love you; that he's the best you'll ever get; that you're damaged, crazy, or psycho. Maybe he—or your girlfriends or mother—have told you that men aren't looking for women your age; they want them younger and firmer. Maybe these same people have told you to stick with what you have because at least he's the "devil you know" rather than the "devil you don't" and the "pickings are slim" out there. Possibly, other divorced gals have told you that the whole dating game has changed and it's scary in the world. Maybe this marriage has worn you down and taken away your optimism and confidence in yourself and your future.

These are all valid concerns . . . but they may not be true. Maybe they were true for your friend—or maybe they are true in general—but that doesn't mean that they will be true for you. You are a unique woman with special gifts and the ability to love is one of them. I can understand if that gift is switched off now. Maybe you've had to switch it off to survive in your marriage. But that doesn't mean it's gone. I suspect that when you feel emotionally safe in your life—whether or not that's with another partner—you will reignite the sexual and partnering side of yourself in many and wonderful ways.

You are not a damaged person. Your spirit may have been damaged by this marriage, but you are a whole and complete person capable of love, of growth, and of contributing to your world and everyone who is presently in it, including those who have not yet appeared.

Not Wanting to Give Up the Fantasy/Illusion of Your Marriage

"Ever since I was four years old, I remember wanting to be married. I played dress-up as a bride and made my little brother play the groom. Whenever people asked what I wanted to be when I grew up, it was always a wife and mommy. I still thought that way in high school and that was in the 1980s when you didn't dare say anything that might be perceived as 'anti-feminist.' Girls were told they could be anything they wanted to be,

which was great, and what I wanted was to be married and have a family. It was my highest goal in life. I went to community college and truthfully, I was hoping to meet my husband there. Yes, I was planning on getting my 'MRS degree.' Maybe that sounds pathetic to other people, but I really didn't care at the time.

"When I met the guy who became my husband, I was nineteen. I was ecstatic and relieved. We got married a couple of years later. My life plan was about to start. We had two boys one after the other right away and I loved being a stay-at-home mom. I felt fulfilled. My life was everything I hoped it would be. Just after our ten-year anniversary, my husband became more and more distant and started spending less time at home. Our intimate life fell off a cliff. I tried to engage him and have him talk to me, but he said everything was fine, that he was just stressed at work. I tried harder and harder to be the woman I thought he wanted, but nothing worked. I felt lost, confused, and desperate. Our boys were growing up and didn't need me as much.

"When our youngest son went to college last fall, my husband told me that he hadn't loved me in years, but he felt sorry for me and didn't want to hurt me anymore than I already was. Apparently, he had found another woman and been involved with her for several years. I was crushed. I couldn't breathe and became very ill for weeks. I begged him to go to couples counseling with me. I asked him to go back to church with me and talk with our pastor. He wouldn't do any of it. He was done and he said there was no going back.

"I can't believe this is my life. I can't give up. I won't give up. This is our family. I thought it was perfect. How is this happening to me?" —Monica, age forty-four, married twenty-two years

I have known many women like Monica and they are all lovely people with noble intentions. There is absolutely nothing wrong with a career as a wife and mother. Monica knew from an early age that this was her life path and she visualized it into existence. We don't know what her criteria were for a husband and if she chose wisely or if she was just determined to be married. Either way, she was happily married for many years and committed to her marriage.

If you're like Monica, here's the problem: You may have been so committed to the idea or fantasy of a marriage that you have not actually looked at *your* marriage and your husband aside from the fantasy or illusion. Many of us want to be married, no matter what. Perhaps no matter what he does . . . no matter what he says . . . no matter how he treats you . . .

no matter what his values are, you will not scream "Uncle." You are so invested in the idea of marriage that you fail to see that *your* marriage is not viable any longer.

When you are determined to be married even though your marriage no longer sustains you—or worse, depletes you—you are in a fantasy state rather than living in reality. That works when you are four, like Monica when she was playing dress-up with her brother, but not when you live in an adult world with adult responsibilities. When your fantasy doesn't intersect with your reality, it is time to take uncomfortable looks at what your life is like today and make real-life decisions.

Wondering "What if he changes?"

"I think I can let this marriage go now, but I have this one bad idea going on in my head: What happens if I've gone through all this heartache and tried so hard all this time and then he goes and is the perfect man for some other woman?" —*Shonda, age forty, married sixteen years.*

The hope for change. It's powerful and it's what keeps many women in marriages long after love or happiness is gone. Maybe your uncle was an angry old coot until he was sixty-five and then, magically, he softened and now he's the perfect husband? Maybe your father-in-law stopped drinking or suddenly became nicer when he was older, or got sick, or his wife threatened divorce? It does happen, but it doesn't happen as often as you might think. And it may not happen for you.

There is a saying: *Hope is not a strategy.* If you have begged, pleaded, cajoled, and truly tried everything possible to help your husband understand what you need in your marriage and he's been unwilling or unable to do those things, it would be unrealistic to think that the problem is you. That means that while he may meet someone else and temporarily have a softer attitude with her—he was softer with you when you met him, wasn't he? —the truth is that permanent change requires a lot of work and determination. For you to stay with him and remain miserable for fear that he may go on to someone else and be a better partner is not a bet you ought to take. I will leave that decision up to you. Just know that if you remain married to him change may NEVER occur.

I hope you've received some clarification and validation that your fears are legitimate. Almost all women who are considering divorce—for whatever reason—experience at least a few of those same fears. It doesn't mean that you're weak, petty, or superficial. They are all very big considerations, which you should acknowledge, rather than deny, and work through to make the correct decision for yourself and your children. Allow them to have a voice in your head; don't push them away or keep them in a dark, secret place. But don't let them have free reign over your feeling of power over your own decisions.

Now that we've looked at the reasons why the decision to divorce may be difficult for you to make, let's examine the signs that your marriage may be in trouble.

CHAPTER 3

Is Your Marriage in Trouble?

DR. JILL

"For the first four years of my marriage, I thought it was a really good one. I didn't have any big complaints. Sometimes, I was kind of sad that my husband didn't take me out to dinner and for some reason he couldn't seem to remember my birthday. But you know, life gets busy and he was tired a lot. He worked hard and we were both doing whatever we had to for the kids. Over time he withdrew more and more from all of us. He was secretive about where he was after work. We drifted apart. We stopped having sex. He hardly looked at me. I suggested marriage counseling, but he wouldn't go. We went on for another seven years this way. I don't really know how. He wouldn't talk about anything. I felt completely alone. Finally, I asked him if he wanted to separate and he said he did. I was stunned by his answer. I had only asked the question because I thought it would shake him up. He said he'd give me whatever I wanted and I could have the kids if I let him see them regularly. So, that's what we did.

"The whole thing was surreal. I've been divorced for three years now and I still don't know what happened to our marriage or to him." —Corrie, age forty-four, married twelve years

As you are making the decision whether to divorce, you may wonder: *Is my marriage really that bad? Am I just being dramatic? Am I merely bored? Am I asking for too much?* Sure, you can look around and see other marriages that are worse than yours. Perhaps you look at those marriages and think, *What do I have to complain about? Maybe I just can't be satisfied. My grandmother told me that my grandfather was a mean, old coot and she stuck it out with him—and if she could do it, shouldn't I?*

We can always find situations that are direr than our own, and often looking at these is a fine way to gain perspective and gratitude for what we have. When it comes to relationships, however, bad is bad. You don't need to quantify *bad*.

When I assess relationships, I look at the three big As.

- Abuse
- Adultery
- Addictions

If your husband has been or is currently involved in any of those behaviors and refuses to get help, the chance of you alone having the ability to repair your marriage is nil. No matter how hard you try, it cannot become a healthy relationship. I realize that sounds extreme, so let's look at the reasons for that statement, plus a few more indications that your marriage is in trouble.

Abuse

"Greg used to tell me I was stupid so often I believed him, even though I graduated with honors from my college. He told me I was fat even when I thought I was thin, so after going on crazy diets for three years without any acknowledgment from him, I finally let myself go and gained a bunch of weight just to see if he'd notice. If I was going to be called fat anyway, why was I killing myself eating carrot sticks when I could have pie? He criticized everything I did.

"After a day of being cruel to me he'd want sex at night and I felt that I couldn't say no. I mean, he wasn't raping me, but if I said I didn't want it he'd tell me he could find ten women 'just like that' who would want him. Or he'd pout or be extra mean to me—so what was my choice? He never hit me or anything like that or I would have left him in a heartbeat." —Cassandra, age fifty-one, married twenty-two years

Abusive relationship. That sounds scary, doesn't it? When we think of an abusive marriage, we usually envision a woman with a black eye or a broken jaw. She has bruises on her body and maybe a broken bone she can't explain. While that may be true, the vast majority of abusive relationships aren't physically abusive. Most are verbally or emotionally abusive, and some are sexually abusive. So that you can be clear about what your marriage is—or isn't—let's look at the behaviors that constitute abuse.

Name calling. The names you get called might be *ugly, fat, lazy, stupid, psycho, bitch, whore, idiot, gold digger, loser, pathetic,* or any number of other horrible names. Name calling is never okay. You may have gotten used to the names—and you may even believe them now—but that doesn't make it alright.

Isolation. Perhaps you used to have more friends than you do now. Slowly, but surely, most or all your friends have disappeared. Maybe it's because they don't like your husband or it could be because he inhibits you from seeing them—sometimes with outright verbiage, but more often, in sneaky ways, such as having something for you to do whenever you have plans with your friends, accusing you of doing something with them that you haven't done, acting hurt that you'd rather spend time with them, or picking a fight with you after you've been with your friends. You may have decided that it's just not worth what you have to go through to have lunch with a girlfriend, so you put her off time after time until she stops calling.

Maybe your husband has isolated you from your family, telling you that they don't like him and he is your family now. Perhaps he's taken you away from activities and hobbies you used to enjoy, but he's chosen new ones for you. He may have isolated you from your house of worship and spiritual community, strongly suggesting you go to his. All these isolation tactics are designed to create a dependence on him so that he is the only thing in your life, making it more difficult to leave him.

Criticism. A few years ago, I saw a woman at my office who was smart, accomplished, beautiful, a good mom, and appeared to be very kind and thoughtful. Yet she was married to a man who critiqued the way she wore her hair and the lovely clothes she wore (even though he picked them out and bought them for her); berated her for keeping a light turned on when she left a room, using "too much" water to wash dishes, and wearing "too much" (or "too little") makeup; and was harshly critical of her parenting skills. She couldn't please him no matter what she did. One day, rule X was in force and the next day it was rule Y. She never knew which end was up. She was constantly nervous and fearful of doing something—anything—wrong.

This type of criticism affects you when you are with your husband, and even when you aren't. You live in a state of constant fear and degradation.

Blame. You may be the subject of your husband's unending blame. It's your fault that he was late to work, he didn't have a clean shirt, he's doing poorly at work, your daughter isn't doing well at school, your son struck out at the Little League game, you forgot HIS mother's birthday, there are dishes in the sink, and the Yankees didn't win the World Series. This is a guy who doesn't take responsibility for anything, but freely assigns all blame to you.

He justifies his behavior. He had to do this because you did that. If you hadn't done that, he wouldn't have to have done this. Do you understand what I'm saying? He says or does unkind things and justifies them by saying that you started it and he was only responding as anyone would. His hands are always clean. He's just the poor sap who puts up with you although you apparently drive him to take actions he really doesn't want to take—but if he's to be believed, what choice do you give him?

You are afraid of his temper. Maybe you're not afraid that he's going to hit you, but you are frightened of the way he flies off the handle, afraid to have a different opinion than his, or fearful of telling him the truth. If you are ever afraid of your husband for any reason, you are in an abusive relationship.

He is unkind or degrading to you sexually. Let's be clear: Your body belongs to you, not your husband. Therefore, you have a right to say no to sex or the way in which you want to have sexual relations. If you feel forced, if you have said no, but he pressures you, if you have sex with your husband to avoid punishment; if he has sex with you in ways that degrade, humiliate, or cause pain, then you are in a sexually abusive marriage. Being married doesn't give him "marital privileges." Rape occurs in marriage as well as outside it.

He "playfully" causes you physical pain. Maybe your husband likes to pull your hair as you pass by or to give you a little jab in the ribs. Perhaps he enjoys pinching and twisting your nipples during sex. He loves to roughhouse with you and hits you hard in the head during pillow fights that he initiates. He loves the "tickle game" during which he holds you down and tickles you long after it's fun for you and you've begged him to stop. When you protest any of these actions, you're told that you're a wet blanket and no fun at all.

He tells jokes at your expense. "Where'd you get that dress? Omar the tent maker? Ha ha ha!" "Did you see Sandi's face? She missed her teenage years so much, she's gone back to having pimples. Ha ha ha!" "Oh, Julie burns every meal she cooks. She must have other talents, if you know what I mean, because why else would I keep her around? Ha ha ha!"

If your husband makes jokes at your expense, especially in front of others, you may want to crawl under a rock, but you don't. You laugh right along with him so that you don't cry. Or maybe you believe that he's correct. Make no mistake: These type of "jokes" are veiled hostility meant to damage you.

Affairs and Lies

"Dave and I were married for less than two years when he told me he was in love with someone else. I couldn't believe it. I thought we had a good marriage. I was pregnant, for heaven's sake! I cried and screamed. I begged him. I asked him to talk to me, to explain this to me. It was completely out of the blue. He hadn't planned it. He asked me to understand. Was he joking?

"In an effort be understanding, I told him I was sure he was just having cold feet about becoming a father because we hadn't really planned it, but it would be okay, as I would take total charge of the baby. Just before the baby was born, the woman broke it off with him, but after our son was born, he told me he was fully committed to me and our family and I forgave him and tried to put it out of my mind. When I was pregnant with our second child—this one was planned—I was afraid he'd do the same thing. I was relieved when it didn't happen, but he did have to travel more and I understood. I was eight months pregnant when he told me he had found someone else and he was truly sorry, but he needed to be with her. I was flabbergasted. Once again, I begged him to stop the affair, but this time it didn't work. Then, I just got angry and asked him how he could do this to his children, how he was such a monster, and if he even had a conscience!

"We divorced right after that and he's never looked back. Not once. He sends the kids presents for their birthdays, but moved to another state with the new woman, who he eventually married. I should have known better the first time and kicked him out then, but I was too afraid." —Cynthia, age thirty-one, married six years

I have counseled countless women whose husbands have had sexual or emotional affairs. Often, the husband makes a hasty apology and promises never to do it again and she believes him because she loves him and doesn't want a divorce. Sometimes, he does some work on himself—attends a few therapy sessions, reads a couple of chapters in a self-help book, goes to a men's group—and sometimes he does no work at all and his apology suffices. With any luck, this behavior doesn't occur again.

Unfortunately, I've seen far too many women who deal with this several times in their marriage, choosing to believe their husbands' apologies and initial wonderful and attentive behavior. By the time I see these women, they are depressed, wrung out, believe the affairs are their fault, and feel degraded as women. They feel foolish for having believed their husbands' lies in the first place.

I do believe that an affair in a marriage doesn't always signal the end. For many women it does, but for others, it is an opportunity for a couple to look at the loose ends in their relationship and where it went off track. It gives a couple a chance to ask for what they need and evaluate their communication skills. It lets them reboot their marriage.

There is a lot of work to do to repair a marriage in which infidelity has occurred. Regaining trust and respect is not instantaneous, and it is a long road of both partners looking at themselves and their marriage.

If your husband has had an affair and doesn't want to commit to the hard work of individual therapy as well as couples counseling, if he tells you the affair is done "so get over it," if he continues to work with the person with whom he had an affair or frequent the same places she does, if he doesn't do all the work his therapist or AA sponsor asks of him, then he will have another affair, and another, and another.

Recovering from infidelity requires the person who has had the affair not only to be remorseful, but also to demonstrate true contrition. He will want to know how you felt then and feel now. He will welcome being accountable for his time. He will answer every question you have until you don't have any more questions. He will change his cell number. He will give you all his passwords. He will not only apologize to you, but also to your parents and siblings.

If your husband refuses these actions or continues to remain secretive or you catch him in lies—even if they are unrelated to the affair—you have a big problem. Many men who have affairs have arrogance and entitlement issues that can be resolved with a commitment to long-term therapy, but without that, you are looking at the strong possibility of another affair.

Addictions

There are many types of addictions, including addictions to:

- Alcohol.
- Drugs: including marijuana, prescription drugs, and steroids.
- Pornography: via the internet, films/videos, magazines, strip clubs, phone.
- Gambling: through the internet or in person.
- Shopping: one type of item or many.
- Sex: with you or with many others.

Sometimes, these types of addictions are tricky to identify. You might think, *Hey, what's wrong with smoking a little weed every now and again? Don't lots of couples watch X-rated films together to spice up their love lives? What's wrong with a few beers after work? Is fantasy football really so bad? He likes Tommy Bahama shirts . . . a lot. Wouldn't lots of women envy a marriage with a husband who wants to have sex twice a day every day? Why am I complaining? It means he still finds me attractive, right?*

You see what I'm after here? When it comes to addictions, the line between what's acceptable and addictive, compulsive behaviors can be a little muddy. Oftentimes, what's acceptable may be based on your culture or what you find personally okay. I have a friend, for example, who grew up in an alcoholic family. If her husband wants more than a couple of glasses of wine per week, it sends her into a state of terror. Many people would find her behavior unreasonable and tell her that her husband isn't her parents, that what he's asking for is acceptable and not indicative of alcoholism. They might think she should just get over it and not blame her husband for her parents' actions. However, she and her husband have come to an agreement that satisfies them, with an understanding that if he doesn't hold up his end of the bargain she has a right to call him out on it. In return, he has a right to have a glass of wine without her giving him the evil eye.

Clearly, two glasses of wine per week is not an addiction. Two bottles of wine per night is a problem. Drinking alone, early in the day, or to cope with difficulties is a problem. Becoming argumentative or difficult to deal with when drinking is a problem. Missing work because of a bender the night before is a problem. Making your spouse or children uncomfortable or afraid because of drinking is a problem. Troubles with the law due to drinking is a problem. Compromising health due to drinking is a problem. Not knowing when or how to stop is a problem. Binge drinking is a problem. Not knowing what you did when you were drinking is a problem. Alienating family or friends because of drinking is a problem.

All these behaviors hold true for drug use as well, whether the drugs are prescription medication or illegal "recreational" drugs.

Many couples find that viewing X-rated videos, reading books of a sexual nature, or perusing computer sites dedicated to these adventures are not only alright, but do much to stimulate their love lives. If this is consensual—not secretive—behavior, that's fine for them. However, what is not fine is your husband viewing these items secretly, compulsively, or replacing your intimate life with such behaviors. Then, that becomes not only problematic, but many women I see find it degrading and insulting. Internet pornography is now the biggest money-making enterprise on the internet and the fastest growing addiction in the world. We all have computers or access to computers and at the touch of a keystroke, any number of people, fetishes, or behaviors are there at our command.

The same can be said for compulsive sexual behavior. You may have seen celebrities, such as Tiger Woods, reveal that they have addictive/ compulsive sexual behavior. In Woods' case, compulsive behavior destroyed his marriage. If your husband consistently wants or demands sex with you at a frequency that you consider problematic, it is time to discuss this with him. This is not to be mistaken with a lack of desire on your part for emotional or physical reasons. Asking for sex once or twice a week (or three or four) is not compulsive behavior, even if you yourself don't care for it that often.

Seeming to be insatiable on a daily basis is a problem. Seeking out other forms of sexual gratification, such as affairs, compulsive masturbation, phone sex, and so on, is a problem. Oftentimes, what you are experiencing is a man with a sexual addiction or perhaps bipolar disorder, as many people act out sexually when they're in a manic phase. Sometimes, sex is used to quell feelings of anxiety or cover difficulties connecting to a partner emotionally.

It's not possible for me to diagnose your husband in a book, but if you feel uncomfortable with his sexual behavior, you have a right to discuss it. If you've discussed it ad nauseum and the behavior hasn't changed and/or he won't seek help, you may need to consider divorce.

Gambling and compulsive shopping are also reasons why women feel compelled to divorce, particularly when they have exhausted all other avenues of help. If this is a problem in your marriage, your husband may have depleted your family's savings, charged up credit cards, or been secretive or lied about your family's finances. Again, if you've sought help for him, but he hasn't availed himself of those services or the behavior hasn't changed, you may have no other choice other than to end your marriage before his compulsions bankrupt your family.

Let me be clear that all addictions can be helped if your husband truly wants to save your marriage. I'm sure that if you are reading this book, you have begged, cajoled, pleaded, and threatened without any success. It is a horrible shame that your husband is putting his addictions ahead of you or his children. This is perhaps the most difficult reason to seek divorce. I would encourage you to seek out support groups such as Al-Anon (for those having a loved one dealing with alcohol or drug dependency) or CODA (Codependents Anonymous). These wonderful organizations that host meetings at which you can learn more about your husband's behaviors and find true support, understanding, and education for yourself.

Feeling Alone in Your Marriage

"It's not that my husband is a bad guy. He has never cheated on me that I know of. He doesn't hit me or call me names. He doesn't use drugs and only drinks socially, if you could ever call him social. What he does is neglect me. I don't feel like I exist. I guess it has always been this way to some extent, and I make excuses for it. Like that he is too busy or doing something more important. His father wasn't emotional so I figured he didn't know how to express his feelings either. I thought I could teach him that. I tried, honestly, I did. I thought I could get used to it, but I want more. Don't I deserve more? Doesn't my son deserve a father that pays attention to him? He's only two now, but soon it's going to start affecting him, isn't it?" —Keri, age thirty-six, married five years*

Do you understand how Keri is feeling? I've always thought that being alone in your marriage is possibly the loneliest place on Earth. When you marry, you believe that you will be with your best friend for the rest of your life, someone with whom you share experiences large and small. But what happens when you give and give and receive little in return?

Like Keri's husband, your man may not be a bad guy. To the rest of the world, he may seem like a nice person and may be attentive to them—and even to you—when out in public. It makes it difficult to come to terms with the fact that the reality of your marriage is far different than his public persona. You may feel like you're going crazy or that you're a bad wife. Why is it that he can act so gracious when you are with your extended family or your friends, but you feel ignored when you are alone? You may believe that if you separate from your husband, all these people will think you're nuts or just impossibly high maintenance.

Yes, that's true—they may think that way—but they don't have to live with him, do they? They don't know the man that you do. And that's all that matters. You know the truth and that's the only truth that counts.

If you have tried to talk to your husband about your feelings of loneliness and despair, if you have tried to encourage him to come to couples counseling with you or suggested reading self-help books together and there is still no positive response from him, you may have to consider your options, as he is giving you no choice.

Disrespect and Hostility

"When things are good, he tells me how much he loves me. I feel that he does. But when things aren't going well, he can be so mean. He insults my intelligence, my appearance, how I act, whatever he can find. It crushes me to my core. How can someone who loves me treat me like that?" —Marissa, age thirty-four, married eight years

When women tell me some of the ways their husbands talk to them, I'm amazed that they think it's normal, or just not that bad for him to belittle and insult them, or tell them to "shut up." I might ask if the comments hurt their feelings or if they think it's okay, and what I frequently hear is, "No, doesn't every man talk like that?" "Well, I used to think it was a little mean, but now I'm just used to it," or "He's right, I am pretty stupid a lot of the time. He's a lot smarter than I am."

You may or may not think insulting comments and nasty little digs are unusual. Either way, I will tell you that while they may be common in your marriage, they are not alright and they are *verbally abusive* behaviors.

There is little that can kill a marriage—or a woman's self-worth—like disrespectful, hostile words or behaviors. You may feel that you are lower than an earthworm, that you don't matter, and that your voice and mere being aren't worth a thing. I'm here to tell you that there is no excuse for this type of behavior and you have done nothing to warrant it.

Let me repeat that last sentence: *You have done nothing to warrant that type of behavior.* There is no reason for unkind behavior from a man who has pledged to love and honor you.

Remember: *Love is a behavior.* You and I both agree that disrespectful, hostile behavior is not indicative of a person who loves you.

You Are Not a Full Partner in Your Marriage If . . .

"I don't have access to money unless he gives it to me. He decides what my credit card limit is and if he's mad at me, he closes the card. There have been so many times when I've gone out to get something important for the kids, like shoes or a team uniform, and when I go to charge it, the card is declined because he decided to close it when I wouldn't have sex with him. I don't have enough cash with me because he gives me an allowance that he thinks is enough for me. I'm not on the checking account so I don't have a way

to pay for these things and it's so embarrassing." —Kaley, age thirty-nine, married sixteen years

Let me be crystal clear about one thing right now: You are an adult in this marriage, not his child. You have a right to be an equal partner in all financial decisions and financial access.

I have counseled many, many women who are not on the titles to their homes. ("It's for tax purposes. It's better this way.") They are given "allowances" by their husbands. ("Don't I give you enough? Why would you need more?") They don't have access to finances either through a checking account, a debit card, or a savings account. ("I give you everything you need. All you have to do is ask me if you need more.") Their names are not on the pink slips of the cars they drive. ("Why does it matter so much to you?") They are told to sign the back pages of their joint tax returns without an opportunity to look at the documents first. ("Why would you need to do that? Don't you trust me?"). They may be told not to get the mail ("You know how you lose things. You might throw away something important.") Every bill is in the husband's name. ("You don't appreciate the favor I'm doing you.")

You are a grown woman and your spouse is not your father. You are an equal partner with equal rights. If you are married to a man like this—in any of those scenarios—you can ask for these things to be changed, but you may not get them. You are married to a highly controlling, secretive man who doesn't view you as his full partner. He makes the rules and you follow them. This may not be what you signed up for.

There is a difference between wanting to be taken care of emotionally, and perhaps financially, and having no rights and no voice. Don't fall for the line that you are being well taken care of, therefore you don't need to know the details, or that your spouse is doing you a favor by sparing you the responsibility or liability. If you want an equal voice, you need to decide to be and act like an equal adult partner in this marriage. And if he refuses to allow you to partner in the finances of your household, you may need to consider divorcing him.

Exercise: Is Your Marriage in Trouble?

If you are reading this book, you have inklings that your marriage isn't healthy. Hopefully, after reading this chapter, you are clearer on the signs that may indicate you are correct in considering divorce.

Frequently, I discuss these indicators with women and they recognize that they are in a marriage that no longer serves them. However, their thinking becomes fuzzy shortly thereafter. I understand: Considering divorce can be the scariest thought you've ever had. So, to crystalize your thinking and make a record of what you've learned and recognized, I encourage you to perform the following exercise.

Get out a pad of paper and a pen, or a journal, and handwrite the following categories at the top of a bunch of pages, making long, vertical column spaces.

- Abuse
- Affairs and Lies
- Addictions
- Feeling Alone
- Disrespect and Hostility
- Not Being an Equal Partner

Now, in the columns under each heading that applies to your marriage, place a checkmark. Even if it happened once. Once is not acceptable behavior.

In each category you checked, write as many examples of these behaviors that you can think of off the top of your head. This may take a while and it may become extremely difficult when faced with what your marriage has looked like in black and white. As you think of more examples in the days ahead, go back to the list and write those down as well. After several days of writing, look at the list in its entirety and read it out loud. Read it again, slowly and out loud. Read it a third time, louder and listening to your voice as you read it. Take it in. Don't be afraid of it. The behavior has already happened.

This list is not only *your* truth, it's *the* truth. This is what your marriage is. This is what it has become. Read the list again.

You don't have to make a permanent decision today or tomorrow. You just need to know that this is true and you cannot deny the truth any longer.

I realize that this has been a difficult—even excruciating—chapter to read. You may now recognize what your marriage *is*, but possibly you don't yet understand the ways in which your relationship has harmed you physically, emotionally, and spiritually.

When you feel ready to investigate those ideas, move on to the next chapter. As always with this process, there is no rush. You may want to sit with the information you just learned a while longer. That's fine. I'll be here when you're ready.

CHAPTER 4

How Has Your Relationship Affected You Emotionally and Physically?

DR. JILL

There are some emotional situations we'd rather not deal with because they are too painful and inconvenient, or because we know that if we address them we must make a decision. When we go through emotional difficulties such as these, the entire body is affected. While you may not notice your body's signals—either because you are distracted or you're actively denying your feelings—your body is trying to tell you something. Your body sends you a variety of messages revealing that the emotional issues you are or are not dealing with are hurting you physically. While your mind may let you slide, your body certainly makes itself known in both big and small ways.

The ways in which I most often see my patients suffering physically and emotionally from a difficult relationship are below. Do any of these resonate with your experience?

- Depression
- Anxiety
- Sleep disorders: hypersomnia and insomnia
- Heart symptoms
- High blood pressure
- Headaches/migraines
- Gastric distress
- Lethargy/fatigue
- Eating disorders
- Poor concentration/lack of focus

Depression

"I just don't see my life getting any better, whether I stay with my husband. Nothing feels good. It's like my whole life hurts. I've lost my ability to be happy and wouldn't even know what does make me happy anymore. I know I should say that my daughter makes me happy, and it makes me feel worse to admit that she doesn't. She deserves a mother who is happy to see her and be with her. Maybe she would be better without me and living with her dad. He likes to barbeque and go to the movies. I'd rather just sit on the couch and watch mindless TV. He's told me that if I divorce him, he'll take Lexi full time, and maybe he should. It would be better for her than a mother who can't get herself together. I'm pretty worthless, to tell you the truth." —Angela, age thirty-eight, married ten years

Emotional ups and downs are common in life and normal reactions to stress and disappointment. Often, people inaccurately use the word *depression* when they are referring to temporary sadness. But depression is more severe than a response to a bad day. Depression takes many forms and the psychological world classifies this state into two categories: *vegetative depression* and *agitated depression*, with the former being much more common and easily identifiable.

Look at the signs and symptoms of depression and see if you can relate to any, or many.

- **Feelings of helplessness and hopelessness.** Many people describe this state as living in a "black hole" or of impending doom. You feel that your life won't ever be better than the way you feel right now, and as if there's nothing you can do to improve your situation.

- **Appetite or weight changes.** When people are depressed they often have no appetite whatsoever—sometimes referred to as the "stress diet" or "divorce diet" —and others eat compulsively, or stress eat for comfort. A change of more than 5 percent of your body weight in a month should be a benchmark used to alert you to a significant change, at which point I strongly advise you to contact a doctor.

- **Sleep changes.** You may find that you sleep more than usual—known as *hypersomnia*—to escape your life or your thoughts. Or perhaps you have *insomnia*, which includes difficulty falling asleep, waking several times in the night, or waking in the early hours of the morning and being unable to go back to sleep.

- **Loss of interest in daily activities.** You've lost your ability to feel joy or pleasure—also known as *anhedonia*—in former hobbies, social activities, or anything else that used to give you a feeling of happiness or excitement.

- **Loss of energy.** Even if you can sleep six or seven hours, you still feel tired, sluggish, and physically exhausted. Your whole body feels heavy and drained so that attempting even small tasks seems impossible.

- **Anger or irritability.** Your tolerance level may be low and your temper short. Everyone gets on your last nerve and you don't have patience for anyone or anything. You may feel agitated, restless, or sometimes even violent.

- **Self-loathing.** Maybe you are experiencing strong feelings of guilt and worthlessness, often without even knowing why. You criticize yourself for every action and decide that whatever has gone wrong in your marriage is entirely your fault. You categorize all your mistakes as a wife, parent, daughter, friend, and human being.

- **Concentration problems.** You may have trouble focusing, reading the same thing over and over, making decisions, or remembering details.

- **Compulsive/addictive behaviors.** In order to escape your brain or numb your feelings, you engage compulsively in behaviors such as substance use (prescription or illegal drugs, or alcohol), shopping, risky sexual practices, gambling, or reckless driving. You may also use self-harming techniques, such as cutting, burning, or starving yourself.

- **Doing too much.** This may sound odd, considering the former symptoms, however while agitated depression has many of the signs above, the major difference is that instead of feeling a loss of energy, you begin working fifty hours per week or cleaning and recleaning your home, organizing your house over and over, and similar things. This is done as a distraction and coping technique, just as other compulsive behaviors listed above can become. If you just keep moving, you can't think about your problems. While you may feel incredibly productive—and your boss or friends my reward you—it is still unhealthy. There is a saying: *What you resist persists.* When you are going as fast as you can, you are resisting dealing with the cause of your depression. As long as you do this, you will not be able to resolve the issue.

Anxiety

"I'm nervous all the time. I mean, nervous like I think I'm going crazy. You know what I do? I'll be driving home from work and I'll start having an entire conversation in my head. Because my husband cheated on me early in our marriage, I've decided that whenever he doesn't answer my text or call within a few minutes he's cheating on me again and making plans to leave me." —Surinda, age twenty-nine, married five years

Anxiety is a tricky emotion. It often masquerades as stomach problems, headaches, or even a heart attack. You know the feeling: nervous tummy, sweaty palms, racing heart, body shaking, head swimming. It is horrible to feel anxious. When you're very anxious, you don't feel like you have control of your thoughts—like Surinda—or even your body.

Because deciding to divorce is extremely anxiety provoking, it's important for you to understand what anxiety really is: *fear of loss in the future.* It's just as simple as that. Anxiety isn't related to anything that's currently happening, it is about something that hasn't happened yet—and may never happen. You have decided that this loss is going to occur.

What kind of loss am I referring to? There are only three that our bodies and brains register in an anxious state.

- Loss of affection
- Loss of finances
- Loss of esteem: our own or another's

If you are considering divorce, it is understandable that you would be worried about all three types of loss. You and your husband have fallen out of the type of love you once had that you were planning on experiencing for the rest of your life. As a result, perhaps you have told yourself that no one will ever love you again or that you are unlovable.

You worry about your financial situation. How much will you have? What types of lifestyle changes may you have to make? Will you have to get a job or a different job? Will you have to sell your home? Will you have to struggle for money?

You may have a lowered opinion of yourself and worry about how others see you, especially your husband. Will you lose friends in this divorce? Will others think you're crazy for divorcing him? Will your children blame you? Will your family stand by you? What if you're making a hasty decision and will regret it later?

You may have entire conversations in your head about the loss you fear—like Surinda—and the more you have them, the more your anxiety makes sense to you. You start believing your own story, even if you have no evidence for your beliefs. But do you really know what the future will hold? If you do, you should be buying Powerball tickets or reading crystal balls.

I believe that the mind-body connection is very strong. Oftentimes, our brain wants to deny what is staring us in the face due to our fear of loss. However, our bodies don't lie. Think of these connections and decide if you're facing them while you make this difficult decision:

- **Stomach issues.** Have you ever heard the phrase, 'I can't stomach this situation'? There's a reason why that is so true. When we are facing a decision or life situation that feels intolerable, the stomach—which is often referred to as the second brain—reacts in ways that meant to wake us up. This could include acid reflux, indigestion, and diarrhea.

- **Sore throat.** Yes, certainly you may have a cold or virus that has attached itself to your throat. But sometimes there are words caught in your throat—tightness or an ache. How many times have you wanted to tell your husband how you feel, but don't do so for fear of his reaction? Or maybe you've told him a dozen times, but nothing had changed, so you figure, *Why tell him again?* Words trapped in your throat may be causing you pain.

- **Back pain.** This is a common problem and may truly be an issue to have a doctor check out. However, I find that frequently back pain is your body's way of telling you to "Get a spine" or "Stand up for yourself."

I recall a client at Laura's House, the domestic violence shelter at which I was a psychological intern twenty years ago, and where I still do counseling. This woman was in the shelter with two young children, having fled the very scary guy who was the father of her kids. The day before she was to go to court with our legal advocate to file a restraining order against him, her hands suddenly and inexplicably became like claws. That morning she couldn't open them without great pain to pick anything up, so she was having trouble taking care of her children. It all seemed very mysterious and upsetting to her until I helped her recognize how her fear was impacting her body. We sat quietly for a few minutes as she breathed and visualized her children playing at a playground happily. Slowly, her hands opened. The next day she went to court as scheduled, returning to the shelter afterward victorious and empowered.

This simple incident has always illustrated to me how powerful anxiety can be and the ways it controls our bodies and thoughts. The next time you feel pain or upset in your body, ask yourself if a fear of loss of some kind may be at play that's making you anxious.

The rest of the items on the list at the beginning of the chapter all are the result of experiencing depression and anxiety, including sleep disorders, gastric problems, headaches/migraines, isolation, high blood pressure, eating disorders, lack of focus and poor concentration, and feeling irritable and sensitive to comments. You may have experienced some of these symptoms and explained them away as something else, not realizing that you were depressed or anxious. It's amazing, isn't it?

If it is unaddressed, anxiety and depression can interfere with the things that matter most in your life, such as how you parent your children and your work performance. It may lead you to isolate yourself, like an injured animal hunkering down in its cave to hide from predators. Lack of sleep, fatigue, pain, poor concentration—these types of symptoms can also make you very ineffective.

Before we move on, let's touch on another of the symptoms listed earlier, as it offers us a very important concept to understand.

Heart Symptoms

While you've been going through what may be the end stages of your marriage or making a decision whether to divorce, you may have had a fluttering heart or irregular heartbeat. You may have had actual pain in your chest and thought, *Am I having a heart attack? Is there something horrible going on with my heart?* It's a scary thought. I get it. Let me tell you my story and how my heart was trying to tell me what I refused to acknowledge.

I was married to the father of my twins for almost twenty years. We met in high school, went through college together, had our children, and shared a life with a lot of experiences, some great, many others not so much. During years twelve through nineteen, I had a lot of illness. I felt like I had the flu a good bit of time, and I also had days in which I had pain in my chest and an abnormal heartbeat. I was taking an antibiotic two weeks of every month. This period was frightening and a very bad time emotionally and physically.

My doctor referred me to a cardiologist who ran a couple of tests and told me there was nothing wrong with me, except maybe I was just high strung. Another cardiologist told me that I should relax more and have sex with my husband more frequently, as he felt that would make me feel better. A third cardiologist—they were all male, as you may have guessed already—told me that he was certain I was having symptoms, and since none of the doctors thus far could figure out what was wrong, in his opinion exploratory heart surgery was in order. All this news was upsetting and I still didn't feel any better.

Starting to wonder if I was going crazy, I went to a female cardiologist, who wisely told me this. "Well, you have very disturbing symptoms, but I can't find a physical cause, so I'd like you to think about something. I don't know you or what's going on in your personal life, but my suggestion is that you take a look at something that may be going on in your home or in your relationships that you do not want to deal with. Your heart may be trying to deal with it for you."

Well, that remark certainly made me stop in my tracks. I recall very clearly that I went home very calmly, sat on my bed, and waited for my husband to come home so I could speak to him. My mind was racing, but at the same time very clear.

When my husband saw me sitting in our bedroom, he rolled his eyes and said, "What?"

I told him, "I figured out what's wrong with me. *You've broken my heart.* I now understand what it means to have a broken heart. I can't die and leave my children, so I'm telling you now that you will no longer break my heart. It's time for our marriage to end." That was it. It was finally over.

You may have a *broken heart*. Your heart may be *in pieces*. You may have *heartache*. All this is true. There is a reason expressions such as these exist. Today, tomorrow, or the next day, you will have the opportunity to make the same decision I did to begin to repair your heart. In case you're wondering, I never had another heart episode after that night.

Now that you understand the ways in which your unhealthy marriage has taken its toll on you physically as well as emotionally, let's take the next step in decision making. How have you tried to repair your relationship? Are you really at the end or is your marriage still salvageable?

DR. JILL

CHAPTER 5

What Have You Tried?

"I can't believe it's over. Why can't we fix it? Why won't he try to fix it? Aren't I important enough for him to try? We went to marriage counseling one time and he didn't like the therapist and refused to go back. He told me I could go alone if I wanted to, but I told him it was for both of us. He wouldn't. He says counseling is a waste of time and if we can't get along then it's a sign that we shouldn't be married. How can he just give up like that? Don't I have something to say about it ending or does he just get to decide like he does everything else? I can't fix this alone and I don't want it to end." —Marcia, age thirty-seven, married eight years

Making a decision to end your marriage is a difficult process—and it should be. I don't think anyone should enter a marriage lightly. Nor should anyone end one impulsively. I believe anyone contemplating this idea should *earn* his or her divorce. What I mean is that you and your husband made a promise to love and respect each other and if you are contemplating breaking that promise, there should be a real effort to understand if there is a way to repair the marriage before taking that final step. If you do decide to divorce, I want you to know that you did absolutely everything possible to prevent it so that you will have fewer regrets in the end. Wondering, two or ten years post-divorce, if you could have saved your marriage or if you made a crucial mistake is not a feeling I want you to be left with.

So, what have you tried? Are you really at the end or is your marriage still salvageable? Here are four ideas you may not have thought of.

- Marriage counseling
- Pastoral counseling
- Marriage retreat
- Self-help books

Let's take a brief look at each of these positive interventions and perhaps you will decide to try something different before you make a final decision.

Marriage Counseling

I've counseled hundreds of couples who come to me with any level of difficulty in their relationships. Some need help communicating more effectively because one or both are frustrated that they can't seem to make their partner behave the way they'd like. They don't feel understood or listened to. Some couples come in because they don't feel loved or adored as they once did. Others believe their partners have large character defects and no longer respect them. Some complain about their partners' hygiene, lack of attention, poor parenting, or lack of affection or sex. All of them feel very alone and crushingly sad. Some disguise their sadness with anger, which intimidates their partners or causes their partners to feel unimportant or frightened. They back up and back away from one another, which increases the loneliness both partners feel. Oftentimes, I find that each partner has personal difficulties that need to be dealt with individually, and once that work is accomplished, the marriage flourishes.

If you have tried one or two joint counseling sessions without luck, there may be several reasons why therapy hasn't worked for you yet. Possibly:

- **You didn't give it enough time.** Your marriage didn't become unhealthy in two weeks and it can't be repaired in two sessions either. It may take a few sessions just for the therapist to fully understand your challenges. Either one of you may have come into the therapy scared, intimidated by the process or by your partner, or trying to put on a good "face" for the therapist, and/or feeling anxious about where the therapy will lead. I usually ask couples to commit to at least six sessions so that we can all assess their dynamics accurately before we start working through a game plan.

- **One of you doesn't want to be there.** I don't mind if one partner forces the other to attend the first session. Many times, both partners don't feel the same degree of urgency to fix the problems in their marriage, or even agree that their marriage is in such dire straits. Some people are fine with going along the way a marriage is, because while they aren't happy, the marriage is working well enough for them that they don't want to stir anything up. If you are the only person willing to work on your marriage and can't get enough cooperation from your husband to join you each session, then your therapist may end up working solely with you, which might be a good option. If your husband is lazy about attending therapy or doesn't see the need for it—or he won't attend strictly because it is important to you—then couples therapy cannot work.

- **You don't like your therapist.** It's important for you and your therapist to click. You should feel that he or she understands what you are saying and feeling, and instills realistic hope that he or she can help you. You want to know that there is trust and mutual respect. Your therapist should tell you what he or she thinks about your marriage, be able to pinpoint the issues, and have opinions on what would help. Personally, I am a very directive therapist. I don't sit across from my patients nodding and saying, "That's interesting. What do you think?" I offer active discussions in which I give opinions and call out where I believe my patients are deluding themselves, are being uncharitable to their partners, or are just simply wrong. I give advice and homework. I see both partners separately prior to our first joint session to understand what their own difficulties are with the marriage and listen to their stories as well as assess their desire to fix things. I understand that not every therapist works the way that I do, but it is what I believe is helpful. What is important for you is that you feel comfortable talking with your therapist, you trust the therapist's expertise, and have a sense of hope that the therapist can help you.

- **One or both of you have individual challenges that affect your marriage.** We all have "stuff" that we bring into our marriages and develop more stuff while we're in them. That's to be expected. However, when your stuff is unresolved childhood abuse, an alcoholic parent, an abusive former relationship, low self-esteem, childhood neglect, a personality disorder, or an addictive behavior, you need individual therapy before you can possibly begin to address your marriage. It is easy to point the finger at your partner, but as we all know, when we are pointing at someone else, three fingers are pointing back at us. I would encourage you to look deeply into yourself—rather than at your husband—and ask yourself if there are unresolved issues that your partner's behavior may just be bringing out or enhancing. If so, I strongly advise you to embark on a course of individual therapy. It may resolve issues in your marriage, and at the very least, make you a more complete woman. You may see the same sort of difficulties in your husband and encourage him to accept therapy on his own, but as you may have already discovered, you can't force anyone to accept help if he doesn't think he has a problem.

Pastoral Counseling

If you are a couple of a shared religious faith, this may be the sort of therapy that will speak to you. Pastoral counseling is conducted by either a therapist or clergy person of your faith that uses your religious book and principles as a cornerstone of the work that you do. It is often very effective because I have found that oftentimes people espouse a religious faith, but don't conduct their marriages according to the principles of that faith. In understanding how your higher power expects you to live your marriage and utilizing tools for forming a true faith-based union, marital issues often can be resolved in a loving and respectful manner.

Going on a Marriage Retreat

How about combining a vacation with marriage counseling? The idea behind a marriage retreat is taking you and your husband away from your conflictual environment as well as from the responsibilities and obligations you have. This is usually done by going to a peaceful setting where you and other couples who are also having difficulties work on these problems in a very specific way. There is a curriculum and agenda to each day's activities that may give you a sense of camaraderie and purpose that allows you to see measurable change fairly quickly.

A marriage retreat may have a theme—such as improving communication skills—or it might be affiliated with a house of worship or religious faith. You may have one therapist/facilitator or several. A marriage retreat might take place over the course of a weekend or be a weeklong process. Because this type of therapy is often quite intense and goes deeply into problems, it can also be very effective, provided both partners participate, and are honest and forthcoming in their actions.

There is, of course, a fee involved, and while some retreats may be relatively inexpensive, others are quite costly, depending upon the location, the duration, the agency or institution running it, and whether you will be working with well-known therapists. Looking up marriage retreats on the internet is a good place to start your investigation.

Reading Self-help Books

I encourage couples in my counseling practice to engage in *bibliotherapy*—that is, reading a book or several books I feel would benefit them—and to read the book together, with each partner reading aloud part of a chapter and then discussing the ways in which the material applies to them personally or their marriage. This not only speeds up the process of therapy, but brings them closer together. With or without therapy, if you have not tried this strategy with your husband, I highly encourage you to do so.

As an author of several self-help books—including the one you're reading—I may be biased in my positive opinion of these types of books. I am not bashful to tell you that I have received literally thousands of emails from people who have read my previous books, telling me how or how much they have helped their lives. I am hopeful that this book will help you as well.

There are hundreds of books about self-esteem, raising children, communication skills, love, and relationships. Some are better than others, but all have a point of view that may be helpful to you. Reading a book—especially a book that is also a workbook—is an inexpensive way for you to look at the difficulties facing you now. A book may not be the complete solution, as individual or joint counseling with your husband still may be required, but often a good self-help book that speaks to you will help you to clarify, magnify, or open yourself to ideas you hadn't thought of before. This might be all that you need.

If you look at relationship books on an online bookstore, you will find too many to scroll through in a day. You may want to refine your search according to the difficulty you're facing and then cull the list down to half a dozen books. Show these books (or as a first step before ordering online, their descriptions) to your husband and ask if he would be willing to read one of them with you. If so, you may be on your way to understanding the problems you face and more importantly, acquire new tools to improve your marriage.

As you can see, there are many avenues to explore before you decide to end your marriage. All hope may not be lost. However, if you are still contemplating the pros and cons, let's think about what would happen if you didn't divorce. There is so much to consider and I'd like to help you ferret out the difference between irrational fears and a true possibility.

CHAPTER 6

What If You Don't Divorce?

DR. JILL

"The thought of divorcing my husband is scary. I feel like my brain has a ping-pong ball bouncing around in it. I keep going back and forth about the decision. I know the right answer for me is to divorce him. Nothing changes no matter how much I talk. My fourteen-year-old daughter tells me things like, "Dad isn't nice to you," and "I don't know why you put up with him," or lately, "You should divorce him." But my nine-year-old boy will say, "I only want Dad to read to me," or "Dad didn't mean that," or in the past few weeks, "You and Dad are always going to be together, right?" I think he senses something's up and he really adores his father. How could I take him away from the man?

"Things have gotten worse and I'm fairly certain Jim's having an affair. I don't know if it's emotional or sexual, and I guess it doesn't really matter. He doesn't love me and I don't love our marriage, but I do love our family. I wish someone would just make this decision for me and then I wouldn't have to feel responsible." —Karen, age forty-six, married sixteen years

Like Karen, I'm sure you've gone back and forth in your head a hundred times about the idea of divorce. Maybe you've made up a pros and cons list, talked to friends or a therapist. You are frightened and confused. Divorce isn't just a little jump, it's a huge leap.

I speak to women in my practice who are contemplating divorce for several reasons. All of them are reasonable reasons, but they still doubt if they have a *right* to divorce. Most are at the end of their rope . . . but then they seem to find a little more rope. Here's what I've discovered: You can never be 100 percent sure if you are making the correct decision. You can only be sure *enough*.

I am certainly not here to pressure you or convince you to divorce. I am only another voice that wants to present all the options to you so that you feel empowered to make the decision that is correct for you. You have the right to chart the course of your own life.

You already know what it's like to be in your marriage. You don't know what it would be like if you weren't. We will discuss that later. However, right now, let's talk about what would happen if you didn't divorce.

- How would you continue to live your life?
- What would your children's futures look like?
- What would your life look like in six months, one year, five years, or ten years?
- How would your senior years look with your husband by your side?

Do these questions make your head swim? There's no need to be anxious. Nothing has happened. I just want you to make the best decision possible with as much realistic information as you can find.

How Would You Continue to Live Your Life?

Picture your life today: the joys and the struggles, the routines, the financial security (or lack of it), who you talk to, the tensions, your emotions, all of it. See yourself waking up in the morning: Is your husband next to you or are you alone? Is he next to you, but you feel alone? Do you feel happy or sad when you wake up? Anxious? Scared of another day? Not certain what mood he will be in or what he will say to you?

If you have children, do you wake them up and get them ready for school or day care? Does your husband help you with these tasks? If you work outside your home, are you exhausted by the time you get there or preoccupied with thoughts about your marriage? If you are a homemaker, do you rush to get everything accomplished before your husband gets home or dread what he's going to say? Are you so depleted that you lie on your couch and watch *The Today Show* and *The Price is Right* so that you don't have to think or move?

What is your evening like? Are you responsible for dinner and cleanup? Helping your children with homework, refereeing squabbles, bedtime routine? How much does your husband contribute to your children's routine or dinner and home activities/maintenance?

When you get into bed, have you had any time to yourself or do you feel depleted? Are there arguments with your husband, angry silence, withdrawal, attempts at conversation that go nowhere, or do you shirk from conversation because it will make you feel worse later? Are there critiques of what you've done wrong today or implications that your efforts weren't good enough? Do you go to sleep just grateful that another day has ended?

That may have been a lot to absorb. The point is, I want you to take a good look at the reality of your marriage without sugarcoating it or telling yourself *It's not all bad* or *Sometimes I can be a lot to handle too.* Of course, that's true. Nothing, including your marriage, is black and white. I'm not attempting to make you defensive about your marriage, force you to explain your reasons for being there, or feel compelled to defend your husband. I'm absolutely certain that all your reasons are valid and have been correct for you for quite a while. Right now, however, you are questioning if your reasons are still good enough.

Let's look back on the details of your day-to-day life that you just went through. If you stay in your marriage, there is no reason to believe that it will improve. If you've examined the possibilities in the previous chapter, you have already tried most anything available to you, including months or years of trying to explain how you feel, crying, shouting, pleading. You've made your case as to why things must change. You can try all those ideas again for the 1,038th time to see if it will make the difference. However, assuming it doesn't, we can predict that your marriage will only continue to deteriorate.

How much worse can it get? I'm not sure. Your husband could have an affair . . . or another affair. He could become emotionally or physically violent (I see you shaking your head, but trust me that it's true). He could withdraw even more than he already has. He might start—or increase— hiding money or being punitive with finances. He could start or increase his drinking or drug use. He may become more and more depressed. He could lose his job or develop an illness that would require you to care for him . . . without appreciation.

What will you do and how will you conduct your life if any of those things happen? How will you cope on a day-to-day basis if they do? If we assume that you are not ready to divorce in the immediate future you have a couple of options.

You can live a life separate from your husband, meaning you live parallel lives. You don't consult with him about your plans and neither does he. You have your activities and your friendships and the only things you discuss with him are your children, household finances, or if you (not both of you) are planning a vacation. Time spent away from the house isn't questioned unless one of you must take a business trip and children or pets must be considered in your absence. Essentially, you live as if you were single except that you remain married and living in the same house. You can decide if sex is a part of this plan or not.

Additionally, if you earn a salary, you should decide how much of that income goes into a joint account for marital obligations and how much is your personal income, since you won't be consulting your husband about your own expenditures. You don't expect him to have conversation with you or help with the children, if he doesn't help now. If he does, you can keep the same routine.

You may be asking yourself: *Wait a minute, if he doesn't do anything, what do I get out of this plan?* It makes your life easier, even though you may be doing a bit more of the work. If you must beg him to help with the kids and it leads to angry words or resentment, isn't it just easier to do it yourself? I'm not saying it's fair, but that's your marriage. The only thing that changes with this plan is your expectations. You just eliminate the angry exchanges that aren't changing the outcome.

You may think this idea of living parallel lives is a crazy one, but I assure you many couples live this way and quite peaceably. It is not marriage in the traditional sense, as very little is shared. However, if you look at what your marriage looks like now and take out the anger, resentment, fear, and sadness, you may be able to stay married in the technical sense. Your family can remain under one roof and your children can see their father daily or as often as they see him now. He can still participate at his desire and you continue to stay as financially secure as you are now, which may be a source of anxiety to you if you divorce. This is more of a "business arrangement marriage" rather than a traditional "romantic partner marriage."

You develop your outside life (friendships, hobbies, activities), so that you aren't seeking your husband's company or support for entertainment or validation. Many times, our marriages are full of what the man wants to do or who his friends are. I find that women in unhappy marriages have given so much of themselves that they have few friends and have forgotten what they used to like to do or what interested them. So, let me ask, when was the last time you did something—or nothing—simply because it was your choice? When was the last time you had lunch or took in a movie with a friend? When did you last sing or play guitar or tennis or even went for a walk without children or the dog? *How much of yourself have you given up so you could stay in this marriage?*

Go look in a mirror right now. What do you see? Do you look tired? Worn out? Sad? Frightened? Old? Do you even recognize yourself? What I'm suggesting is that you find yourself or even just a small part of yourself again. If you are going to remain in your marriage, you need *you* to be in this marriage so that no matter what happens, you have you back.

Don't look to your husband to define you or tell you what you want or who you are. Improve your own life because you have the power to do that. Make yourself happy outside of your marriage and don't depend on it to be your be-all and end-all.

What Would Your Children's Future Look Like?

The primary reason women stay in their unhappy marriages is because they don't want to cause their children pain. It might be an acceptable reason to stay in yours. I'd like you to consider what your children experience in their home on a daily or a weekly basis. Do they see you crying or upset or worse yet, pretending to be happy and put on a brave face? Do you tell them that nothing is wrong when it is? Do they hear angry words between you and your husband? Does he call you names or withdraw into another room without participating in daily family life? Do they see their father miserable? Is either one of you drinking more than the occasional social drink? When either of you drinks, do you fight more or do your arguments escalate? Do they see you sleeping more than usual? When Dad is angry, does he leave the house angrily? Has he stopped coming to the children's events or family vacations?

The reason I'd like you to think about these scenarios is because, despite what you might think, children notice every one of these actions. You aren't fooling them at all. Even if you fight when you think they are sleeping, they wake up and know. Even if you cry when they are at school, they know. They don't believe your excuses about Daddy's mood or Daddy's drinking. They don't buy that he has to work late so couldn't attend their baseball game, piano recital, or school play. They know when there is tension between the two of you. As a matter of fact, they may understand more than you do!

You may want to consider what you are teaching your children by staying in your marriage. On one hand, you may be teaching them that when you make a promise you keep your promise, no matter how difficult it may be. On the other hand, you may also be teaching them that you— or they—don't deserve to be treated with love and respect. They might therefore begin to equate love with pain or great sadness. You also may be telling your daughters that it's alright for a man to treat her the way your husband treats you, and you may be telling your sons that it's okay to treat women in that manner.

Ask yourself this question right now: How would I feel if my child/ children found themselves in a marriage just like mine? Does your answer make you feel queasy? Ashamed? Fearful?

Now ask yourself another question: If my son grew up to be exactly like his dad, or my daughter grew up to be just like I am now, would I feel that I'd done the very best job I could as their mother? Do I think their father and I are the best role models for relationship success? If the answer to any or all these questions is no, then you must ask yourself why you continue to keep your children in this toxic environment.

If you want better for your children, start by wanting better for yourself.

What Would Your Life Look Like in Six Months, One Year, Five Years, or Ten Years?

If you stay in your marriage, what do you anticipate your life to look like in the short term and long term? The reason I ask according to these time frames is this: Many women put a timeline on their suffering or when they feel it's acceptable to leave the marriage. They plan to leave their husbands . . . when the baby is out of diapers, when I get a better job, when my last child goes to school full time, when my kids are old enough to understand, when the oldest child can drive, when the last one leaves for college.

I am frequently asked what the "best" age is for children to experience divorce. Is it better when they are too young to remember their parents together? Is it better when they are in elementary school because they develop friendships and a life apart from their parents? Is it better when they are in middle school since they are so awkward and angry a good bit of time anyway? Is it better in high school when they have more independence and their friends appear to be more important than their parents?

The fact is that there is no "best" time and no good age. Divorce is difficult for kids no matter when it occurs. There, I've said it. If you were expecting me to tell you that divorce doesn't harm kids, I would be lying to you. Some kids understand it better than others and some kids are more resilient. But all kids are narcissistic and their worlds revolve around them, not their parents. Sure, your kids care a lot about you, but they are more interested in what you've planned for dinner and whether you are going to let them have a sleepover next weekend. They care about birthday parties and going to their friends' houses after school more than they care about your upsets with your husband.

Here is a good rule to follow: If Mom is okay, the kids are okay. It's like the advice I give to my patients who are nervous about airline travel: Look at the flight attendants. If they aren't worried, we don't need to be, because they know a lot more than we do about what's going on in the air and in the flight deck.

So, what would your life and your marriage look like half a year from now? Can you stick it out for six months? Alright, maybe you can, but should you?

How about a year from today? What happens to your life if nothing changes in your marriage? You will be a year older. Will you be a year happier?

Five years from now, your children will be five years older. What will they have experienced in those five years? Are they more stressed? More tense?

Ten years will go by whether you stay in your marriage or not. If your marriage stays the same as it is now, 3,650 days from today will you feel as if the last ten years have treated you well? Will you feel more accomplished? Those will be ten years of your life you can never get back. Nor will your children be able to reclaim their childhood at that point. They will have lived the most carefree years of their lives looking at two adults who don't like each other, have bitterness and contempt. You can't take that away from them.

You have one go-round at life. You have one shot with each of your kids. While you don't have all the answers to life's questions, if you don't see your marriage changing, I strongly advise you to consider what your life will look like in the future.

What Do Your Senior Years Look Like with Your Husband at Your Side?

When we marry, we plan for a lifetime together and often dream of playing with grandchildren, what retirement will look like, growing old together, and looking back at a lifetime of precious memories with the person we love. Divorce takes that all away from us and I think that, quite possibly, that knowledge is the very worst part of ending a marriage. It's the destruction of a dream or a fantasy.

Knowing that you may not have your "golden years" with your husband may be a crushing blow. Not sharing grandchildren in the way you dreamed of is a depressing idea.

While it's true that sometimes a mean younger man mellows into a kinder older man, this is not always the case. It is also sometimes true that a poor father becomes a better grandfather, but that is also not always the case. Oftentimes, a cruel guy is an even crueler older guy and an uninvolved father becomes a crotchety grandpa who is so annoyed with his grandchildren that it makes it impossible for Grandma to have as much time with them as she would like.

Here's the real deal: Illness and some level of dementia is going to happen to all of us. When you become ill or incapacitated, how well is your husband going to take care of you? Will he be kind, patient, and tolerant? Will he help you to the bathroom, answer the same question over and over, change your bandages, and sit by your bedside? Will he tell you that you're beautiful if you have a mastectomy? Will he be devoted to you if you can no longer do for yourself, much less him?

I'm not asking you fantasy questions. I'm asking you questions about events that WILL occur in your lifetime. Look at the man your husband is today, and allowing for some weathering and continued hard feelings, consider the answers to those questions.

Also, ask yourself if you will have felt that your life was the best it could have been as you celebrate your fiftieth anniversary. Will you feel proud of that milestone or just angry because you have wasted most of your life, rather than seeking happiness and personal fulfillment.

I also see women who have taken care of the home, the children, and everything else during their entire marriages. They were married to men who didn't appreciate all their hard work and were critical of every little thing. These men rarely said, "Thank you," and went through their marriages with a sense of entitlement. This type of woman was living from day to day with a sense of dread and unhappiness. Then, the old bugger got sick and she was stuck playing nurse to a man who still didn't appreciate her. Worse yet, he became mean when he was old and ill. Now she was really stuck because how was she going to leave him now? This is a common theme among women in their sixties and seventies.

You may wonder what will happen to you if you divorce your husband and you still have to go through any of the scenarios I presented. I heard you thinking. Then, you imagine, you will be alone and isn't it better to have Old Faithful (or maybe not so faithful) rather than experience old age by yourself? That's a good question. What I will pose to you is this: If you have children and you are unmarried, they will most likely want to help you much more than if your husband is available. I would also ask you to consider—I said *consider*—if you might remarry and whether your new husband would be capable of taking care of you. If you choose wisely the next time around and find a man who truly loves you and unselfishly wants to spend the rest of his life taking care of you in every way, then you have found the perfect partner in your old age.

You are not too young to think about yourself in your fifties, sixties, and beyond. You are going to become that age one day whether or not you remain married to your husband. Your children will leave home and make homes for themselves, and their new lives will supersede the life they had with you. It is important for you to plan for the rest of your life in the way you'd like to see it, and ask yourself if your husband is part of that plan.

CHAPTER 7

What Do You and Your Children Deserve in Your Lives?

DR. JILL

"I have to honestly admit that I don't even know who I am anymore. I know who I was before I married Mark. So, I don't know if I changed because, you know, you do change as you get older. But what I really don't know is if living in this marriage and being so sad is what changed me. All I know is that I don't laugh like I used to and I just seem to be kind of flat most of the time. —Clare, age forty-nine, married eighteen years

When you are unhappy or mistreated in a marriage, it eventually changes your view of the world as well as your belief in yourself. You go through life from day to day merely existing rather than living fully. A patient of mine once told me, "I live every day for the time I can go to sleep at night because it means another day is over." I can't tell you how sad that made me, but then I heard similar feelings from many other women. They felt that their lives and marriages were something to endure. They didn't think there was any other way. Oh sure, there was a way out of that misery for other women, but not for them—they thought.

Another patient of mine saw her identity being gobbled up by her husband and begged him, "Please, I like who I am. Don't work so hard to change me. You used to like who I was, too. I don't want to become that other person you want me to be. 'Me' is starting to fade away into you." That was incredibly powerful and heartfelt.

Perhaps, at this stage in your marriage, you don't even know that you deserve any more than you have right now. Yes, that's right, I said *DESERVE*. You may have forgotten that you are entitled to life, liberty, and the pursuit of happiness.

Let's think about that right for a moment: Do you feel that you are living life fully or living your best life? Do you possess emotional freedom? Are you free to express yourself? Are you free to be who you truly are? Are you happy? Do you feel joy, contentment, optimism, peace, and tranquility? These are your rights, not a preference.

As we've discussed previously, many women stay in unhappy marriages for their children. That's an important consideration. Let's talk about what you and your children truly deserve in your lives.

- Feelings of emotional safety and security
- Feelings of contentment and optimism
- Being accepted without criticism
- The ability to express your thoughts and opinions freely
- Setting a good example for your children of what their future relationships should look like

You may not have known that you and your children are entitled to every one of those freedoms. Let's investigate what each of those would look like in your lives.

Feelings of Emotional Safety and Security

If you ever had the warm feeling of safety when you were a child being snuggled by a loved one, you know the feeling of emotional safety and security. At that moment, the outside world stopped and all you felt was love and acceptance. You may have felt that way many times in your marriage—or at least, during your courtship—and the feelings were so profound as to be primal, meaning that they instinctively called up that childhood memory. Often, it is those wonderful memories of your husband—those beautiful almost-forgotten thoughts of the emotional safety and security he provided—that are now so difficult to come to terms with.

How could he have made you feel so protected and loved once upon a time and now he doesn't? Can you get the man who made you feel that way back again? After all, if he was capable of being a protector and "hero" at one point, surely he is capable of being that for you now? But why won't he act chivalrous and attentive like he used to?

I know all those thoughts are swimming in your head and have for quite a while. This is one of the reasons why you may feel so betrayed, cheated, and confused.

You may have been going about this all wrong. Emotional safety and security actually comes from within you. Your husband can't *give* it to you like a Christmas present. It comes from not being afraid of knowing what you're feeling and then taking the risk of feeling them. In a marriage, emotional safety and security allows you to be open and vulnerable with your husband. In your marriage, days, weeks, months may have been so turbulent that it wasn't safe to feel your feelings. This may have caused you to shut off, shut down, and put a barrier between you and your unpleasant feelings. That's understandable and in the case of your marriage, it may have been a smart survival skill, but that doesn't mean that you don't *deserve* to have these wonderful feelings in your life every day.

Likewise, your children may have felt secure and safe with you, but do they feel that way every day with your husband? Sure, your children may seem attached to him—that is, they like spending time with him—but who do they come to when they really need nurturing? Your husband may be unpredictable with your kids. He may be Fun and Nice Daddy one moment and Angry Daddy the next. He may lash out for no reason. And they may never know which dad is going to show up.

They *deserve* to feel emotionally safe and secure from both of their parents every day.

Feelings of Contentment and Optimism

A feeling of contentment is necessary to feeling happy. Contentment is feeling satisfied, feeling peaceful and serene, having ease of mind. Do you feel that way most of the time? Or do you feel discomfort in your life and in your own skin, sadness, a feeling of pervasive misery? You *deserve* contentment and so do your children.

We all want to raise optimistic kids, children who look on the favorable side of events or conditions in their lives and have an expectation that most situations will have a good outcome, even if it's not exactly the outcome they would like. Raising optimistic children gives them resilience and a sense of buoyancy in difficult times. Their childhood doesn't need to be one of those difficult times. If your life and marriage make you feel hopeless, pessimistic, and you have a general gloom about your days, your children will pick that up and see it as a natural way of life. You can't tell your children to "be happy" when you have very little happiness yourself.

Being Accepted Without Criticism

How long has it been since you were truly yourself and not a clone of the person your husband wanted you to be? How many critiques do you receive in a week? Think about that number for a moment. Perhaps there are too many to count, but I'd like you sincerely to try to remember every single critique you received last week. Perhaps, some of them weren't even out loud; maybe several were looks, sighs, eye rolls. Do you even notice these anymore or are they just a part of your everyday life? "You can't do anything right," "You aren't good enough," "You'll never get it," "What's the point?"

Do your husband's comments extend to your children? Maybe he critiques them directly and kills their little spirits, or maybe he uses them to criticize you: "Mommy can't find her way out of a paper bag. Ha, ha, ha," "No wonder you got a bad grade on your math quiz, Mom helped you with your homework," "I know the hamburgers are dried out. Mommy never really learned to cook. But we should eat them anyway so she's not so sad," and so forth. Sound familiar? This kind of putdown may seem harmless on a superficial level—he even might make jokes at your expense or use sarcasm in front of the kids—but it is confusing and upsetting to children. Your kids love you, and hopefully love your husband as well. But when he makes these types of remarks, he is forcing your children to take sides and to see you as a buffoon, something they really don't want to do.

It undermines your authority and ability to parent them. It makes you appear to be less than him. Do you know what I mean?

You are a lovely person. I heard where your head went right there: *Oh, if only she knew. I'm not that lovely. I'm actually a pretty bad person.* I don't believe that and I believe that your feelings about yourself are a direct product of your husband's criticism and who he's told you that you are. Maybe you heard this kind of critiquing in your childhood home between your parents as well, so you know how damaging it is for your own children.

Both you and your children *deserve* to be who you are and to feel accepted and loved. If you don't know who you are besides being a wife, mother, coworker, sister, daughter, friend, then you have the opportunity—no, the obligation—to find out who YOU are. This may be with your husband or without him, ultimately, but nevertheless, no one must live the rest of your life with you except you. Children move on to have their own lives, your marriage may or may not last the rest of your life, parents pass away, siblings have their own families, and friends move away or develop other friendships. You always have you. When you realize that you only need your own acceptance and that the nasty things your husband says about you are incorrect, then you will come closer to deciding what to do about your marriage.

The Ability to Express Your Thoughts and Opinions Freely

Here is my general rule: If you are afraid to express your thoughts, feelings or opinions you are in an abusive relationship. You have the *right* to tell someone what you think and how you feel, in a respectful manner of course. If you are afraid to do this because your husband may shout, sneer, pretend he can't hear you, bang or throw things, laugh, call you names, withdraw, punish you financially, or strike you then you are in an abusive marriage, not merely an unhappy marriage. You should NEVER be afraid of your partner for any reason. Likewise, you children should NEVER be afraid of dad, ever. They shouldn't be afraid to say how they feel or what they think. They should never be afraid to express themselves. I know you want to raise your children to be expressive and be able to say how they feel. When they were toddlers, didn't you tell them, "Use your words?"

Are you going to force them to remain in an environment that squelches that? Think about that and think about it hard.

Setting a Good Example for Your Children of What Their Future Relationships Should Look Like

I cannot say this powerfully enough or repeat this point too much in this book: If you want something better for your children, you should show them an example of a better relationship and a happier, more confident, and optimistic mom. I can't count the number of teenagers I see in my practice who tell me, "My mom wants me to be out of my relationship, but you can't believe what goes on in my home. She's such a hypocrite."

Yup, that's it. I see countless women who tell me they stay in a miserable marriage because "I can't break up my family," "My children need a father, especially my little boy," "Girls who grow up without fathers will find any guy for attention," "My children love their daddy. How can I take him away from them?" and on and on.

As I've said before, and will likely say again, you can't want more for your children than you want for yourself and you can't want more for your children than what you are showing them. You can't force them to live in an unhappy home and then expect they will find kind and generous partners. You can't show your daughter that you can take it, but tell her she shouldn't. You can't show your son that he can treat a woman this way without consequences. You can't show them that you just endure life, but tell them they should go out and be happy and accomplished. You can't show them that this is okay for *you,* but not for *them.* Children learn what they live.

Let me invite you to look up the research on children and divorce instead of making proclamations that may not be accurate. Let me reiterate: If you decide to divorce, *you* are not breaking up your marriage, behaviors are breaking up your marriage. Yes, some of them—even many of them—may be your own behaviors. This is why I encourage you to seek counseling. But some of the problematic behaviors are also your husband's behaviors, and at this point, you may have reached a stalemate where further improvement may not be possible.

It isn't necessarily true that children need a father in their home. What they need are kind and emotionally healthy male role models who show them good examples of life and behavior. You are not taking away their dad. Your children will most certainly see their father, providing he hasn't done emotionally damaging or illegal things in their presence.

What children really need is you, all of you: emotionally present you, happy you, honest you, determined you, confident you, loving you. That's all children need to succeed in life: a parent who shows them, through her actions, what she wants for them. She describes it not only in her talk, but in her actual conduct. I would hope your husband would do the same, but if he doesn't, you can do it for them. And while you're at it, do it for yourself.

CHAPTER 8
Seeking Consultation

DR. JILL

"I don't know who to believe. I tell my friends what's going on in my life and they tell me to 'ditch the bum.' I know they care about me, but it's a bigger decision than that. It's easy for them to say; all but one of them is married and if any has ever considered divorce, I sure don't know about it. Then, I talk to my mom, who tells me I need to stick it out and fix it. She tells me that ninety percent of marriage is the woman doing the work and said I should have a baby and I'd see what a difference that would make. How am I supposed to have a baby with a man who treats me like dirt? Her input makes me feel like a huge failure.

"I talked to my pastor once and he was not sympathetic at all. Let me correct that: He sounded sympathetic, but told me that I made a promise before God so that was it. He told me to pray for wisdom and suggested I come talk to him with my husband—who wouldn't do that.

"Is this really it? Am I just supposed to pray and work harder? I feel stuck and sad and that I should feel that I'm wrong and failing, and shouldn't be thinking or feeling like I do. It's a hopeless situation."—Maya, age thirty-four, married seven years

Divorce is, of course, a huge decision and not one to be considered impulsively. I know that you agree with that concept, which is the reason you're reading this book. I'm sure you've gone back and forth in your head and maybe talked to several people about your feelings and received many different opinions. Which ideas make the most sense? That may change with the day or the wind.

On the other hand, perhaps you haven't talked to anyone because you believe that even thinking of divorce is shameful. Or maybe you've presented a perfect image of your life and marriage to the world and the idea of admitting that you're thinking of divorce would mean that you're admitting you've been a huge fraud. Take it from me, girl, I personally know what I'm talking about with that one!

What I'd like to discuss with you in this chapter is the idea of talking with people who can truly help you make this enormous decision. In the end, of course, yours is the only opinion that counts. You are the only person who has to live in your life, and so while others may offer well-meaning suggestions, they don't have to live with the consequences, positive and negative. They are living their own lives and yours is not on the top of their list.

The first thing I'd like you to consider before going further in this chapter is whether you can allow yourself to be open and honest with your feelings without feeling ashamed that you are considering divorce. Divorce, in and of itself, is not a shameful event. It is the personal feelings we and others put on it that causes us shame. Divorce is a legal process that ends a marriage and certainly, there are many feelings attached to it. However, you are not bad or wrong as a person for considering divorce.

What I know for certain is that women don't impulsively or quickly decide to end their marriages. It is not a split-second decision and it is often a grueling emotional process. Anyone who asks you, "Have you really thought about this?" is just a fool and you needn't listen to the words that follow.

Let's talk about people from whom it might be safe and wise to seek consultation.

- A nonjudgmental family member whose opinion you trust
- A non-gossipy friend who has made difficult decisions you admire
- A clergy member who will listen without making you feel badly about yourself
- A therapist who can give you unbiased advice

- A family law attorney who will answer questions you have and questions you didn't know you needed to ask

Talking to a Family Member

Your family should be composed of people with whom you may have automatic trust and belief. I hope that is true for you. What I have found time and again with my patients is that approval from family lasts as long as you are meeting their expectations of what they believe your life should look like. I am not meaning to disparage your family. Likely they want what they believe is best for you and what they believe is best is, quite naturally, a family atmosphere and you doing well emotionally. They don't want your life to be difficult. To that extent, marriage would seem to fulfill those expectations.

Of course, you had hoped for the exact same thing and the fact that you are contemplating divorce means that you have tried everything in your power to achieve this and it has not worked. It means that you don't have the emotional security and stability that you and your husband agreed to.

Your family may be resistant to the idea of you divorcing. I can tell you with certainty, as a once-divorced woman, that if either of my children came to me and told me that they were considering divorce, I would be heartbroken for them. If you are going to talk to a family member, you will want to choose one who has shown that she or he has not judged you or another person harshly. You will want one whose opinion you've trusted in the past who has given you reasonable advice. This is not to say that your family member has to agree with everything you say. Perhaps this individual will kindly point out a snafu in your thinking or show you another side to what you feel. You don't have to agree, but you might get food for thought.

You also want to choose a family member who trusts *your* judgment and believes in you as an adult woman. You need assurances that the information you share is confidential until or unless you want to tell others in your family. That must be your decision, not this individual's. If there is pressure to tell other family members, be sure that you can assure the person you're talking to that you will tell whom you wish when you decide and thank him or her for the help and concern. Understand that you have told this person very difficult feelings and given the person a tremendous amount of responsibility within the family.

Perhaps too much responsibility. Let's say, for example, that you talk to an aunt or uncle who is a sibling to one of your parents. After talking with this family member, and after searching yourself, you decide to divorce. If your parent discovers that you spoke to their sibling first, there may be very hard feelings. You might be asked, "Why did you talk to him/her instead of me?" Did you divorce because he/she influenced you to do so? This may come back as bitterness to the sibling who was only helping you at your request.

These are important ideas to think about before going to any close family member.

Talking to a Friend

As Maya expressed in the beginning of this chapter, friends love you, but they may also have an ulterior motive for their advice. They may also be people who see you for who you really are. They may have socialized with you and your husband and seen behaviors you've made excuses for.

If you talk with a friend, you will want to choose one whose decision making you've admired in the past. If you've seen her make good and clear-headed decisions in difficult situations, she may be a candidate to be an advisor. If you've known her not to gossip, even better. You need to make sure that your information won't go any further than her. You know, the friend to whom you say, "I need this to be between just the two of us," only to find out that she told her husband? Her customary answer to this is, "I tell him everything. He's not going to tell anyone else." That's not the friend to talk to.

If you say, "No one," that means *not anyone else*. Lips sealed.

Sometimes, in crisis and in pain, we talk to any and every girlfriend we've got, thinking that because she's female and she's known you for some time—it could be as little as two months—she will understand and have loyalty. Sadly, that is very often not the case at all. I've seen lives and friendships crushed at the exact time that you need your girl squad the most.

Talking to a Clergy Member

If you are a person of faith and practice regularly at a house of worship, speaking to your clergy member may be an excellent option. The clergy can reinforce what your holy book decrees, and just as importantly, they can give you a perspective that the secular world may not consider. This type of counsel may give you great clarity and comfort.

I will offer you some suggestions about talking to a clergy member, gleaned from speaking about relationships at many clergy conferences and having been an invited speaker at multiple houses of worship belonging to different faiths. Make sure that—while the person you're speaking to has a specific point of view—he or she is not so strictly adhered to that faith that he or she cannot look at you as an individual and will counsel you nonjudgmentally. I have spoken to countless clergy who say, "Well, the Bible says," "The Torah instructs us," or "The Koran decrees," and so on. While that is true and valuable, you are also a human being with your own individual set of circumstances, which are currently extremely difficult, and you need advice that is faith based, but not so stringent that it doesn't allow for your own feelings.

It is a given that you are struggling—both with the correct decision within your faith and for your family—which is the reason you are asking for consultation with your clergy. You should not be shamed. You should not be told or led to believe that you will be damned. You should not be told that there is only one way to deal with this problem. You should not be told that you should just pray about this and God will help you make the decision. You should not be shunned at your house of worship, but rather should be embraced—especially if this church or temple is the source of many of your friendships and social life. You should be assured that your clergy member will keep your conversations confidential.

Talking with a Therapist

As we've already discussed at length, speaking with a therapist—a psychologist, a social worker, or a marriage and family therapist—who can give you unbiased advice and open options you haven't considered is a very good idea. A therapist isn't part of your family, your social network, or your religious community. They are outside your circle and have no personal stake in your decision. You will want to seek out a therapist who demonstrates good boundaries and is an active therapist; that is, someone who gives you feedback other than asking, "What do you think about that?" You need someone who will give you direction and actively participate in a discussion.

Offering you "homework" or other means to increase your knowledge and decision-making skill is important as well. Your therapist right now should be one who can offer you short-term therapy with a focus on helping you make this decision. There certainly may be many factors that contribute to the process, among them imprints from your childhood family life, your self-esteem, your need to confront fears or irrational beliefs, residual feelings from previous relationships with men, and so on, but the focus of these investigations should be that the endpoint is that you understand yourself better and can confidently make the decision about whether a divorce is the best option.

Talking with a Family Law Attorney

In Part Two, Adam is going to give you all the information about the kind of fact-finding you need to do, and he is an expert, so I don't want to go too deeply into this idea. The reason I believe it's crucial to seek legal consultation prior to deciding is because almost every woman I've seen as a therapist who is contemplating divorce doesn't know the first thing about the divorce process or what she can expect. Oftentimes, her husband has told her that if they divorce he will take the children, not give her a dime, she will have to leave her home, she will have to go back to work or take another job that pays more, her children will blame and hate her, and he won't have to pay child support. He states these things with such authority that she believes him and is crippled with fear and paralysis. Here's the real deal, my friend: Your husband is not your attorney and likely doesn't know the first thing as to what he's talking about. He is trying to bully and intimidate you in the ways he knows will frighten you the most.

To prevent your husband from pressing his own agenda and messing with your head is exactly why you need to speak with an attorney who will give you realistic and unbiased counsel as to what you might expect in a divorce process. He will not only answer the questions that Adam will lay out for you shortly, but can answer questions specific to your case that you wouldn't necessarily think to ask. I *highly* advise you to spend at least a half hour with a good attorney before you make a pro or con decision. It will be the best money you've ever spent.

PART TWO
Legal Issues Before Divorce

"Am I really doing this? Am I going to go to a lawyer and talk about divorce? I don't understand how I got here. A few years ago, we were so happy—well, I thought we were happy. More and more ugly things piled up. There wasn't one big thing, but many small things. I thought we would be married forever. I didn't marry him with the idea that we would ever divorce. I'm just so sad. This is real now. I don't know how I'm going to survive this divorce." —April, age thirty-one, married seven years

Contemplating the legal side of divorce can be intimidating. That is why the first chapter in Part Two covers key foundational principles that I call the Seven Legal Rules of Divorce. If you make it your policy to adhere to these rules no matter what, the ground under your feet will feel much more stable than otherwise.

In many ways, however, you could characterize the theme of this section of the book as information gathering. *Information is empowering.* I repeat this assertion to clients all the time. This is particularly true during the period when a woman is contemplating divorce—even if she never goes through with it. Armed with the right information, you put yourself in the position to be successful and achieve your *realistic* goals during the legal dissolution of your marriage.

For your ease, I've separated the information-gathering stage of legal preparation for divorce into three interrelated steps and earmarked a separate chapter to discuss each step.

Step 1. Researching your legal rights

Step 2. Learning how those legal rights apply specifically to your situation, by collecting your personal and financial information

Step 3. Evaluating your options regarding how to get divorced

The final chapter in Part Two is about spending money on your divorce: How much is appropriate and expected? We'll consider a range of possibilities.

If you're ready, let's get started.

ADAM

CHAPTER 9

The Seven Legal Rules of Divorce

I wish I could go back in time and talk to my clients at the precise moment they started thinking about divorce. Even if I only had a few minutes, I would teach them the same seven legal rules I'm about to share with you. Some focus on mindset, others on action. All put you in the position to be successful and avoid common mistakes. This information is critically important at every stage of a divorce, starting from the moment you begin to contemplate it.

Rule #1: Your Actions Are Evidence

Once a divorce is initiated, your life becomes part of the legal system. Things you did or didn't do during your marriage can be used as evidence either for or against you in court.

This idea may take some time to sink in. But you need to get used to it fast. That text you sent yesterday, that post on Instagram, your involvement with the children, your emails, your spending habits, and so much more—all of it is in play.

Why am I telling you this? Evidence you create (aka your actions) can help or hurt you during your divorce. *This means you have the power to influence and control how your divorce case unfolds.* While it is impossible to change the past, you absolutely can have an impact on your case today and in the future.

Your actions are evidence. It is critical always to be mindful of this fact, because divorce is overwhelming and it is easy to forget. I'll cover this rule in more detail later, but to sum it up: Be aware of your actions. Before you do something, remind yourself that the action you are about take is evidence. Decide if it's a good idea or if it could come back and "bite" you later. Get in the habit of doing this and it will become part of your routine.

Also, pay attention to your husband's actions. Keep notes. This rule applies to him too.

Rule #2: Set Realistic Expectations from Day One

Early in my career, I wanted to understand why some outcomes in a divorce devastated my clients in one instance and barely bothered them in others. The answer, more often than not, was traced back to a woman's expectations.

The scenario usually goes something like this: While meeting with a new client (let's call her Megan), I describe how the law treats child custody and support. She reacts calmly to the custody topic, but is extremely upset and distressed about the support topic. Why? It turns out that Megan had read about the custody rules on the court's website, whereas a friend gave her the wrong information about child support. (She thought she would get more money than I did.) Megan had set realistic legal expectations about custody, but she expected something completely unrealistic regarding child support.

Why does this matter? Due to her unrealistic legal expectations, Megan had initiated several actions that would make her divorce more difficult.

The first problem with unrealistic expectations is they often cause emotional setbacks. Divorce is emotional enough without adding to it. Never underestimate the toll your emotions can take on your legal case. With Megan, the emotional setback she suffered caused her to leave our meeting early and miss out on important information that would have helped her. Then, she also was so distraught that she had difficulty remembering everything we discussed.

Emotional setbacks differ in severity, but tend to occur and reoccur throughout divorce. Luckily, many are avoidable.

The second problem is that we tend to make key decisions based on our expectations. When an expectation is inaccurate or based on faulty information (and they often are, especially in the beginning), then our decision making will be flawed. The tricky part is that many of us develop and set these expectations *without realizing it.*

Take the time to ask yourself why you hold a certain legal expectation. Is the underlying reason sound? Maybe you read something somewhere or talked to a friend when she was going through divorce. Expectations are fueled by many sources. The decisions that flow from your expectations will shape your divorce. Understanding this early on is critical.

To sum up, rule #2 is to be aware of your expectations. What are your expectations for your divorce? Where did they come from and why do you have them? When you answer these questions, you can determine if your expectations are putting you on the right path or setting you back.

Rule #3: Your Decisions May Not Always Be Right, but They Should Be Informed (and That Is the Best You Can Do)

Please, always take the time to make an informed decision. While this is a good idea in general, it is never more important than during a divorce. An informed decision means you have 1) taken the time to consider why you are taking a certain course of action, and 2) researched your options. I've seen too many people skip this step and regret it later. And believe me, in divorce it is easy to skip this step. The most challenging cases are littered with uninformed decisions.

Here is an example of an informed decision: Judy hired an attorney after meeting and evaluating several attorneys. Beforehand, she had researched what questions to ask them and knew what she could afford.

And now, an example of an uninformed decision: Judy hired the first attorney she found online because she just wanted to get the process over with and let a professional handle things.

What were the ramifications of Judy's uninformed decision? It turns out she hired an attorney she couldn't afford, one that she didn't personally get along with, who specialized in wealthy divorce cases rather than in the child custody and visitation issues that were central to her case. Failing to make an informed decision added another layer of difficulty to her already challenging divorce.

Now, here's another wrinkle that underscores the importance of taking the time to make an informed decision. Let's say that in both cases Judy hired the same attorney. Was it a waste of time for her to invest the time it took to make an informed decision? Nope.

You should always do your best to make an *informed* decision because you are going to be accountable for this decision throughout the divorce. Even if you end up regretting the decision later, it won't be because you were careless or uninformed. You will always remember that you did what you thought was best based on the information you had at the time, which is the best any of us could do in a similar situation.

Those who make uninformed decisions cannot say the same. They are likely to beat themselves up later for not taking the time to inform themselves at the outset. Striving to do your best is important as you move through this process. Be accountable to yourself for all decisions, good or bad.

If nothing else, remember this: At the moment of decision, the best you can do is to make an informed decision based on the information and circumstances known to you *in that moment.* The most successful people in the world apply this same approach. Tech billionaires. World leaders. Wall Street financial geniuses. All rely on informed decision making, because they know it reduces risk and is more likely to put them in a stronger position. And moving forward, so will you.

Despite it all, this is also where a lot people in divorce get stuck. They are unable to move forward, fearing they are making the wrong decision. To those people, I say this: You can't see the future. No matter what you do, there will always be risk. No one can tell you that in a year you'll look back at a decision as being the absolutely correct move. This goes for you,

Mark Zuckerberg, and Warren Buffet. Put your decisions in perspective and know you are doing the best you can.

To sum up: Take the time to weigh your options and do the research before you make decisions during your divorce. Avoid making snap decisions based on emotions or a lack of information. Remember that the most successful people in the world rely on informed decision making too. You cannot make the perfect decision every time because you can't see into the future.

Rule #4: Think Critically, Not in Absolutes

It's time to stop thinking in absolutes and assuming a certain outcome is predetermined.

- "The mom *always* gets the children"
- "If the wife didn't work during the marriage, the court will make her get a job *immediately*"
- "The judge *always* sides with the husband"

It doesn't work that way. Divorce is seldom ever black and white. It's a nuanced and evolving process that is every shade of gray. There are a lot of moving parts: Laws, legal cases interpreting these laws (called case law), the judge, attorneys, the parties (you and your ex), the children, and the facts are unique in every case. That every case is different means your case is unique!

When we think in absolutes, we close ourselves off to the benefits of critical thinking. By resigning yourself to the fact that an outcome is predetermined, you are missing out on opportunities to impact your divorce in a meaningful way.

So, what do I mean by *thinking critically?*

Ask questions. Let's say Sarah's husband's attorney just told her that she will receive $1,000 per month in child support. She could have accepted this number and moved on. Instead, she challenged herself to think critically. Sarah asked how this amount was calculated and learned it was based on timeshare with the children, her income, her husband's income, and childcare costs. Sarah then looked at the calendar and added up her days with the kids and her husband's days with the kids, and she found an error in the timeshare calculation this attorney was using. Her simple calculation ended up increasing the support payment she was to receive.

Even if she hadn't discovered an error, by going through this exercise Sarah was getting into the habit of thinking critically and understanding how things work. Down the road, if the circumstances changed with respect to any of the factors involved in child support, she would be in position to ensure the support payment was adjusted accordingly.

Don't be afraid to ask questions. You've never done this before, so there are no dumb questions. If you don't understand something or need clarification, that is your mind signaling you to get more information. Just ask!

Be proactive. Don't be passive and allow the divorce to wash over you. In the example with Sarah above, it would have been less effort just to accept what the attorney told her. You couldn't blame her if she did. She was intimidated and emotionally exhausted. She just wanted to get it done. But in all likelihood, Sarah would have regretted this later. Empower yourself, like she did, to be proactive and evaluate an issue.

To sum up, ask questions and listen to your instincts! If something doesn't fit or you feel like you need more information, than you do. Be proactive in getting that information.

Rule #5: Success Does Not Mean "Winning"

I use the word *success* a lot in this book. Typically, I'll say something about a certain mindset or strategy putting you "in the position to be successful." Notice that I don't say it will put you in a position to *win*. This is intentional. Success in divorce does not mean winning. In fact, you shouldn't view divorce in terms of winning or losing at all, particularly when it comes to the law. If you do, you will be making your divorce that much harder.

Success defined: If you look it up, success is generally defined as the "accomplishment of a goal or purpose." I tend to like this definition for divorce, so long as your goal or purpose is *realistic*. Put another way, success can also be summed up like this:

You are successful in divorce when you take action that is designed
to put you and/or your children in a better position.

To accomplish this, your definition of success should always be realistic. For example, let's say you are co-parenting with your ex-husband and he's making it difficult on you. Maybe he's constantly late to pickups and dropoffs or the kids tell you he's saying negative things about you in front of them. If your version of coparenting success is for things to work perfectly, then you are going to be disappointed. It is simply not realistic to believe you can suddenly turn your ex-husband into a super parent. No one can do that, so why put that pressure on yourself?

Of course, you can be successful in the things you can control. You can:

- Choose not to speak negatively about him in front of the children.
- Take care of your emotional health.
- Maintain awareness that your actions are evidence and act accordingly.
- Make sure you are living up to your side of the parenting agreement, even when your he isn't, because structure is good for your children.

By taking these actions, you are accomplishing goals left and right. You are doing right by yourself and your children. In divorce, that is the nature of success.

Even after setting realistic goals, you will still need to address outcomes when it comes to success. BUT, these outcomes should not define your success. This is where critical thinking and perspective come into play.

Let's say Sasha is seeking financial support (sometimes called spousal support or alimony) at a court hearing because her ex is refusing to pay her anything. She asks for and is awarded $800 per month. One could argue that Sasha was successful because of this outcome. What if the amount awarded was lower, say $500? Does that mean she was unsuccessful because she asked for $800? Not so fast.

First, let's focus on her goals. Did she take actions to put herself in a better position?

Yes. She was prepared, said exactly what she needed to say, answered the judge's questions, submitted all her evidence, and followed her plan. She successfully achieved each of those goals. The outcome (the judge's decision) was outside her control and did not factor into her achieving these goals.

Second, let's look at the outcome. Yes, the lower amount was disappointing, but that does not solely define her success. This process was not limited to one outcome ($800 per month), but to several and they are easy to miss. The other outcomes included:

- **Outcome #1:** Her ex, who previously had refused to pay anything, now understood there were consequences to his actions. He had to defend his position in a pubic courtroom. He missed work to go to court. He also paid money to hire an attorney. And his original goal was to pay zero dollars!
- **Outcome #2:** Sasha gained an understanding of her rights under the law. Moving forward, she made sure to retain evidence. In the event another situation arose where she had to go to court, she would be ready.
- **Outcome #3:** Sasha stood up for herself, gained valuable courtroom experience, and felt empowered by making it through her first court hearing.

By thinking critically, Sasha could see that many of the outcomes she experienced were positive. She was successful, even though she didn't achieve the outcome of $800 per month (which was outside her control anyway). She was empowered and on the road to rebuilding her emotional health. All because she took actions designed to put herself in a better position. Had she not taken the time to think critically about the outcomes, she very likely would have thought she "lost." Which leads to my final point about perspective.

Often, my clients are successful and don't even realize it. In fact, they believe they have lost even though they just did something AMAZING to improve their situation. This drives me crazy because I have the advantage of knowing that their situation would have been so much worse if they hadn't acted. Their lives are better because of something they did, yet they don't give themselves any credit.

Perhaps the best way I can illustrate this type of scenario is by way of an example involving two clients, Cindy and Sarah. The first woman, Cindy, was upset because she had sent an angry text to her husband the night before (after an argument) insulting him and saying he couldn't see the children. Her ex would later use the text against Cindy in court, arguing she was alienating him from the kids. (Remember: Actions are evidence!)

Then I met with Sarah, who told me how she had almost sent a similar text to her ex after an argument, but stopped herself from sending it. Even though she had done a smart thing from a legal perspective, she was upset because her husband was antagonizing her.

I took this opportunity to provide some perspective on success for Sarah. I told her about Cindy's text and how it later became evidence against her in court. In that moment, Sarah realized that she had *succeeded* by not sending that text and how her case would have been more difficult if she hadn't applied the "actions are evidence" rule. Afterward, she still had a difficult time with her ex, but instead of focusing on how hard she had it, she was able to give herself some credit.

With Cindy, I reminded her that we all make mistakes and encouraged her to learn from hers moving forward. I can tell you this, she never made that mistake again—but her ex did, and she was able to utilize his text messages as evidence down the line.

What am I saying here? What does perspective really have to do with the legalities of your divorce? Everything actually. When you are thrown off balance emotionally you can make poor legal decisions. So, stop and give yourself some credit. Focus on your successes and own your mistakes. And when you mess up, take it as an opportunity to learn.

Are there times when a legal result is very bad? Of course. I'm not saying that these concepts will turn every disappointing outcome into a success. However, a less competitive attitude will help you keep things in perspective and move forward in a healthier and realistic way.

To sum up: Maintain realistic goals and remember that although outcomes matter, they shouldn't be the only goal. Take *actions* to put yourself in a better position and at the end of the day, keep things in perspective. You may have accomplished something incredible and not even know it.

Rule #6: Focus Your Energy on What You *Can* Control

You cannot control other people or events. Anyone who tries will drive herself crazy. Focusing your energy and attention on controlling your own actions, on the other hand, is incredibly powerful—and it makes you feel sane.

Take my clients who represent themselves in court, for example. They put the weight of the world on their shoulders (often without realizing it), convincing themselves that they must somehow control everything that is about to happen. That's simply impossible. So, I remind them, "The best you can do is put the information you have in the judge's hands so that the judge can make the right decision for you."

Instead of focusing on the judge and your ex-husband, and putting pressure on yourself, redirect your energy on what you can control: being prepared, following your plan, telling the judge exactly what happened, introducing the evidence, and so on.

And do your best to remember that goals within your control are *realistic goals*. Yes, if you don't achieve the desired outcome at court, it's a setback. But you can't use mind control to make the judge do what you want. You can only control your own mind and actions.

Rule #7: Remember That You Are Your Strongest Advocate

Think of the preceding six rules as tools in your divorce toolkit. All are extremely valuable. One of the main goals I have in this book is to get you in the habit of using them regularly. If you do that, you'll realize that you yourself are by far the most powerful resource you possess.

It will take work on your part to keep follow these rules through your divorce. You will very likely stray and suffer emotional setbacks. That is totally normal. I just ask that you take a step back occasionally and reflect on this chapter. See if each rule still reflects your behavior. If not, take the opportunity to reacquaint yourself.

CHAPTER 10

Researching Divorce

ADAM

I don't love using analogies. As you will soon recognize, I prefer to throw out examples to illustrate a concept. In this part of the book, however, I'm breaking with tradition and going with an analogy because I think it's helpful. Plus, this one makes sense to me because I like to cook . . . and eat. When it comes to information gathering, I want you to think of your preparation for a possible divorce as planning a meal.

Let's say you're making lasagna. Step 1, the *legal research*, the subject of this chapter, is the recipe you've chosen. Step 2, your *information*, is your list of ingredients. Step 3, your *legal options* are how you want to set the table.

The goal of these three steps is not necessarily to make the meal, which will come later. Right now, you are only *planning* and *preparing for* the meal. You are not implementing plans yet, just thumbing through a cookbook. This is the "contemplating divorce" part of the book. The goal is to learn a recipe, collect all the ingredients available to you, and figure out how you want to set the table if you decide to make the leap.

As you can imagine, skipping these steps and going straight to cooking and eating the meal can have disastrous consequences. Without reading a recipe, for example, I wouldn't know the first thing about making lasagna. I'd be making it up. Without the right ingredients, well, I can pretty much guarantee it would taste gross and nothing like lasagna. Then, after I set the table and served it, no one would eat. In fact, they would probably leave the table.

This way of doing things is a bad idea for cooking and very bad when gathering information for your divorce. Do yourself a huge favor and conduct *helpful* research at the outset. Before I explain what I mean by *helpful research* (as well as the idea of *wrong* research), I need to emphasize the importance of getting this part right. Mainly, because I've seen so many people get it wrong. Researching divorce is not easy. It should be, but it isn't. I have worked with too many people whose missteps during this stage haunted them for the rest of the divorce. Luckily, this is *completely avoidable* and I'm prepared to show you how.

This chapter will focus on the opportunity to utilize some extraordinary free and low-cost resources to gain insights and a better understanding of the divorce process. The goal is to empower you by providing you with the skills to meet the challenge of finding the information you need with ease. When done correctly, research can advantage you in your divorce while simultaneously reducing your anxiety about the challenges ahead. This is huge. However, when performed incorrectly, anxiety levels go up and mistakes are made. This is also huge.

What's out there and how can it help or hurt you? Let's look.

Mistakes, Misinformation, and Message Boards

We tend to head straight for the internet when contemplating divorce, which makes perfect sense. It's free. It's fast. It's super convenient. There is a vast, seemingly infinite, amount of information on divorce out there. But this tendency is both a blessing and a curse. Distinguishing the good information from the bad is *tricky*.

Message boards can be a rabbit hole you don't want to go down. For example, Robin (age forty-one, married ten years) was using Google to search for an attorney in Miami when a search result near the bottom of the page caught her eye. When she looked closer, it was an article on hiding assets in a divorce. Robin had always wondered if her husband had been hiding things from her, so she clicked on the article. This led her to another website. Which led her to another. Before she realized it, Robin had clicked through fifteen different websites and found herself reading message board posts from women in other states. Some of those posts were about legal issues that didn't apply in Florida. Some posts were from 2008 and contained outdated advice. Robin didn't notice. She just kept reading, looking for answers.

Robin felt good. The message board topics described exactly what she was going through. It was cathartic to learn that she was not alone. Plus, the advice was free! So, why was this a problem? The risk was that Robin would end up making decisions based on *unverified information* from *nonexperts*. This information had the potential to take root in her mind and end up influencing her approach to divorce with disastrous consequences.

Unverified information is a big problem. Any fact you learn on a message board could be a fiction or a partial truth. Maybe the author is venting and writing a version of her case that she wishes had taken place. Or it could be the truth. In either case, it doesn't mean it applies to you. Odds are that differences—meaningful differences—existed between what Robin was reading and her own situation. Relying on unverified information greatly inhibits the process of making an *informed decision.*

You need to be careful when relying on nonexperts. This is not information from a reliable legal resource. Would you invest all your money in a certain stock because some stranger online said it was a good idea? If you answered no, you likely aren't comfortable with that level of risk regarding something as valuable as all your money. The outcome of your divorce is also extremely valuable too. Don't risk it.

It was easy for Robin to overlook these two problems because the process of sharing with other women on the message board made Robin feel good. Although Robin was benefiting from the exercise emotionally, it was harming her legally. Her story illustrates how it is so easy to forget to utilize legal research only for your legal needs.

Inaccurate or Avaricious Divorce Websites

"I didn't want anyone to know I was thinking about divorcing Ryan, I just wanted to search a little bit while I was at work. I Googled 'starting my divorce' and a bunch of sites came up. The first one looked perfect. It was easy to follow and I clicked on the topic called 'Before you start your divorce, read this!' I started reading and then another window opened with an ad for women's vitamins. I closed that window and before I read

another sentence, I was asked to take a survey. I skipped that! I felt like they had lured me in just to try to get me to buy something. "Later, I tried another site, but it wound up asking for my contact information. I almost gave it, because the information looked amazing. Another link took me to an entirely different website that was advertising services for a life coach." —Cindy, age twenty-eight, married four years

In Robin's situation with the message boards, the problem was that she was relying on unverified information from unknown members of a message board, who were likely not experts.

Now, what about Cindy's visit to official-looking websites offering help and information on divorce? The information on the sites was seemingly verified. Here's where a new set of concerns can arise, so keep your guard up. You need to understand that people researching divorce are often vulnerable (maybe even) desperate), which makes them easier targets for marketers and advertisers. Cindy clicked on a paid advertisement that looked like an article, but was really a site that gave some information for free, but wanted readers to pay for more.

- The top search results or the most highly trafficked websites are not necessarily the best. Companies can pay to ensure their sites are easily searchable and gain more visibility.
- If a site requests your personal information or money, you should take a step back and make sure that it is the right fit for you.
- Divorce sites are inviting and relatable. They look good and are designed to make you want to visit and stay awhile. They are almost certainly more user friendly than the government websites that contain helpful information (we'll get there in a bit).
- Some attorney websites offer loads of free information about divorce. This isn't necessarily a bad thing, but keep in mind that while this information may be helpful, the attorney isn't giving it away out of the goodness of her or his heart. The law firm wants you to hire them.

The point I'm trying to make is here is don't be an *easy target* for people out to make a quick buck. The goal here is straightforward: Avoid wasting your time and money on the wrong information. Your time is precious. Be aware during your research because it is easy to get sucked in. Your money is precious. If you are going to spend it, be selective.

Friends and Family "Legal Advice"

"I told my best friend Holly that I was thinking about divorcing Tom. She knew how unhappy I was and wasn't surprised. She could see how unhealthy our marriage had been. I was so relieved that someone else saw it too. Then Holly told me I needed to file for divorce first. She said, 'Don't wait, just do it,' because her aunt didn't file first and her uncle basically won the divorce. He was able to get more money. Doesn't the judge always give the person who files first the benefit of the doubt?" —Sarah, age twenty-eight, married five years

Situations like this are *extremely* common. Sarah, like many women contemplating divorce for the first time, sought emotional support from someone close to her. Very often, however, something that sounds suspiciously like legal advice gets weaved into these types of conversations, such as "File for divorce first."

Maybe your support person has been through divorce personally or knows someone who has gone through it. No matter how amazing they are, this experience doesn't make them an expert or qualify them to dispense legal advice. Or maybe they just have an opinion. Many of us do. Whatever the case, Holly's "legal advice" did Sarah more harm than good. It stressed Sarah out. Suddenly, there was a sense of urgency to divorce. Making decisions, critically important decisions, based on faulty legal advice can be catastrophic.

Once the word goes out that you are considering or going through divorce, suddenly everyone has "legal advice" for you. By everyone, I mean friends, friends of friends, family members, coworkers, neighbors, and on and on. And by "legal advice," I mean, it's not legal at all. Actual legal advice is professional advice provided directly from an attorney.

In the interest of being honest with you, I want you to know that I'm assuming these individuals are not attorneys with a background in divorce law. (If your friends and relatives are, then I'm happy to be wrong . . . because that would be awesome.)

Simply put, non-attorneys cannot provide legal advice. What you are getting, then, is *sham* legal advice, which is based on that individual's personal experience (their divorce, their marriage, or their research) or the experience of someone they know—perhaps a friend, a family member, or a coworker.

Maybe your friend says his or her advice came straight from an attorney. In that case, you should talk to the attorney directly because this is still not legal advice. The information is not coming directly from an attorney if it is coming from your friend.

Never forget that every case and situation is different. Divorce law is not one size fits all. This process, when a friend relays legal advice from an attorney, distorts the information you are receiving, again making it sham legal advice. True legal advice must be objective. Therefore, attorneys with no personal interest in your life are qualified to give it, and friends who are biased are not.

You should be very careful when you are contemplating a divorce. When you are flooded with sham legal advice at the outset, it is difficult to move forward and can lead you to develop unrealistic expectations.

Now, I also want to point out that advice from friends and family isn't necessarily wrong. The information may correct and helpful. But it also may be completely inaccurate and damage your case. That is a huge risk you need to consider. Whatever you do, your decision to rely on or reject advice from friends and family should be informed.

Here are some strategies to help you navigate the challenges of phony legal advice.

Determine what is useful and applicable to you by thinking critically. Do not simply rely on unverified "legal" advice. Take steps to verify if the information is accurate through research. The verification process can be productive, regardless of the result, because it gets you asking questions and being proactive. Get in the habit of making informed decisions.

Your Life Experience

Without realizing it, you may be drawing from your life experience to guide your legal divorce. Maybe your parents, or someone else you know, went through divorce. Maybe years of watching the news, television, and movies has subtly (or not so subtly) influenced you. Or it may have been a book or article you read. They all contribute to your life experience. This may create problems with your legal divorce. Take Michelle, for example.

When I met with Michelle, she knew exactly what was causing all her anxiety and stress about her legal divorce. She told me her husband was deeply religious would never agree to a divorce. Michelle told me how she felt trapped and defeated, but finally decided she needed to talk to someone about it. When I informed her that, in California, you don't need your spouse's permission to get divorced, she was stunned, frustrated, and bewildered. Where had her belief come from? We set about answering that question by examining her life experiences. In the end, the answer was simple: television. She couldn't remember exactly when or on what show, but it was about a woman whose husband wouldn't give her a divorce who was forced to stay married. For whatever reason, it stayed with her. It stayed with her so long that it became something she believed without question.

The facts of Michelle's case are very specific, but illustrate how life experience can and does play a role in your legal divorce. It may have only a small part to play or it could have a significant impact, like with Michelle, who stayed married longer than she wanted. Either way, your beliefs are worth examining. Simply questioning why you believe something is the first step.

So, What Is Helpful Research?

Don't worry. The information your need is out there, you just need to know how to look for it. The sources of helpful information fall into three categories.

- **Type 1:** Verified and not trying to make money off you
- **Type 2:** Verified and trying to make money off you
- **Type 3:** Maybe verified and maybe trying to make money off you

Here's a quick breakdown of our terms.

Verified source. A resource is *verified* when you can confirm it is legitimate, reliable, and appropriate. Resources that pass this test include state and county courts, state bar associations, licensed attorneys, certain legal clinics, law libraries, and nonprofit legal aid organizations.

Not trying to make money off you. This means, well, that it's *free*. There are no financial strings attached. The information is available at no cost.

Type 1 Resources: Verified and Not Trying to Make Money of You

Look for websites that are 1) *verified* and 2) *not trying to make money off you*. That's it. If a resource passes this two-part test, you're good to go. By starting here, you don't have to question the authenticity or accuracy of the information. This will help you to lay a strong foundation for your case from the beginning.

Here are some examples of informational resources you can trust.

Online Resources

The following websites are state and county government operated, making them available to the public at no cost

- **County Court Websites.** A straightforward internet search ("name of your county" + the word *courthouse*) should bring up the correct website. These sites offer a combination of information, self-help resources, videos, and workshops specific to your location.
- **State Judicial Websites.** All state judicial websites are listed on the National Center for State Courts website. Visit: http://www. ncsc.org/information-and-resources/browse-by-state/state-court-websites.aspx. Depending on the state, a judicial website may offer a similar selection of services as county court websites.
- **State Bar Association Websites.** The state licensing boards for attorneys, called state bar associations, often post helpful information on their websites. Similarly, local county bar associations may offer information online or be able to direct

you to free legal clinics in your area covering divorce. You can find links to all the state bar associations on the American Bar Association website. Visit: https://shop.americanbar.org/ebus/abagroups/divisionforbarservices/barassociationdirectories/statelocalbarassociations.aspx

In-Person Resources

If you want to look beyond the computer screen, there may be several resources in your area.

- **Self-help Clinics.** There are free clinics offered by courts, county bar associations, or nonprofit agencies that offer you a great opportunity to meet with a legal professional to discuss your divorce options and obtain guidance.
- **Non-profit Legal Clinics.** Free legal assistance may be available at local agencies that also give referrals to pro bono attorneys. These clinics were established to provide free information, advice, legal representation, and more. They are often referred to as Legal Aid organizations, and may provide online information and help as well. You can visit them by entering the search terms "legal aid" and "your state or county." The website address should have a ".org" at the end, signifying it's a non-profit organization.
- **Law Libraries.** See if your county has a law library and head to the family law section for self-help materials specific to the laws in your county and state.

Type 2 Resources: Verified and Trying to Make Money Off You

I learned a valuable lesson after I once sat in with Judy, age thirty-four, during her free consultation with an attorney. For the entire hour, I listened to her ask smart questions about the divorce process. The attorney was awesome. She answered each of Judy's questions, providing tons of information in a way that was clear and easy to follow. Judy left the attorney's office that day feeling empowered, like she finally had a grasp of the divorce process. I was thrilled for her. Except, a few days after the consultation, something began bothering me.

It didn't take me long to figure it out. I realized I had let Judy down. I pulled up the family law page of the county court's website and my concerns were confirmed: Eighty percent of the information Judy received at the consultation was available on the court's free website. If she had reviewed this in advance, Judy would have generated an entirely new list of questions specific to her situation that would have been perfect to ask the attorney. And sure enough, the following week, Judy came to the clinic and had a list of new questions.

Free Consultations

Many divorce attorneys and law firms will offer free consultations to discuss your case. Even though these consults are free, they fall under the category of *verified* and *trying to make money off you* because the lawyers are offering you advice with the goal of being hired. These meetings can be great. The information received is verified if you are meeting with a licensed (and hopefully experienced) family law attorney. You can look the attorney up on your state's bar website to confirm they are, in fact, licensed and have no disciplinary history because of misconduct. It is fine if they would like to make money off you. It's a very common and accepted practice to find new clients in this way.

So how does this tie in with Judy's story? My point is that you should maximize the value of the attorney consultation. Don't ask questions you can easily answer for free on the court's website. If you do this, you will be able to ask very advanced and specific questions tailored to the unique facts of your case, the answers to which are likely not available online.

Type 3 Resources: *Maybe* Verified and *Maybe* Trying to Make Money Off You

This one is tricky. There may be value here, but you need to evaluate this information differently.

Answer Websites

Some websites, like AVVO.com (an attorney rating service) and Yahoo Answers, provide opportunities for visitors to ask questions for a "legal expert" to answer. You can read through past answers given to other legal questions or ask your own questions. I would not recommend you begin your divorce research on these sites. The questions asked by others are typically very specific and the facts and law may not apply to your situation. Also, if you post your own questions, you must keep in mind that the answer may not be accurate, complete, or authored by an attorney or a qualified expert in the field.

Attorney Blogs

Attorneys often write blogs about certain divorce issues that read like advice columns. Their goal is for you to hire them, and I would recommend against starting your research with a blog because laws change frequently and these sites may not always be current. That said, you can always supplement your knowledge on these sites. Again, it is advisable to confirm that the attorney is in good standing with the state bar and you may want to research them online first.

Setting Realistic Expectations with Research

Jessica had a plan. She spent the past few nights researching divorce and was energized. She researched that a divorce takes six months to complete in California and marked that date on her calendar. Jessica envisioned the new plans she would make after that date. Her new life would start. For the first time in a long time, Jessica felt hopeful. Then I told her this was the minimum period, and explained that her divorce could take much longer. Devastated and deflated, she went home and threw the calendar away.

Before researching divorce online, make a commitment to set *realistic expectations*. I cannot emphasize this enough. Online research, even when done right, will only take you so far. The key is to understand what online research can and cannot give you. Jessica's mistake was interpreting her research to conclude with 100 percent "certainty": Six months and she would be done. In divorce, laws and rules are seldom this black and white. She conducted helpful research, but drew the wrong conclusion. Many people make this mistake. Luckily, if you set *realistic expectations* and understand that this information is just a starting point, it's totally avoidable.

Online research will give you a road map, but is not a crystal ball. Spending minutes, hours, or days on the internet will not predict exactly how your divorce will unfold. It will not tell you exactly how much financial support, property, debt, or money you will receive. *It will tell you what the law allows.* It will not be able to tell you exactly how long your divorce will take. *It will tell you the earliest date possible.* And this is extremely valuable information.

The truth is no one knows exactly how your divorce will unfold. The process is fluid and can veer in different directions depending on your spouse, the judge, the attorneys, the court's schedule, life events, finances, emotions, physical health, children, and more. Knowing this at the outset will put you at an advantage and allow you to move forward effectively.

Knowledge Is Empowering

"My husband has always said he won't give me a divorce. And even if he did agree, he says he'll ruin me. He keeps saying he knows I've cheated on him and the judge is going to take the kids from me and I won't get any financial support. I didn't cheat, but I'm terrified he'll convince the judge I did and I'll lose the kids and everything. I don't know what to do." —Julie, age forty-three, married fourteen years

There's an old saying, "Knowledge is power." In divorce, especially in the beginning, "Knowledge is *empowering*." After Julie told me this, I turned my computer screen to face her and had her read a one-page section on the Superior Court of California, County of Orange, court website (www. occourts.org) entitled "What Must I Know about Divorce in California?" Here's what she read.

Both persons do not have to agree to the divorce. One partner can't force the other to stay in the relationship. Either spouse can decide to end the marriage. The spouse who does not want to get a divorce cannot stop the process by refusing to participate in the case.

If the parties cannot reach an agreement to the divorce and all issues of the marriage or partnership, the court will make final decisions regarding how the couple will divide what they owe, divide property, determine whether one person will receive financial support from the other regarding the minor children, and make other orders on related issues.

There is a no-fault divorce law in California. There is no need to prove "fault" of one or the other spouse or partner in the deterioration of marriage or partnership from the court's point of view. The grounds for divorce in California are that there are irreconcilable differences or incurable insanity.

Note from Adam: This information is used to illustrate an example only and not meant to substitute for your own legal research, as the laws may have been updated or changed.

When Julie finished reading the last paragraph, she stared at the screen for a while and then looked at me. It was as if a fog had been lifted. California is a no-fault state and allegations that she cheated were not relevant! She now had options. *This knowledge empowered her.* Not only was Julie able to separate her husband's threats from reality, but for the first time she removed some of the mystery from her divorce that had paralyzed her for so long. Julie now had confidence, and most importantly, accurate information, with which to start realistically planning her divorce.

The Right Website Can Still Be Confusing—and That's OK!

You've found your county or state court website and are ready to research. Then frustration sets in as finding the information becomes a chore. The reality is that even *verified* court websites can be confusing. Often, in my experience, these sites are not always intuitive or easy navigate. The truth is that government or court websites are likely not going to be state of the art or user friendly. However, if I had become frustrated or walked away, I would have missed out on a ton of valuable information. Take your time and erase instant gratification from your plan. Be patient. There is a lot of legal information on these sites, not just for divorce, so you may have to hunt for it, but it's worth it.

Not all the answers were laid out neatly when I visit a county court website. Some information is easier to find. But for other answers, I had to invest some time. Look in sections entitled "family law," "divorce," "dissolution," "custody," "self-help," "frequently asked questions," "FAQs," and "forms." You can also use the SEARCH feature on the website (although this sometimes returns too many results).

Your Pre-Divorce To-Do List

Now you know what to avoid and where to go get some answers. First, go visit your local county court website (or state court website if the county court website is limited) and spend twenty minutes exploring the website. Then see if you can get explicit answers to the questions below. These are the common introductory questions many people have at the outset of divorce. The answers will provide you with a strong foundation moving forward. To find the answers, look for sections on the website entitled: "What must I know about dissolution/divorce in [name of your state]?" or another category of interest (see above).

Use the blank spaces below to record the answers you find.

- Does your state follow the law of *community property* or *equitable division* for dividing property? Include your state's definition for these terms below.

- Do I need to prove "fault" in my state (in other words, does it matter if someone cheated)?

- Does the petitioner's spouse need to agree?

- How long will it take for my divorce to be final?

- What forms do I need to file to start the process?

- Where do I file them?

- How much does it cost to file for divorce?

- What happens after I file?

- How do I tell my husband?

- How do I get orders for support, custody, visitation, and so on?

CHAPTER 11

Gathering Your Personal Information

ADAM

It's time for step 2 of "making lasagna." Now that you have done your research, you know the recipe for divorce in your state. That means it's time to move on to gathering the "ingredients" (your personal information), which requires a different approach. To identify the correct recipe, we focused our discussion on outside sources of information (websites, legal clinics, and the like). To collect the ingredients, you will need to shift your focus inward. The recipe calls for specific ingredients, and the quicker you gather them, the better.

The importance of gathering personal information shines brightest when I am participating in pro bono legal clinics. Inevitably, there will be at least one person in attendance who has no idea about the detail of her own or her spouse's finances, property, debt, income, and so forth. Right away, I know this session will be limited to explanations of the law, but not how it applies to her specific circumstances. It is great to know how spousal support works, but most women really want to know the amount they could receive or will have to pay! If the woman had collected pay stubs and tax returns ahead of the legal clinic, then the lawyer possibly might be able to help her to determine the amount of spousal support she is entitled to.

The belief that anyone could determine the amount of spousal support without collecting financial information falls into the *unrealistic expectations* category. That's like trying to make lasagna without any ingredients. It just doesn't work.

Recipes and ingredients always work together. In reality, you may start collecting ingredients before the reading the recipe, rather than vice versa. And sometimes, these two steps are completed simultaneously. My advice is not to get hung up the order of the steps; the important part is accomplishing them.

What's the difference between taking the step of gathering information or skipping it? Here are how these scenarios could play out for a woman named Brittany, age twenty-nine, who has been married for eight years.

Brittany takes the time to look at her car payment, bills, rent, and expenses and concludes she needs $3,500 per month to live on. If she gets a smaller apartment, she can get that down to $3,200. She decides to talk to an attorney, who tells her she entitled to spousal and child support of $2,600 per month. **Reaction:** Brittany knows how much she needs to make up the difference ($600) and starts looking for part-time work to make up the difference so she can go ahead confidently with her divorce.	Brittany has no idea what her monthly expenses are. Her husband handles all the bills and she doesn't want to think about it. He tells her that his salary won't pay for two households, so good luck leaving him. She decides to talk to an attorney, who tells her she entitled to spousal and child support of $2,600 per month. **Reaction:** Brittany has no idea if this is enough, but she keeps thinking about how her husband says it's not enough. Frustrated and defeated, she decides to avoid it all and stays married.

The good news is that identifying what information you need is straightforward. The same laws and requirements apply to both people in a divorce, to your husband and to you. Put another way, if everyone in your state must follow the same recipe for their divorces, then everyone must collect the same list of ingredients. There is no mystery here.

Holding this fact in mind, you should pursue the following two *realistic goals.*

Goal #1: Identify What Should Be on Your "Shopping List"

Why do this? Before anything can be divided, you'll first need a complete and current list of all your property and debts. Before any support can be ordered, you'll need to know specific information like both spouses' incomes. Luckily, your state's divorce forms are perfect for this step. *These forms literally are the ingredient list.*

While the names of the forms you need will vary depending on where you live, they are commonly referred to as a *financial statement*, a *statement of assets and debts*, a *schedule of assets and debts*, a *property declaration*, an *income and expense declaration*, or something similar. These forms itemize EXACTLY what you need to produce for your divorce.

As discussed in Chapter 10, these financial forms are available online from your county or state court website. And you may be able to pick up hard copies at your local courthouse, a self-help center, a nonprofit legal aid organization, or the office of an attorney. You may also find additional forms designed to help get you ready to complete these forms.

Regardless of the actual forms you use, the information requested typically breaks down into two types: *Assets and Debts* and *Income and Expenses.* This is a helpful way to think about categorizing your information. Below is an example of a worksheet demonstrating what is typically requested. This will get you thinking about what you need to gather, the information you have at your fingertips and create questions about what else might be out there.

Sample Worksheet for Assets and Debts

Description	Separate Property	Date Acquired	Fair Market Value	Amount of money owed (debt, encumbrance, etc.)
1. Real Estate				
2. Household furnishings, furniture, appliances, etc.				
3. Jewelry, Antiques, Art, Collections, etc.				
4. Vehicles, Boats, etc.				
5. Savings Accounts (list account number and balance)				
6. Checking Accounts (list account number and balance)				

7. Credit Union and other Bank Accounts (list account number and balance)				
8. Cash				
9. Tax Refunds				
10. Life Insurance with cash surrender or loan value				
11. Stocks, Bonds, etc.				
12. Retirement & Pensions				
13: Profit Sharing, Annuities, IRAs, Deferred Compensation				

14. Accounts receivable and other unsecured notes				
15. Partnerships and Other Business Interests:				
16. Other Assets				
Total Assets			$_____	$_____

For your income and expenses, rather than filling in my sample worksheet, it's time to start getting familiar with your real forms. Here are your marching orders: Visit your local county court website, search for a form that covers income and expenses, and then do your best to fill it out.

Filling out the forms should create questions—that's normal. Getting the questions answered correctly utilizing the tools covered in the legal research chapters is how you can move forward in the right way.

Goal #2: Gather the Ingredients on Your "Shopping List"

Some items of information you need to fill out the financial forms will be easier to gather than others. Since everyone's situation is different, there isn't one specific way to proceed, so long as you gather everything in the end. Feel free to start with the first item on your list and work through the entire list or to move through it at random. Another suggestion is the following three-step approach.

Step 1: Easy Information. Start data collection with the easier items, which are the items that you can input off the top of your head. For example:

Identifying Assets

- *Cash.* List your bank accounts—checking and savings, shared and individual—and where these accounts are located and the account numbers.
- *Real estate.* List the address of your home and any other real estate owned.
- *Vehicle(s).* List the year, make, and model. Include cars, motorcycles, RVs, boats, and so forth.
- *Household items.* Furniture, appliances, art, and décor.

Step 2: Modest Effort. Then move on to the items may not be at your fingertips, but are attainable with a little effort. Continuing with the examples from above:

Determining Asset Values

- *Cash.* What are the balances of the checking and savings accounts?
- *Real Estate Value.* Free websites like Zillow or others will provide a ballpark value if you own your home or other real estate. An appraisal will ultimately be necessary, but this will give you a starting point.

Vehicle Value. Again, free websites like Kelly Blue Book will provide you with a value.

Identifying Debts

- *Mortgage.* List the remaining balance and the name and location of the lender, plus the account number.

- *Car loan.* List the balance on your car loan and the name and location of the lender.
- *Credit cards.* List the balances on your credit cards—and the name and contact information for the company that holds them, as well as the account numbers.

Step 3: Diligent Effort. Finally, there will be items on your list that aren't available . . . yet. These ingredients are "out of stock at the grocery store." This doesn't mean you won't get them eventually, but you may have to "special order" them. Maybe you are missing a bank statement for a checking account and you don't have access at the beginning. Or maybe there is a debt you don't know about yet, like a credit card your husband carries in his wallet.

This step may trigger a bunch of stress-inducing questions like: "What if I can't find everything? What if my husband hides information from me or cheats?" My suggestion here, if you're contemplating such ideas, is to slow it down and remember you cannot *control* what any other person says or does. Plus, in divorce, there are options to request this information.

Tip: This would be a great question to answer through legal research.

In general, your husband and/or his lawyer may produce the information you need voluntarily, in response to the court's request, or turn it over based on a formal request made by you or your attorney. In whatever way it happens, at this preliminary stage, it isn't *realistic* to believe you can gather every single piece of information required immediately.

This is a starting point. Just fill out your financial forms to the best of your ability. You can't be expected to get everything, so don't put that pressure on yourself. This should be your *realistic goal.*

A Few More Things to Think About During this Process

First, don't assume any numbers without verifying them. I have had clients who were so proud that they had no credit card debt or that they didn't live paycheck to paycheck, and who believed they were growing their savings or investments every month, only to find out the opposite was true. Moving forward with divorce based on *assumed* financial information is risky. Take the time to obtain accurate and verified information.

Also, be safe! Do not put yourself in an uncomfortable, unsafe, or illegal position in order to gather the information you need.

In the end, the information-gathering process should give you a partial snapshot of your finances, property, debts, and so on. Remember, this is a snapshot of how things stand today. The divorce process likely will take some time, therefore some of this information will need to be updated periodically because it may change. This is totally normal. But you have to start somewhere. Everyone does!

Unexpected benefits you can experience when collecting your information are:

- **Confidence.** You will be able to speak knowledgably and confidently about your case. Remember, *informed decision-making* is impossible without the information. This process will put you on the path to making informed decisions and moving forward.
- **Evening the playing field!** This information will help to keep the "playing field" even. Let's say you want to discuss spousal support, but don't have your husband's most recent paystubs or tax return. Obviously, you cannot engage in a productive or fair dialogue if he possesses this information and you do not. In fact, it puts you at an immediate legal disadvantage. You eliminate this disadvantage, and even the playing field, when you also possess the information.
- **Avoid delays.** Your ability to move forward could stall if you don't possess the necessary information. This creates an inability to make an informed decision and/or plan for your future. Gathering this information will allow you to push past or entirely prevent these sorts of delays.
- **Eliminating uncertainty.** Not having information causes uncertainty about your case, which can lead to anxiety and stress that might compromise your emotional health.
- **Empowerment.** It's not just beneficial to your legal divorce to have this information, knowledge itself is *empowering.*

ADAM

Chapter 12
Evaluating Your Legal Options

Yes! Finally! We've reached the last stage of preparation for your meal. You have the recipe you want to follow and you have gathered the ingredients. Now you just need to decide who will have a seat at the dinner table. Will it just be you and your husband? Are attorneys invited too? Or will a mediator be joining you? It's time to "set the table."

This chapter will cover different options for completing your divorce, including the decision to invite (or not invite) legal professionals to be involved. The goal here is simple: Understand your options so you can make an *informed decision.* Your main options include litigation, mediation, and negotiation. I'll also go over a few others below.

Keep in mind, there is no one right way to get a divorce. In fact, when all is said and done, you may end up utilizing all three options.

Litigation

This is the divorce option everyone seems to recognize. It's where you and your spouse cannot agree, you oppose each other in a court of law and let the judge decide. This is a contested approach to divorce, where issues you cannot agree on, like property division, child support, spousal support, and custody arrangements are argued (litigated) before a judge.

If you were setting an actual dining table, your place would be at one end of the table, as far away as possible from your husband's place. And if one or both of you retained an attorney, the table would include a place setting for a lawyer next to you and another for a lawyer next to your husband.

Benefits to litigation. When two people cannot agree, there needs to be an option that allows them to move forward and finalize their divorce. Litigation is that option. Without it, parties in disagreement would be stuck in limbo and unable to divorce, until they either agreed or reconciled. Can you imagine that? Litigation is how you move your divorce toward the finish line, whether your husband wants to or not. You have a neutral third party, the judge, listen to both sides and make a decision.

Downside to litigation. I'm not going to sugarcoat it, litigation can be rough. It can be expensive if you hire an attorney. And it can be a long process because the courts must accommodate a lot of people. Emotionally, it is very taxing. Courtrooms, judges, and attorneys can be intimidating and frustrating. Placing the decision-making power for your divorce in the judge's hands can be anxiety inducing because you are losing *control* of making decisions about your case. It is important to know these challenges in advance, because if litigation is your only option, you can set *realistic expectations* about the process.

If you elect to litigate your divorce, you are not alone. Millions of people litigate their divorces and you can too.

Mediation

This is where you both try to agree, with help. You and your husband agree to work with a mediator to assist you in negotiating the terms of the divorce. Through mediation, parties are attempting to avoid litigation and opposing each other in contested court proceedings. Mediators are neutral and are on neither person's side. They typically have a background in family law to help reach a resolution that is consistent with the law. They are often attorneys themselves.

Mediation isn't an option for everyone. Hiring a mediator costs money and both parties must agree to mediate the divorce.

When setting the table, you'll seat each spouse on opposite ends of the dining table, with the mediator sitting exactly in the middle between them. Or if you are in a good place with your soon-to-be-ex, each party could be seated on either side of the mediator in the middle of the table.

Benefits to mediation. This is a low-conflict and collaborative option, which allows you to avoid the downside of litigation (listed above) while saving time and money. It is also less emotionally taxing and keeps you out of clashes at court. By avoiding litigation, parties can pursue a collaborative result.

Downside to mediation. Mediation is voluntary. Since it is not a binding process, either party can walk away at any time. You may spend time and money on this process for a while, only to realize it's not right for you. Or your husband may walk away from it for some reason. For example, he may be all for mediation until he hears something he doesn't like or doesn't agree with, or he doesn't get along with the mediator. Maybe he thinks it's *unfair* (even if it's the law). In any event, he may exit the mediation process—as may you. You (or the mediator) cannot *control* the other party in this regard.

Informal Negotiation (You Both Agree)

Yes, negotiation is an option. This is the one where you both work towards a resolution of your marriage without help—no mediator, just two consenting adults who want to amicably work out the details of their divorce, such as dividing the property, setting a custody schedule for the kids, setting a dollar-figure for monthly child support payments, and more. When I meet with clients for the first time, they often haven't even considered this option, falsely assuming they have to jump straight into litigation. Everyone contemplating divorce should at least consider this option before ruling it out.

For negotiation to work, you must be informed. *Informed decision-making* is at the center of this option if you are going it alone. You don't want to agree to anything without knowing your rights. You can always consult with an attorney during the process, however. Or you can take your negotiated agreement to an attorney afterwards to verify that it is consistent with the law. You may choose to educate yourself via legal research. Ultimately, a combination of all three of these things might happen or it could be something completely different. There's no right way to handle a negotiation, but it is critical that you are *informed*.

I want you to consider one more thing when it comes to this option. Very often, parties will agree to things informally, such as a visitation schedule or support, without making it a court order. People do this all the time and it works fine—that is until it doesn't. Let's say you go to pick up your child from your ex-husband, as you agreed, and he refuses to let your child go with you. What would you do? You can't *control* the other parent and forcibly make him return your child. You also wouldn't have a court order that you could rely upon, which is what the police will likely ask for if you call them.

The point I'm making is that informal agreements, while often very convenient and useful when things are friendly, are probably not enforceable like a court order would be. I'm not saying you should never utilize an informal agreement, but you should be informed so you can set realistic expectations in the event they are not followed.

To set the table for an amicable negotiation, seat both parties next to one another.

Benefits to negotiation. Like mediation, negotiation can be a low-conflict option. In fact, the benefits are like those of mediation (avoiding litigation, keeping things collaborative, and so on), with the added benefit that you are saving on the cost of hiring a mediator.

Downside to negotiation. Again, like mediation, negotiation is voluntary. But you must be sure to get informed, because you will not have the guidance of a mediator trained in family law. Otherwise you risk agreeing to something that is not in your best interests. Also, without a third party present, there is a risk that the process can become unpleasant (argumentative, intimidating, unproductive) without someone there to keep the peace.

A Blended Approach

Sometimes what begins as litigation turns into mediation. Sometimes when trying to negotiate, a woman ends up needing to litigate her divorce agreement in court. This process is fluid and you are not locked into a particular option.

For example, two parties may have lawyers, cannot agree and go to court for a hearing before the judge. Then, in the hallway before the hearing, the attorneys start talking. They in turn talk to their clients about negotiating a potential resolution. They go back and forth for a while, and in the end, they come to an agreement. Judges appreciate it when parties can work things out because it likely takes something off their already very busy plate. If a change like this does happen, you won't be caught off guard because you set realistic expectations about the process from the get-go. You may set the table one way, but rearrange everything before it is over.

CHAPTER 13

Spending Money
on Divorce

ADAM

Most of us would love to hire the best divorce attorney in town, have the attorney handle everything, and get the best result humanly possible. Simple, right? This is an attractive option, *if* you have the financial resources, which many people don't. In fact, my experience is that most cannot afford an attorney at all. Even so, when you are emotionally drained and intimidated by the divorce process, the thought of hiring an attorney starts to look *really good* even when it's not in the budget. If this happens, alarm bells should start ringing! I've witnessed many women struggle with this decision and made two observations: 1) the lure of hiring an attorney is strong before and during divorce, and 2) impulsively acting upon this urge has pushed many women into financial trouble.

Clients often recount some version of the same story to me. They are now seeking free legal assistance because they spent their remaining savings (or went into debt) to hire an attorney they can no longer afford. They hired the attorney without thinking it all the way through. It was entirely (or partially) an emotional or compulsive decision. When the money ran out, they were on their own. When they reflect on the services received and the money spent, frustration sets in. They wish they had done things differently.

How does this happen? The reasons vary. For example:

- They felt like it was something they were supposed to do.
- Their friends or family members hired divorce attorneys.
- Someone told them they had to do it.
- Some panicked when their spouse hired one.
- They were overwhelmed.

Whatever the reason, they often regret not weighing their options before taking this expensive step. Sound familiar? It should. They didn't make an *informed decision.*

Here's something to keep in mind when taking stock of your ability to spend money on your divorce. Most people cannot afford to hire an attorney to represent them. For example, in California, 67 percent of parties are self-represented (without an attorney) when the divorce is filed, and this number rises to 80 percent by the time the divorce is finalized.[1] That is a crazy high number of people getting divorced without attorneys! If you fall into this category, take a breath and remind yourself that you are not alone and you have options.

This chapter is going to focus on the considerations you should consider before spending money on legal assistance. Your *realistic goals* are to ensure 1) this decision is an *informed* one, and 2) makes sense based on your financial situation, rather than on your emotions or what others say or do. No matter what you can afford (even if it's $0), there are options.

As a starting point, consider what kind of divorce assistance you can afford, if any. This is a critically important question to ask and answer before you deplete your funds, take on debt, or both.

Step 1: What Can You Afford?

Hiring an attorney should not be an impulse buy! Even though it usually is asked a lot later, your first question should always be: What can I afford?

---

[1] "California Statewide Action Plan for Self-Represented Litigants," California Judicial Council Task Force on Self-Represented Litigants (2004).

When you think about it, the process of hiring an attorney is like budgeting for any big purchase. For example, let's say Amanda is buying a car. She walks into the car dealership and the salesperson tells her that her dream car is going to cost $1,000 down and $199 per month for thirty-six months. If Amanda has no idea what she can afford, she may make an emotional decision and drive off the lot in a new car she can't afford to keep, putting her in financial jeopardy and causing her stress and anxiety later.

On the other hand, if she knows her budget in advance, Amanda can confidently decide to agree, negotiate, or move on when the dealer tells her the price. Amanda takes control of the process. Emotion may play into her decision (she loves convertibles), but she isn't deciding blindly. In fact, Amanda may still drive off the lot in a car she can't easily afford, but the decision will be informed and there won't be any surprises down the road.

This example illustrates another important point. You may very well decide that hiring an attorney, even if it means going into debt, is right for you. This chapter is not about a particular decision in this area being right or wrong. It's about the process you utilize to arrive at that conclusion. Be thoughtful in the decision-making process so you can own the decision, whatever it may be, and be accountable to yourself.

Review your finances: cash on hand, credit card balances, anticipated income, routine monthly charges (rent, mortgage, utilities, estimated taxes), and savings. With that information, here are some questions to ask yourself:

- If you can't afford a lump sum, what can you afford to pay monthly? (Maybe the attorney takes payment plans.)
- If you plan to borrow money, how much can you borrow? How will it need to be repaid?
- How much does it cost to file for divorce in your county, and do you qualify for a fee waiver? (Look up this information on your court's website.)

Two questions to ask an attorney (pro bono or otherwise) are:

- Can you use money from your joint bank accounts or use a joint credit card to hire an attorney?
- Can you ask the court to order your spouse to pay your attorney's fees?

No matter the answers you come up with, you will gain clarity about your options after moving through this process. Reducing uncertainty is key. Believe me, this is better than being in a constant state of anxiety about your legal bills.

Step 2: Based on What You Can Afford, What's the Plan?

Your legal budget will bring your options into focus. Some cost money and some don't. So, which approach is right for you?

Attorney representation. Unfortunately, there is no easy way to find out how much this will cost in the end. Attorneys charge different amounts and the cost of each case is different. You will have to meet with an attorney to get an idea of the exact cost. Ask if they will accept a flat fee for the entire divorce.

Mediation. If you choose to hire a mediator, the same rule about hiring an attorney applies here too. Rates vary and you will need to get this information from the mediator.

Limited scope representation. Did you know that some attorneys can be hired for parts of a divorce? Attorneys that offer limited scope representation or *unbundled* legal services allow for clients to hire them for specific tasks like filing or reviewing paperwork, consultations, or representation at a hearing. Again, you will need to discuss cost and rates with the attorney.

Do-it-yourself (DIY) divorce. Depending on what is available in your area, a variety of no-cost legal resources are available to assist with divorce. See Chapter 10 for ideas.

A blended approach. No decision is written in stone. For a variety of reasons, you may choose to start with one plan and then change to something else. Your budget may change. You may meet with an amazing attorney and reevaluate the decision not to go into debt. You may come into some money or get a higher-paying job and reconsider your options.

If your calculations in Step 1 have led to the realization that you can spend little to no money on legal assistance, you now have some specific options to consider.

- Do you pursue pro bono legal assistance?
- Do you pursue the DIY divorce option?
- Can your spouse pay for your legal fees?
- Can you (and do you want to) borrow money to pay for legal assistance?

Every answer and calculation may lead to more questions and calculations, but going through this process *before* you start a divorce is necessary. It means you are forming a plan on how to move through your divorce should you decide to move forward. Remember, if you decide to stay married for the time being, you can always revisit the subject later.

ADAM

CHAPTER 14

How Is a Divorce Accomplished?

As has hopefully become clear by now, a primary goal of this book is to empower you with the tools and resources to educate yourself on the fundamentals of divorce in your state. With that said, understanding how the overall divorce process works can be something of a mystery. In this chapter, I share a bird's eye view of a generic divorce process from beginning to end. We often focus so much on the details, I find it's helpful to take a step back and view the whole journey. Keep in mind that this is a general overview, inspired in part by California, and the rules and laws of your state will be unique. You will need to verify them. Nevertheless, this framework should hopefully provide a "big picture" from which you can then fill in the details.

Completing the forms. The person initiating the divorce (usually called the *petitioner* or *plaintiff*) acquires and completes all the required forms she will need. This may include special local forms specific to the county in which she resides. Remember, forms may be found on online, at the courthouse, legal aid non-profits or via the other resources we have covered.

Filing the completed forms. *Filing* means taking the forms to the courthouse and turning them in to a court clerk. The clerk will review the forms and use them to create a file that initiates a case with the court. The case will be assigned a unique case number. Stamped copies are returned to the person who filed them. Find out in advance how many copies you'll need to bring to court.

Officially notifying the other party. After the court case is filed, the other party has a right to be notified. This means someone (a third party who is not the petitioner) must give (typically called *serving*) the other party copies of the court forms. That person then completes a form certifying that the forms were *served* and that form is then filed with the court.

The other party (called the **respondent** *or* **defendant)** *has a decision to make.* Once served, the respondent typically has a specified amount of time to respond. If he chooses not to respond, then you will need to determine your state's requirements to proceed without his participation. Or, the respondent may choose to fill out a response (by obtaining the correct response forms), file them with the court clerk and have the petitioner served with those forms.

Exchanging information. This is where each state will have very specific requirements. Generally speaking, both parties will then need to exchange financial forms and documents (often with proof) that show what they own and owe, along with their incomes and expenses. This process provides a rough framework for what will need to be divided and how much support (if any) will be paid.

Completing the divorce. In the end, for a couple to be officially divorced, a judge must approve and sign off on what is typically called a *judgment.* The judgment will include all the specific details of the divorce—everything ordered by the judge and/or agreed upon by the parties. Who gets what, how much support is to be paid, child visitation schedules and more are contained in the judgment. It is the official order of the court and can be relied upon by either party to enforce the terms of the divorce.

Now, how the parties arrive at the final judgment can vary greatly. For example, if a wife and husband can come to an agreement about all their issues (like through negotiation or mediation), they may not have to appear before a judge or go to court at all. On the other hand, if they cannot agree on everything (or anything!), they will have to pursue litigation and go before a judge (typically called a 'trial') to handle any outstanding issues.

Timing . . . and temporary orders. Even if the parties agree and file everything as quickly as possible, there is usually a minimum amount of time that must pass before the divorce can be final. In California, the minimum amount of time is six months, starting from the time the case is filed and the respondent is served with the forms. A very common question typically arises here: What if I can't wait six months for certain orders like financial support and custody? Never fear, there are options. Parties may agree to temporary orders before the divorce is finalized or, if they can't agree, go before a judge to litigate specific issues (typically called a *hearing*, which is like a mini-trial) that become temporary orders of the court until the judgment is finalized.

PART THREE

Legal Issues During Divorce

Up to this point, we have covered the tools to research and, if you so choose, proceed with the divorce process. In Chapter 14, we concluded with an overview of that process, which shows us that ending up in court, while not always a certainty (Dr. Jill avoided it, for example), is a distinct possibility. It may be solely to file paperwork, for a trial on all the issues in your divorce or something in between. And I want you to be ready. First, we will begin with a primer on legal threats, and how to address them, as these can influence your decision-making in and outside of the courthouse. Thereafter, we devote significant attention to navigating around the challenges of the courthouse. Whatever path you follow, I cannot overstate the importance of understanding the courthouse environment before you step foot inside.

For most people, a courthouse is a foreign, intimidating, and unpleasant place. Moving forward, I want you to think of your journey to the courtroom as you would an obstacle course. The idea of an obstacle course began to form after I had witnessed countless clients being tripped up by the same obstacles at court, which made a challenging day for them that much harder. These obstacles are not obvious and are not listed on a sign at any courthouse. Yet they stand between you and your ability to be successful.

The course is completed in three stages, each covered in its own chapter.

- **Stage 1:** From your bedroom to the courthouse entrance.
- **Stage 2:** From the courthouse entrance to the door of your courtroom.
- **Stage 3:** Inside the courtroom.

The last two chapters of Part Three are devoted to courtroom behavior and principles of organization, areas that are often overlooked but can be absolute game changers in your divorce journey.

ADAM

CHAPTER 15

Legal Threats and How to Respond to Them

Throughout divorce, but particularly in the beginning of a breakup, women are susceptible to legal threats from the men they are divorcing. They often believe the assertions their husband makes about the law, even though he's not an expert or bears them malice. If your goal is to advantage yourself in divorce, then legal threats are your enemy. If you don't address threats head on, they will not go away.

Legal Threats: The Great Paralyzer

The root of an *unrealistic expectation* or an *uninformed decision* often is an actual or perceived legal threat made by a husband. A legal threat is a "statement that something bad will happen regarding your divorce if you do not do what the other person wants." Legal threats are utilized to prevent you from filing for divorce, make you not ask questions so you will remain ignorant of your legal rights, and cause you to believe life will be worse if you take an action that your husband doesn't want you to take, such as requesting financial support.

This is what I've heard from women dealing with legal threats.

"I haven't left because he said the courts would give him custody if we got divorced since he makes all the money in our household."

"If I file for financial support, he said he'll quit his job and I'll have to pay him support."

"I don't know what he makes and he pays all the bills. He says we can barely afford one household and if we got divorced the children will suffer."

"He says if I divorce him he'll tell our family and friends that I cheated on him."

These are examples of *direct legal threats,* intended to prevent a woman from taking legal action or moving forward. Sound familiar?

Sometimes legal threats are direct, and in other instances, they are subtle and harder to identify. This second type of threat is called an *indirect legal threat.* Let's use my meeting with Sarah to demonstrate.

During our first meeting, Sarah was behaving like a legal threat was in play. Yet, when she would think about it, she couldn't think of a single time a threat was made. This was a signal to me to encourage her to think *critically* and see if an *indirect* legal threat was responsible that was delivered in a roundabout way. In this example, we finally figured it out when Sarah mentioned that her close friend was also going through a divorce (the wife had filed for divorce). Every time it came up, Sarah's husband would talk about how the wife in the other couple's marriage would get destroyed in court and how much worse off she would be, because her husband was the breadwinner. Or he would say that Sarah's friend was being selfish, thinking only of herself and not the children.

From Sarah's point of view, her husband might as well have been saying these things directly about her because his remarks had the same effect: Sarah was terrified to do anything due to painful expectations. Her fears prevented her from even bothering to research divorce.

Legal threats are particularly effective at planting seeds of doubt. Plant enough of them and you may find yourself paralyzed and unable to move forward.

By the way, I want to be clear about something: I am not demonizing someone because they made a legal threat. Divorce is challenging and things are often said in the heat of the moment, out of desperation and frustration, or for countless other reasons. Some legal threats are calculated, some are not. Threats may be made intentionally or unintentionally. However, the *intent* behind the legal threat isn't the issue in this chapter. It is the effect of the legal threat that we are worried about.

So how can you overcome a legal threat?

Step 1: Recognize the nature of the legal threat. This is critical. When you break them down, legal threats may be nothing more than a smokescreen. With this understanding, you can move on to the next step.

Step 2: Verify the accuracy of the threat and then make an informed decision. It is important to challenge the accuracy of any threat. Having assessed a threat, you will be empowered to overcome it.

Step 1: Recognizing and Understanding Legal Threats

Understanding a legal threat and why they are so common is straightforward. When you understand them, you can take action. There are just four characteristics of legal threats that you need to know:

Legal threats require almost zero effort. How much effort is required to say a few words in a few seconds? The answer: minimal effort. Other reasonable answers include: barely any, marginal, negligible, nominal, and insignificant. Making a threat usually is slightly easier than ordering a cup of coffee at Starbucks. You get my point. It's not hard. In fact, it's so easy that people are sometimes unaware they are making threats at all.

Legal threats are incredibly effective. For a few seconds of effort, the payoff is huge. People will remain in a marriage for months or years based on a single legal threat. Or maybe you've heard a series of threats, as part of an ongoing dialogue that you've been having with your husband for years. The threat may be altering your course of action or plan. It is amazing how hypothetical statements about what someone is going to do, if a divorce happens, can influence the other person. Maybe your husband is just venting. Or maybe his statements are designed to intimidate you. Either way, if you remain uninformed, the impact will fall somewhere between making you uncomfortable and paralyzing you from acting to improve your situation. Neither outcome is acceptable.

Legal threats are low-risk/high-reward actions. Just as the effort required to make a legal threat is minimal, the risk to the person making the threat is also minimal. When you think about it, what is the risk involved? Take the following threat, for example: "If you file for divorce, the court will give me all our savings." There is no risk to your ex in telling you this. If you ignore him and move forward, nothing changes. No downside to him. You do what you were going to do anyway.

Your ex has wasted a few seconds of his time. No big deal, right? Well, it could be a big deal to you. The upside of the threat is that it makes you change your plan. Maybe you hesitate for a week or start to question yourself. During that time, he could be moving funds around in your bank accounts. Or maybe you stay in the marriage for months and question everything. The point is that the person making the legal threat really has nothing to lose and potentially a lot to gain. It costs him nothing, but can cost you something or even everything.

Legal threats are often hollow. There are two very big reasons why legal threats are often hollow. First, most legal threats have no basis in reality. You must ask yourself, is what I'm hearing even consistent with the law? Does the person know what he is talking about? Has he spoken to an attorney or done the research or is he making this stuff up? Posturing and make-believe are particularly common in the early phases of a breakup. Clients of mine have relayed some wildly inaccurate legal threats to me over the years. You should know that legal outcomes are complex and these types of threats often oversimplify divorce outcomes to a ridiculous degree.

Second, threatening to do something is extremely easy, whereas following through and acting upon a threat is not. It requires effort, money, time, and conviction to follow through on a threatened course of action.

Step 2: Overcoming Legal Threats

Uninformed decisions and legal threats often go hand in hand. Doing or not doing something based on an unverified legal threat is an *uninformed decision*. You need to identify and verify the details in a threat so you can transition to an informed decision.

Example: Carla came to me to discuss how to get out of her marriage because she was stuck and didn't know what to do to get started. She had talked to her husband about separating six months earlier, and he threatened that he would quit his job if she filed for divorce. He also told her the court would make her get a job and pay him support since he had worked and supported her and the kids for the previous fifteen years. Carla had been a stay-at-home mom who hadn't worked in over fifteen years. Because these consequences were upsetting ideas, she hadn't done anything since that initial conversation. After she finished speaking with me, we went to work overcoming her husband's legal threats.

First: Identify the threats. In Carla's example, there were several. These included:

Direct Threats

- He would quit his job if she filed for divorce.
- She would have to get a job because he quit, even though she hadn't worked in fifteen years, and because he supported the family during that time.
- She would have to pay him spousal support while he didn't work.

Indirect Threats

- The kids would suffer because she would likely not earn as much.
- She would not see her kids as much because she would have to get a job.

Second: Verify the threats. Do not take any threat at face value. Instead, take action to verify if any of what is being threatened is true. Go back to Chapter 13 to learn research techniques to complete this step. Empower yourself. In our example, Carla researched these issues on her court's website and spoke to an attorney at a legal clinic and came to the following conclusions.

Direct Threats

- Would he quit his job? After thinking critically about it and discussing it with the attorney, Carla considered this very unlikely: He had been at his company for fifteen years, had seniority, made a good income, all his friends were there, and he still would need to work for several years to be eligible for his pension and full retirement benefits. Plus, the attorney pointed out that the law in her state did not look favorably on someone quitting his or her job to avoid paying spousal or child support.
- Would she have to get a job because he quit his and make enough to support him and the kids, even though she hadn't worked in fifteen years? She learned this was also unlikely based on her work experience, her role as primary caretaker of the children and what the attorney told her about him quitting to avoid paying support. Now, she may choose to or need to get job at some point, but it wouldn't be under the one-sided circumstances described in this threat.

Indirect Threats

- Would her kids suffer because she would likely not earn as much as her husband? Since she considered the direct threats to be unlikely, she could dismiss this indirect threat as well.
- Would she be unable to see her kids as much because she would have to get a job? Same as above.

Remember, the facts and law in Carla's hypothetical case are for illustration purposes only and aren't meant as legal advice for your situation. The law in your state may be different and your facts certainly are unique, meaning you should follow the same steps to verify a threat (research, consulting with an attorney, and so on) as Carla did.

Third: Make an informed decision. Based on the results from the second step, you can proceed on a course of action that is consistent with the law and your circumstances. In other words, you can make an *informed decision.* In Carla's case, she relied on the information she gathered information to move forward with filing for divorce despite her husband's legal threats. In a year, would she look back on this decision as being 100 percent correct? Maybe. Maybe not. She made the best decision she could, using the information available.

Remember that nobody can see into the future and your decisions may not always be perfect, but they should be informed—that is the best anyone can do. You are successful by simply refusing to take a legal threat at face value. Don't be afraid to act: Identify, verify, and make an informed decision.

Top 10 Most-Heard Predivorce Legal Threats

- I'll fight you on everything.
- You won't get a dime.
- I'm going to hire the best lawyer.
- I'll quit my job.
- The judge will make you get a job.
- I'm taking the kids.
- This will destroy the kids.
- We can't afford it.
- I won't give you a divorce.
- I'll tell everyone you cheated on me.

ADAM

CHAPTER 16

Divorce Obstacle Course Stage 1: Navigating from Your Bedroom to the Courthouse

Whether you have been to the courthouse countless times or it's your first visit, there are a variety of strategies you can deploy to avoid or address the obstacles that pop up between your bedroom and the courtroom.

If you have an attorney or plan to hire one, you may be wondering if you should be concerned with knowing what to expect in court beforehand. The answer is yes. You can have the best plan or attorney going into court and still be thrown off by something unexpected.

Of course, you can't prepare for everything. However, there are a lot of circumstances that occur regularly at court but are unknown to the average person. I want them to be known to you. The less you are caught off guard, the more capable you will be to execute your plan at court. If you have an attorney, knowing the lay of the land will make you a better client. If you are self-represented, you will be a better advocate for yourself.

From Your Bedroom to the Courthouse Entrance

Your journey of navigating your court proceedings successfully begins at home.

Obstacle 1: Hunger. Yes, I realize I may sound like a nagging grandparent with this one. Believe me. I get it: You're stressed and the thought of eating makes you sick. Lack of an appetite on the morning of court is extremely common. Just as common, however, is watching people who don't eat crash, lose focus, become irritable, or are generally less able to deal with adversity once they're in court. No food plus a stressful day at court is a terrible combination. Time can move very slowly at court and delays are common.

Solution 1: Eat something. Try and eat something in the morning. Anything. If you simply can't do it, at least bring a protein bar or some trail mix with you. Both are portable and have enough calories to get you through. Not coincidentally, I always carry bags of trail mix and protein bars for my clients on court days. And mints. I always have mints. A breakfast of coffee with a side of stress can have some unpleasant consequences. I've seen clients fixate on having bad breath, when then should be focused on their cases.

Obstacle 2: Dehydration. Dehydration is the enemy. According to the Mayo Clinic, even mild dehydration can cause tiredness, sleepiness, headaches, dizziness, and lightheadedness. Do you want to be feeling any of these at court just because you didn't drink some water?

Solution 2: Drink something. Do yourself a favor, drink water in the morning. Bring a bottle of water with you. And use courthouse water fountains throughout the day.

Obstacle 3: Effects (or side effects) of medication. Medication—whether prescription or over-the-counter—can make you feel sick, drowsy, or impaired, which is not going to put you in a position to be successful. The last thing you want is for the judge to suspect that you are impaired due to drugs or alcohol. An innocent mistake can have damaging consequences.

Solution 3: Be careful with medication. If you have never taken the medication you're planning to take, be sure you understand the side effects in advance. Also check if the medication should be taken with or without food. Nausea is a common side effect I see, since so many people have trouble eating the day they go to court.

Obstacle 4: Hangovers. I've seen this problem too, many times. A night of drinking before a court appearance manifests as a hangover the next day. Not only does a hangover inhibit a person's ability to think clearly, it can influence the judge's opinion of you. If judges remotely suspect it, they may call you out or make judgments about your character. This is particularly bad when child custody and visitation are at issue.

Solution 4: Be mindful of what you imbibe the night before. A glass of wine to calm your nerves is one thing, but heavy drinking the night before your important day in court can do some serious damage to your case. Think about the consequences that being impaired could have on your case and be mindful when consuming alcohol.

Obstacle 5: Getting to court. I have found myself waiting for many clients at court because they got lost or were stuck in traffic. Sometimes their tardiness is excusable and sometimes it's simply because they did not put in the effort to be on time. Furthermore, lateness creates anxiety and stress, which are enemies of your plan to be successful.

Solution 5: Plan your route and departure time ahead. Do not wait until the day of your court appearance to get directions to the courthouse. Figure out the details in advance. Program the court's address in your GPS or print out a map. This way, getting to the courthouse will be one less thing you have to worry about that morning and allow you to focus on your case. Plan to get there early in case there are delays due to traffic. Also make sure there is enough gas in your car, as you don't want to make any extra stops.

Similarly, if you're going to be taking public transportation, figure out the schedule and arrival times of your bus or train in advance and plan accordingly. Then hope for the best. Delays can derail the best laid plans, so don't be too hard on yourself.

Obstacle 6: Parking. Will you be using a parking lot or a parking structure? Sometimes courthouses are located among multiple government buildings and different parking lots, which can be confusing. If you need to enter a parking structure, you may have to drive at a crawl all the way to the top before you find an open space, which can be slow! There may even be a line to enter the parking lot or structure in the morning.

Solution 6: Plan ahead. See if you can get information about the parking situation from the court website in advance. Allow for an extra ten minutes of travel time just for parking and assume that you will have to pay for the parking when you arrive or leave.

Obstacle 7: A security line. You will likely not be able to breeze through the front door of the courthouse without going through security first. Not in our violent day and age. Security lines can be long and slow, as people pass through a metal detector and their bags are run through an X-ray machine so that security guards can scan for weapons. When I'm in a hurry, I always seem to run into a long line. It's not unlike going to the airport.

Solution 7: Plan for security delays. I honestly can't say what the security protocols are at every courthouse in the country, but you do not want to get sent back to your car to return an item because you tried to bring something prohibited through. Usually if you don't want to return something, the security personnel will keep it. I've seen clients really upset about allowing an item to be confiscated because they did not want to be late. I'm telling you, it's the little things that sneak up on you and trip you up.

Leave the scissors, mace, knives, firearms, and anything else that's remotely weapon-like in the car or at home. Also, even though most phones nowadays take pictures and record video, some courthouses will not allow cameras through. Keep that in mind.

Extra Solutions to Avoid Being Late

Running late happens to the best of us, even when we allow plenty of time. The stress and crushing fear that comes from being late is something we all want to avoid. *Will they dismiss my case? Will the judge be mad at me? Will this hurt my case?* I have seen so many people freak out in the situation and it causes them to lose focus and limits their ability to be effective in court.

Plan to arrive thirty minutes early no matter what. When you consider all the ways delays may occur (traffic, parking issues, security, and more), don't cut it close. Play it safe. If everything goes smoothly and you arrive without issues, you can use the extra time to get prepared. It's much better to be in this situation, then the alternative.

If you're running late, call the courtroom. Try requesting the number of the courtroom in advance by calling the main courthouse number (not on the day of your hearing) and ask for the number to your courtroom. This number may also be available online. If you are running late and do not have an attorney, it may be a good idea to let the courtroom clerk know you're on your way. Attorneys do this all the time, yet I seldom see self-represented parties do the same. Calling in and getting reassurance from the clerk that your case will put on "second call" (meaning it will be heard later in the morning) is huge.

ADAM

CHAPTER 17

Divorce Obstacle Course Stage 2: Navigating from the Courthouse Entrance to the Courtroom Door

OK, you're in. Stage 1 is complete. Unfortunately, the obstacle course does not end here. Plenty of obstacles remain in play after you enter the courthouse that can trip you up, slow you down, or set you back emotionally. Fortunately, you are going to be ready for Stage 2 and arrive prepared with *realistic expectations* for what is to come. Use this to your advantage.

Obstacle 1: Where is your courtroom? Finding your courtroom can be confusing and cause delays, adding unneeded stress on a day when you want to stay relaxed. Is it on the fifth floor down the hallway to the right or just a few feet away? Depending on the size of the courthouse, your path to the courtroom may be direct or more complicated. Courthouse layouts can be maze like. While this may seem like a trivial obstacle, on stressful days, it can take just one hindrance to push you into panic mode.

Solution 1: Get the lay of the land in advance. If you can, find out in advance where your courtroom is located by calling the court or looking up the location online. You can also ask court staff or security when you arrive or look for it listed on a monitor or a floor plan map at the courthouse. In fact, some courts have monitors that list every case being heard on a given day and you can look for your name on this monitor, like looking at a flight departure monitor at the airport. When emotions are running high, even getting a little lost can be traumatic and stressful. You will be much calmer if you know where you are going and how to get there. Again, it's the little things that can get you.

Obstacle 2: Elevators. This may also seem trivial, but riding elevators throws people off all the time. Much like the lines to get into the parking lot or go through security, elevators in courthouses cause a surprising amount of delays. Expect to wait for the elevator during busy times of the day (like the morning). It's usually not a huge delay, but it can feel like an eternity and induce stress. Plus, getting a spot on an elevator can be competitive. Big groups of people sometimes mass around the elevator entrance board. And it doesn't help that most government buildings have older elevators that either run slow or can't hold many people.

Solution 2: Set realistic expectations. Expect a small delay at the elevator, and don't worry about it. If you are really in a hurry, the court should have a stairway that can get you to the floor you need if you're willing to walk up one or more flights of stairs.

Obstacle 3: Temperature. Some courthouses are freezing inside, which can make people uncomfortable and amplify anxiety and stress. I've had to give my jacket to many a client who was cold. Other courthouses are too hot, which causes the same issues. You should be comfortable and the last thing you should be worried about is the thermostat.

Solution 3: Dress accordingly. Bring something warm to wear that you can take off it gets too hot. Even if it's summertime, bring something warm just in case the courthouse is like a freezer.

Obstacle 4: Your ex's support people. You should not expect your ex to come to court alone. I have seen people bring an entire entourage to court. This will no doubt affect you, but I don't want you to be blindsided and waste valuable energy recovering from the shock. While his support people are typically near the courtroom, don't be surprised if you run into them elsewhere, like the bathroom, the security line, the elevator, and so on.

Solution 4: Be ready for whoever shows up and bring your own support team. No matter how much you prepare for this possibility, it can be tough. It will likely feel awkward to see your ex with his supporters. Maybe you had a great relationship with one of them. You may love these folks like family, but in the courtroom hallways they may treat you like a stranger or an enemy.

Typically, three types of support people bother my clients the most.

- **The ex's family.** This can be hard, particularly when you have had a close bond. In reality, these family members may agree with you! However, family is family, so they will tend to back your ex, even if he is in the wrong. Now, they may come over to talk to you—even try to comfort you. Be careful. Limit what you tell them. Assume they will communicate any information you give them to your ex, and he may try to use it against you. *Your actions are evidence,* even in the courthouse hallways.

- **Mutual friends.** You may be shocked to see a mutual friend siding with your ex. Unfortunately, this happens all the time. Be wary of friends who try to play both sides. Assume that anything you say will not be kept confidential. I know it sucks to think like this, but the risk is real.

- **A new significant other.** This may be the hardest one. Even if you know about the new love interest, seeing her in person could rattle you.

Think about bringing some support people of your own. Being alone at court is not ideal, so I always recommend bringing someone for emotional support.

Obstacle 5: The opposing attorney. What if your ex has an attorney?

Solution 5: Know this is normal and be ready with your plan. First, do not be shocked if your ex shows up with an attorney. This is something out of your control. The best you can do is acknowledge that it's a possibility and be ready for it. You might be thinking, *How can he afford it? He said he was broke and couldn't pay me anything!* Well, the more time you spend fixating on these ideas, the less you will be able to focus on your goals for the day.

If your court has online case access, you may be able to look up your case ahead of time to see if your ex hired an attorney. You can also call the courtroom clerk and ask. However, neither method of verification is full proof. He may just show up with one.

Second, do not be surprised if his attorney approaches you. This is *extremely* common. Attorneys talk to each other about their cases in the hallway all the time. If you are acting as your own attorney, your ex's attorney will likely want to speak with you directly. You may have the urge to vilify his attorney, which is totally normal. But whether this attorney is reasonable and honest or aggressive and shady, you can expect the attorney to try to talk to you in the hallway.

Below are some common reasons why an opposing attorney may want to talk to you.

- **Introductions.** His attorney may simply want to introduce her or himself and give you a business card. Once an attorney is retained, you can communicate through the attorney instead of directly with your ex.
- **Update.** The attorney may have an update for you. For example, she may tell you she was just hired and is not ready to go forward that day, and therefore will be seeking to continue your hearing to another day. The attorney may have some paperwork for you that she has filed, intends to file, or plans to introduce in court. Or the update could be about something else entirely.
- **"Let's work something out."** It is very common for an opposing attorney to explore a resolution with you before your court hearing. Remember, this process is fluid, so what starts as litigation may become negotiation. The courts often encourage this type of collaboration. The attorney may have a proposal to run by you and want to engage in a back-and-forth discussion that will resolve some or all the issues before the court that day. For example, if the court appearance is to litigate financial support, the attorney may suggest a dollar figure. Or the attorney may have a child visitation schedule in mind.

We'll discuss how to prepare for this in the next chapter, which covers Stage 3 of navigating court obstacles, but essentially you should focus on coming to court prepared with a specific plan of how you want the court to rule. Doing so ahead of time will allow you to properly evaluate any proposal made by the opposing attorney.

Do you have to talk to the attorney? No, it's completely up to you—unless the judge orders it. If you refuse to speak with the attorney, be ready for the possibility that the judge may later ask you to go back out in the hallway and see if you can work something out. You can give it a shot, but if you then find that you don't feel comfortable or are intimidated, you can let the court know. Don't feel pressured to make a deal in the hallway.

What if you don't understand something your ex's lawyer says? Don't agree to anything unless you are confident that you completely understand what is being discussed. Ask for clarification or explanation if you are unclear. You do not want to agree to something you didn't fully understand because you were afraid to ask.

Obstacle 6: Hurry up and wait. After you put in all the effort to navigate Stages 1 and 2, and arrive promptly for your hearing, you may find that the courtroom door is locked. Your hearing maybe scheduled for 9:00 AM, but the courtroom may not open until 9:15 AM. Don't be surprised and don't let it get to you. It's better to be in this situation than running late! Of course, being stuck in the hallway with your ex and his entourage is not ideal.

Solution 7: Don't be surprised and use the time productively. Breathe, stay calm, and find a spot to review your plan, your notes, or the court paperwork. Don't stray too far from the courtroom, however, as you want to be on notice for when they open.

Overall Solution for Stage 2: Be Realistic and Trust Yourself

There may be five obstacles waiting for you at court on a given day. There may be ten. You may have planned for all of them, except for the one where his attorney tells you your ex lost his job and can't afford to pay you support or explains that your ex expects spousal support from you. Expect the unexpected. It is impossible to plan for every possibility. No one can do that.

You can't control everything. You can only control how you prepare, plan, and move through the obstacle course. So, plan and then trust yourself to respond in the moment to whatever happens. Remember, avoiding even one of the obstacles in Stage 2 will make you more effective, because it's one less thing added to your plate!

As always, keep your expectations realistic. It's still very likely to be a challenging day, but you may avoid making three mistakes that another person would have been tripped up by. Each obstacle avoided is a success and you should appreciate each and every one.

CHAPTER 18

Divorce Obstacle Course Stage 3: Navigating Inside the Courtroom

ADAM

You made it to the final stage of the obstacle course. Whether it's your first time or fifteenth, appearing before a judge and being your own advocate can be intense. This is true with or without an attorney. Remember, it's okay to be nervous and stressed, or to get emotional. This is normal!

The courtroom is where people get closer to, or further from their goals. It's where decisions are made that will impact your life going forward, and where all your preparation and planning pays off, hopefully. Thousands of people are put in this very same position every day, and you are going to be ready. Remember, you can do this!

Inside the courtroom, when emotions are running high and you are in an unpredictable environment, it is always a good idea to return to the basics: *Holding realistic expectations, making informed decisions, focusing on what you can control, and being well prepared.* In addition, in Chapter 20, we will cover a new one: the incredible power of being organized.

Checking In

Obstacles can emerge right at the threshold of the courtroom.

Obstacle 1: The wrong courtroom. Do not take for granted that you're in the right spot. I've observed people waiting in a courtroom for long stretches, not realizing they were in the wrong place. When they found out, the shock and resulting stress of the discovery were evident in their body language as they raced out of the courtroom, fearing they had missed their hearing.

Solution 1: Confirm you have the right courtroom. Typically, there will be a sheet of paper posted outside the courtroom listing the cases on the courtroom calendar that day. Confirm that your case is listed. If it isn't, double check your paperwork to make sure you have the right courtroom. If your paperwork says you have the right courtroom, check with the bailiff or clerk inside. The absence of your name may simply be an oversight; however, it's possible that your case has been transferred to a different courtroom or judge. The reasons why this might happen can vary, so you'll need to ask the clerk in your new courtroom to get the answer.

Obstacle 2: Closed courtroom. As discussed in Stage 2, the courtroom may not open on time—or it may simply appear closed.

Solution 2: Have your check-in strategy ready. Don't panic. Stay close by the door so you can enter as soon as the courtroom opens. When you arrive, even if the courtroom looks closed, try opening the door to make sure. I have found plenty of clients waiting outside an open courtroom because they thought it looked closed. Once inside, be sure to let the bailiff or the clerk know you are present. If the courtroom remains closed, check to see if there is a notice indicating that hearings are being moved to another courtroom.

Obstacle 3: Where do I sit and what if my ex is already there? Some courtrooms have specific rules about where opposing parties should sit, like on opposite sides of the aisle. Even if there is open seating, issues may arise. If the courtroom is crowded, you might have no choice but to sit near your ex. Maybe just having your ex in your line of sight makes you uneasy. You may be waiting in your seat for a while, making this a long and uncomfortable period.

Solution 3: Sit strategically and ask for guidance. Ask the bailiff or clerk if you need to sit on one side of the audience or the other. If not, take a seat anywhere. If your ex is already in the courtroom, try and sit somewhere where he will be out of your line of sight, such as near the front. If seating is limited, see if the bailiff can accommodate you and seat you away from your ex.

If you came with friends or family, ask if these supporters can sit inside the courtroom with you. If seating is limited, they may have to wait outside until seats open. If one of them is a witness, that individual will likely have to sit outside until being called to testify.

Obstacle 4: When the judge doesn't come out. Once everyone has been checked in and seated, people often expect the judge to appear. When this doesn't happen, time begins to move very slowly. Anticipation builds and stress and anxiety can creep in. You may think: *Is something wrong? Will the judge have enough time for my case today? How long will this take?*

Solution 4: Be ready for anything and understand court hearings are a process. A judge may enter as soon as a courtroom opens or be delayed. When the judge does come out, what happens next may vary. Usually judges hear several cases per day. The judge may take attendance and announce every case to see if both parties are present and ready to move forward. This process may involve conversations with the attorneys and the parties for each case, which can be quick or drawn out, depending on the circumstances. Based on that process, the judge will hear cases in no certain order; it could be alphabetical or something else entirely. Or the judge may skip roll call and jump right into the hearings for the day. This part is unpredictable, so you should be ready to be either the first case called or the last.

Your Hearing

New obstacles arise when your hearing starts.

Obstacle 5: Fearing that your ex will lie. At some point before your hearing begins, both you and your ex will need to take an oath to tell the truth. Despite this oath, "the truth and nothing but the truth" does not always come out of people's mouth. People constantly tell different versions of the truth. Sometimes, these versions are complete opposites. This means someone is not taking the oath seriously. It is the judge's job to determine who is being truthful.

The reality is that people do get away with lying in court. This is one of the main frustrations I hear from my clients after their hearings. They say:

- "But he just lied, and the judge didn't do anything!"
- "Maybe I should just lie too."
- "Why should I bother preparing or telling the truth, he's just going to lie again!"

Solution 5: Focus on telling your truth. Under no circumstances should you attempt to fight fire with fire. If you start thinking that you should make false assertions, there are a few things to keep in mind that can help you maintain perspective. The first is the importance of self-control. You will improve your credibility with the court and perhaps expose false statements in your ex's testimony by being prepared, consistent, organized, and/or having evidence to show to the judge that supports your testimony.

Second, while hearing your ex tell a lie in court can be extremely frustrating, stay realistic when it comes to him being truthful with the judge. If you do, you will be more prepared to deal with lying when it happens and be less likely to suffer an emotional setback.

Third, do not lower yourself to his level. If the judge catches you in a lie, it can have lasting negative consequences on your credibility for the rest of your divorce proceedings.

Obstacle 6: Being asked for a time estimate. Before you begin, the judge may ask you for a time estimate. This means she wants to know how long you think your hearing is going to take. This question catches a lot of self-represented women off guard. They wonder: *How should I know? I've never done this before! What if I give the wrong answer?*

Solution 6: Have an estimate in mind and make your best guess. Relax, even seasoned attorneys get this part wrong. If you aren't sure, you can ask the judge for guidance or let her know what you plan to say. If pressed for an answer, just give your best estimate. It's best not to spend a lot of energy stressing about this part. Make an *informed decision* based on the information you have ("I think I will need thirty minutes to tell my side") and move forward.

Based on the time estimate given, the judge will determine when on the day's schedule your case will be heard. Don't be surprised if the judge gives no indication of when that will be and tells you to take a seat. The judge will also determine if there is sufficient time to hear your case that day. This catches people by surprise. They think: *I scheduled this hearing two months ago. What does the judge mean they don't have time?!*

If the judge determines she doesn't have enough time to hear your case on the day of your scheduled hearing, here are a few possibilities to be prepared for.

- Your case could be transferred to another courtroom to a judge who is available.
- The judge could continue your hearing to another day when she has more time.
- The judge could hear as much of your case as possible and then continue the remainder of the hearing to the same afternoon, the next day, or another open date.

Obstacle 7: *A continuance.* A *continuance* is when a hearing gets postponed to another date or time. They are very common and are a huge source of frustration. People generally expect their cases will be heard in a timely manner and to completion on their court dates. It is important to know in advance that this may not be the case.

Solution 7: *Understanding the process will make you more effective.* A continuance can be frustrating, especially if the rationale for the delay seems unfair. It is important, however, to understand that these are everyday occurrences. Below are some common reasons for them.

- **The judge wants one.** There are a variety of reasons why the judge may need to postpone a hearing. She may need additional information or want the parties to try to negotiate and resolve matters themselves. Another case may have run long and cut into your time. The judge may need to leave early that day or a host of other reasons.

- **The opposing attorney may request one.** She may have a conflict (in other words, be double booked) and need to appear in another courtroom or courthouse to litigate another case. She may have been recently retained by your ex and need more time to get up to speed on the case. She may submit a time estimate that is too long (even though yours is not.) She may claim that you did not provide certain information and the case can't move forward without it. She may call in and say someone on your ex's side of the case cannot appear due to an emergency or illness, or have some other reason. Every case is different and there are a variety of reasons an attorney might seek a continuance.
- **Your ex may want one.** If your ex is self-represented, he could seek a continuance as well. Your guess is as good as mine as to why. Maybe he is confused about the purpose of the hearing, needs more time, is unprepared, needs to collect more information, is purposefully trying to delay things, or thinks you didn't provide enough information, and so on.
- **You may need one yourself.** Yes, if you aren't ready to go forward for some reason—any of the reasons above will do—it might be you asking to postpone.

How long will the continuance be? You are probably sick of hearing this, but *it depends* on the reason and the court's schedule. Your case could be continued to the afternoon, the next day, the next week, the next month, or the next year. You can advocate for an earlier or later date (depending on your goals), but be prepared to explain why. For example, you could say: "I want a court date before August 20th *because* our son starts school on the 21st. We need to have visitation and custody resolved by then so he can have a consistent schedule." Get in the habit of explaining your position.

How does the judge pick a new court date? She often asks all parties their availability. Be sure to have your calendar ready. Know which dates are bad for you due to regularly occurring events (work, school, and so on) and singular events (vacation, birthdays, and so forth). Your first choice may not be an option. Be ready to go through a few dates because your dates may not work for the other party or the court. Always come to court prepared with alternative future dates that work for your schedule. It is better to have this planned, or else you may have to come up with a suggestion on the spot that ends up being inconvenient.

Fair or not, continuances are the reality of our court system. That's why you likely won't see attorneys throw their hands up in exasperation at a continuance, expected or unexpected. They are used to them. Continuances of all kinds are a normal, common practice.

Of course, this doesn't mean you shouldn't advocate for yourself and oppose the continuance if you want the hearing to go on as scheduled. It's not a foregone conclusion that a request for a continuance will be granted. Explain why you need the hearing to go forward that day. For example, stating you can't take off more work, it's difficult to find childcare, this is the second continuance in a row your ex has requested, or that the relief being requested (financial support, custody, and so on) is too important to be delayed further. Advocate for yourself.

Of course, even if you have the best argument on the planet, you may not prevail. There's no easy way to put it other than to say you'll need to just roll with things. Give your argument your best shot and live to advocate another day.

Obstacle 8: Knowing when to stand, sit, and who goes first. When your hearing begins and you are called before the judge, the process can be confusing. How a judge runs her courtroom is entirely up to her and her style may be different from that of other judges. This unpredictability means everything from seating assignments to when you are allowed to speak may be running through your head.

Solution 8: The process will reveal itself, but be ready for anything. Expect to be told whether to remain standing (usually when you're taking the oath to tell the truth or discussing preliminary issues like time estimates) or to sit down. There is usually a long table facing the judge where the opposing parties and their attorneys sit. To keep things consistent, the party who filed for divorce (the *petitioner* or *plaintiff*) typically always sits on one side of the table and the party responding (the *respondent* or *defendant*) sits on the other (which side depends on the courtroom).

As a rule, the party who is seeking the relief that day (in other words, the one who filed the request, requested the hearing, and so forth) will speak first. However, don't be surprised if the judge has questions or

173

directs that the hearing move forward in a different way. For example, I've seen a judge tell the parties, based on what she read in the papers filed, that she was inclined to grant the request, and then to ask the responding party to tell her why the relief shouldn't be granted. The directness of this kind of question catches some people off guard. Expect the unexpected and stay ready, even if it seems like you won. In this kind of scenario, the judge may still require you to present your case or have questions for you.

The Judge

People can be obstacles, too.

Obstacle 9: The judge doesn't care. This reaction often comes after telling the judge details of your life that have shocked your friends and family (for example: Your ex threatened to quit his job to avoid paying support, he has started bringing a new, young love interest around the children, he drinks too much, and so on), and the judge, with a look that says, "Is that all?" appears completely unmoved. The judge literally has no reaction. This can come as quite a shock because you are used to getting a strong reaction to these facts.

In response to the judge's equanimity, I have witnessed people stop trying as hard or lose focus. Typically, they think this means the judge is disinterested or doesn't care.

Solution 9: The judge isn't your friend, so don't expect her to react like one. The truth is, none of us know what the judge is thinking, and it's a futile exercise to try to figure it out based on facial expressions and reactions. Before you become disheartened or outraged, here are a couple thoughts to keep this in perspective.

- **Everything you say is normal and standard to the judge.** While this hearing is likely a unique and emotional experience for you, the judge does this all day, every day. Judges may hear stories like yours all the time. In fact, your judge may have already heard similar facts several times that day. So, just like with any activity or job done repeatedly, the shock factor (if it was ever there) has worn off.

- **Mudslinging is common.** Judges in divorce cases constantly listen to accusations, different versions of the same event, and negative portrayals of the other party. Their job is to figure out who is telling the truth and decide on the issues before them. Do not expect them to ride an emotional roller coaster with you and your ex.

- The judge's familiarity with mudslinging is why evidence that supports your testimony is so important. It is difficult to determine who is telling the truth in a she said/he said case. However, if you can produce text messages or emails, for example, that corroborate your testimony, you are making it easier for the judge to believe you when you tell your stories (There are special rules for introducing evidence, be sure to research them in advance). When you think about it, if you have two friends in a disagreement, and one had evidence to prove her point, who would you believe?

- **Being unbiased is the judge's job.** The role of the judge is to listen to all the testimony and evidence. To be unbiased, judges often do this with a straight face that shows they are serious about their job. This doesn't mean they don't care about your case.

- **Multitasking.** Judges have a lot of responsibilities beyond your divorce. During your hearing, you may see the judge reading, looking at her computer monitor, speaking to her clerk, stopping the hearing to deal with something else, or doing something that makes it appear she is not focusing on you. This doesn't mean the judge is not paying attention. Remember simply to focus on your plan for putting the right information (your testimony and evidence) in the judge's hands.

Obstacle 10: The judge and your ex's attorney are friends. The sight of a judge and an ex's attorney being friendly has sent many a client of mine over the edge. They become defeated and intimidated before their cases even start. I hear things like: "Great, I'll never get my orders now," "Now the judge is going to side with my ex no matter what I do," and "This isn't fair!"

Solution 10: Don't read anything into this. Yes, the judge may be friendly with attorneys in the courtroom. They likely see each other all the time in court and at legal functions, so it's common for them to be friendly and collegial with one another. Don't let this freak you out. In fact, I've seen judges lay into attorneys shortly after some friendly banter. Trust that the judge will not let her relationship with an attorney bias her decision.

Obstacle 11: The judge doesn't like you. Okay, I hear this one a lot. This idea gets in my clients' heads and causes all sorts of issues. They perceive the judge is rude to them or doesn't like them, which results in anxiety, stress, intimidation, and a lack of self-confidence.

Solution 11: Who cares! Advocate for yourself regardless of the judge's demeanor. First, do not assume anything based on the judge's demeanor. I have had clients who obtained positive results tell me afterward that they were surprised because they'd thought the judge was upset with them.

Second, who cares! Yes, it would be great if the judge greeted you with a smile and asked you about your day. But you are not in court to become friends with the judge. The judge has a job to do and so do you. Whatever the judge's feelings are toward you personally, her job is to be impartial and apply the law to the facts in front of her.

Third, even if your judge doesn't like you, which you can't prove one way or the other, worrying about her feelings won't get you anywhere. You cannot control the judge's mood or how she treats you. Focus on factors you can control, like staying prepared and organized.

Your judge may seem different from one court appearance to the next. Judges are people too and variety of circumstances may influence their demeanor. Let's say the judge just dealt with a very emotional and frustrating case and yours is next. It's very possible she may be curt or short when speaking to you. Maybe she is getting over a cold and you confuse that with annoyance. Do not be caught off guard by the judge's demeanor.

Obstacle 12: Your judge is gone. Let's say you show up to court ready to go, but as you walk into the courtroom you find that a stranger wearing a judge's robe is sitting up there. *Huh?* Yes, this may happen. It may be temporary. For example, the judge may be sick, on vacation, had an emergency, had a scheduling conflict, or be absent for a variety of other reasons. Possibly your judge is gone for good. A judge may have retired, transferred to another court, and so on. In which case, this judge may very likely your new judge moving forward. No matter how well you set your *realistic expectations*, this scenario could catch you off guard.

Solution 12: Once you regroup, you'll need to think critically. If this is a temporary judge, here are some questions to consider.

Will this change impact my case? Yes, it is possible. This new judge may rule differently (better or worse) on your matter. As discussed above, every judge is different. I have seen this countless times. A client doesn't get a result with a temporary judge that she would have obtained with her normal judge—and vice versa.

Can you continue the hearing until your original judge returns? Find out if you have this option by asking the temporary judge.

Should you try to continue the case? You may have waited a long time for this hearing and want the issues (custody, support, visitation, and so forth) to be resolved speedily. You have to weigh the risk of an unfamiliar judge presiding over your case against continuing your hearing to a day when your judge is back. How long will you have to wait for a new hearing? What is the hearing about? Weigh your options and make an *informed decision* based on the circumstances.

Now, before you spend any time worrying about this, remember that it may never happen to you. However, it happens with enough frequency that I wanted you to be aware. My goal is to set your expectations so you are not completely blindsided by predictable events when you walk into court. If you are not caught off guard, you will be better able to handle a change in your circumstances and make rational and informed decisions. Of course, you still will be surprised by your judge not being there, but the fact that it can even happen will not be a shock to you.

Your (Soon-to-Be-Ex) Husband

Your ex may be the greatest obstacle of all.

Obstacle 13: There are two sides to every story. When it comes to divorce, sometimes it seems like there are two coexisting worlds. One is the day-to-day world in which you live. The other is the world that exists inside the courtroom. Inside the courtroom, facts can be seemingly distorted from real-life.

For example: Daily, your children may tell you they don't want to go to their dad's for visitation for a variety of reasons (They don't have their own rooms, he brings his girlfriend around, he gets upset if they don't want to spend every minute with him, and so on). You always take the time to explain why it's important they spend time with their dad and go out of your way to make sure the visits go smoothly. Then you get into court and their father claims the visits aren't going well because you are alienating the kids against him.

Solution 13: Actions are evidence. Now use that evidence. Be prepared to explain to the court why any story your ex tells isn't true. In the case of a custody hearing, you could make a point to keep a journal of the types of issues your kids were having before their visits with your ex and what you did to assist them. Parents having disagreements about visitation is a normal issue to the judge. Inside the courtroom, it would be surprising if both parties told the judge that everything was going perfectly and there were zero issues.

Obstacle 14: A tale of two exes. Women often talk about the man they deal with daily being different from the man who shows up at court. Outside of court, your ex may be constantly late, difficult to deal with, unpredictable, unreliable, and irrational. Inside the courtroom, he will do his best to appear responsible, reasonable, reliable, and rational. To put it mildly, this transformation of his character can be frustrating.

Solution 14: Plan to face the courtroom version of your ex. It is valuable to know who is showing up at court so you can tailor your plan to respond to that person. You don't want to be caught off guard when your ex, who hasn't worn a suit in his entire adult life, shows up looking like he walked out of a Men's Warehouse commercial with the persona of a professional.

Remember, you cannot control how your ex looks or behaves in or out of the courtroom. Focus on what you can control: your plan, the evidence, being organized, your own appearance, your own demeanor, and so on.

Five Additional Courtroom Tips

I have just a few more suggestions for you.

Tip 1: Watch and observe. Whenever you are in court, pay attention to the other cases. This is a golden opportunity to gain experience without going before the judge. The fundamentals of a hearing are laid out before you. In fact, I feel strongly that observing court hearings should be a prerequisite for court preparation. Lessons about what to do and what not to do play out before you when you observe other people's cases. I mean, why go first when you can let others go before you and learn from their mistakes and successes?

Observe the judge's demeanor, styles of testimony, how evidence is introduced, where the opposing parties sit and stand, and learn a variety of valuable lessons. How does the judge react to different situations? Did you cringe at the way someone, or both parties, acted when she was before the judge? *Hint:* Make sure this isn't you when it's your turn.

I have learned so much from simply sitting in court and watching. So much so, that you may want to consider observing before your day in court. OK, this would take an investment of effort and time on your part. Most people are trying to avoid going to court as much as humanly possible, and here I am encouraging you to go voluntarily. Yikes! Just hear me out.

You can ask others who have been through divorces (friends, family members, and so on) what court is like, but there is no substitute for observing the real thing. This applies whether this is your first time or tenth time going to court. You can always learn something about:

- **Context.** This is an opportunity to set realistic expectations and dispel any inaccurate or preconceived notions about court hearings or how parties, attorneys, and judges act.
- **Objectivity.** You get to go to court when it's not your life and observe other cases through an objective lens. You can then apply these lessons to your own case.
- **Preparation.** This will mean one less unknown when you go to court for your case, which will help reduce your anxiety. Think of it as a practice run. You'll know where to park, how long it takes to get there, where the entrance is located, how to get through security, how to find the courtrooms, and where the bathrooms are, and learn courtroom procedure. Your calm/objective self

will be removing these items from the plate of your future self who will be dealing with a ton of other issues on the day of your hearing.

- **The real deal.** You will get to see what actual divorce litigation looks like. It's not theoretical anymore. It's not like it is on TV or in the movies.
- **Keep perspective.** Remember that the cases you observe are different than yours, even if they are similar and address the exact same issue. When you visit a court as research, you are not there to predict how your case will turn out based on the results of other cases.

Tip #2: Know exactly what relief is being requested at your hearing. When discussing an upcoming hearing, clients will tell me the hearing is about a specific issue, like child support. However, when I look the case up online, I see that something else, such as modifying visitation or changing the children's school is also being requested. It is surprisingly common for people to show up to court only to find out they misunderstood what was being decided that day.

How does this happen?

- **Inattention to detail.** The person didn't read the paperwork carefully. Yes, it can be this simple. Read every line and double check it as you get closer to your hearing date.
- **You think you know, but you don't.** Sometimes you have a preconceived notion about what is being requested and make an assumption without reading the forms carefully.
- **It's too painful.** Or maybe, you stop reading or don't give it your full attention because it's such a painful experience that you don't want to relive.
- **The passage of time.** The time between the filing of a request and the hearing date can be lengthy—maybe months. During that time, life happens. Before you know it, the hearing date has arrived. You may think you remember everything, but time has a funny way of affecting your memory. Double check the court paperwork in advance.

- **Misunderstanding.** If you are confused about what is being requested, get clarification. This is totally normal. Seek out assistance via no-cost or low-cost legal options.
- **Continuances from a prior hearing.** This is where the law can get really confusing. You may go to court for a hearing and not get to everything, which results in a continuance and a new hearing date for these outstanding issues. It's essential to confirm what is at issue for that next hearing. It may just be for the issues you didn't get to, but the new hearing may also include new issues. When all else fails, ask questions!
- **Failure to stay on point.** There may be several issues before the court at a given hearing (for example: support, visitation, vacation schedule, asset division), and it can get confusing because these issues are often interrelated. For example, a hearing on child support can quickly shift to child custody and visitation. A parent unhappy with the amount of child support may purposefully change the conversation to increasing their visitation time (maybe so he can pay less). If you feel that the hearing is going off track or you are confused about why a certain topic is being discussed, do not be afraid to ask for clarification. Do not interrupt, but wait for an opportunity to ask your question respectfully.

It's important to be on the same page as your ex when you leave your hearing. You don't want to walk out of court and immediately be in a disagreement with your ex about interpreting the judge's order. Use your time before the judge to get all your questions answered and confirm that both you and your ex share the same understanding. For example: If it's unclear, confirm that the Wednesday overnight visits start next week and not that very night.

Tip #3: Be prepared to explain WHY. It's equally important to know what you want as *why* you want it. Here is an example I saw the other day. At a custody hearing, a mother was asking to have her children remain with her during the week and every other weekend. But she seemed surprised when the judge asked her why her ex shouldn't be awarded 50/50 visitation. I could tell that she expected the judge to automatically agree that her request was the right decision since she was a stay-at-home mom.

The woman became flustered and when she spoke her reasons came across as badmouthing the father. She said, "He's never home, he drinks, he can't change a diaper, he doesn't care about the kids, he can't spend five minutes alone with them," and more. While she knew what she wanted, she was not prepared to defend her position by explaining why. Consequently, the judge interpreted her responses as mudslinging and became frustrated.

An alternative way the woman could have responded would have been by stating that she wanted the children with her during the week *because* she had always been their primary caretaker, was responsible for getting the kids ready for school every day, handled pickups and drop-offs, took them to all their medical and dental appointments, volunteered in the classroom, was trained to assist their special-needs son with his homework, and that her children's father worked late and had an unpredictable schedule, and she wanted the kids on a predictable schedule during the school week.

When answering the judge, I cannot stress enough the importance of explaining why you want something. Giving the judge a reason to say yes to you makes the judge's job easier. Instead of the judge probing for answers as to why her proposal is a good idea, the woman in this example could have prepared in advance, enabling her to lay out reasons clearly for the judge.

Get in the habit of saying "I want _____ *because* . . ." This practice applies whether you are in the courtroom, in mediation, or in discussions with your attorney, the opposing attorney, or your ex.

Tip #4: Take amazing notes. You may not have the skill set or experience of an attorney. Even so, you can out-prepare, out-organize, and out-note-take your ex or his attorney. Success during a divorce can be all about the effort you put in. For example: During the end of a hearing, a woman representing herself was quietly reviewing her notes as the judge and the opposing attorney wrapped things up. But they had forgotten an important detail and the woman asked a question about it. Both the judge and attorney were clearly exasperated by the delay, until she pointed out that they hadn't addressed when the new child visitation schedule would begin. Immediately, both the judge and opposing attorney realized they missed it.

This was a small victory, but it avoided some serious confusion later, and the woman was rightly proud of herself. She earned the respect of the professionals in the courtroom, and that was awesome.

Taking notes at your own hearing can be a challenge, whether you have an attorney or are representing yourself. To put it mildly, you'll have a lot on your mind. Do your best to get down what you can (details such as what was ordered and why it was ordered). If you have a friend or family member supporting you at the hearing, ask this individual to take notes too. Sometimes your recollection may be off.

The devil is in the details. Facts in divorce are lost at lightning speed. Any given case may include reams of transcripts, and multiple motions, declarations, court orders, financial documents, and so on. Then add in multiple hearings, negotiations, and correspondence being exchanged over months or years. Sprinkle in the fact that the judge deals with hundreds of cases a year and that the opposing attorney may be on her tenth case of the week. This means details can get easily overlooked, missed, or forgotten.

Sometimes issues that you *know* have been discussed and settled to your satisfaction can be brought up again. Your ability to be organized, thanks to note taking, will cut through this kind of mistake. Don't put it off! Write things down while they're still fresh in your mind.

Tip #5: Use all available resources to prepare. Use the no-cost or low-cost resources we went over in in Chapter 10 to help you prepare for court. Remember, your state or county may provide hearing assistance forms, how-to videos, classes, and clinics. In addition, you can utilize resources like free legal clinics, pro bono attorneys, and public law libraries. And don't forget to explore low-cost legal resources, such as legal aid agencies, attorneys who offer limited scope/unbundled legal services, and so on.

CHAPTER 19

Courtroom Behavior

ADAM

There are a few dos and don'ts we need to cover before you enter the courtroom. How you present yourself in court can absolutely impact your case. In a courtroom, I find it's better to be unremarkable. Unremarkable is a good thing. This means you didn't do anything to catch the judge's ire and made life easy for the judge.

Typically, if your behavior stands out, that's usually a bad sign. For example, the judge may not remember that you were organized or helpful, but she may remember when you interrupted her when you were desperate to make sure she knew a fact that you were certain would influence her decision in your favor. She will remember the bailiff needing to tell you to turn off your cell phone.

You need to be respectful and play by the court rules, no matter how frustrating or difficult your court appearance or divorce may be for you. Following these five simple rules will put you in the position to be successful.

Rule# 1: Body Language

Judges notice everything. Always assume your judge is watching you and what she sees may influence her decision. This makes body language extremely important. You can say a lot without uttering a word. For example, a husband glaring at his wife as she testifies about his temper is going to send a message to the judge that the woman is speaking the truth. It will play a role in the judge's decision-making process.

Other body language mistakes to avoid are: rolling your eyes, throwing up your hands, slumping in your chair, snickering, sneering, shaking your head, yawning, fidgeting, rocking back and forth, sighing, glaring at the judge or your ex or his attorney, falling back into your chair in frustration, and similar behavior. Now, you may be thinking these would never apply to you, but in the heat of the moment, when emotions are running high, anything is possible.

As a rule, sit up straight, don't look at your ex or his attorney, look at the judge when the judge is speaking to you, and try to remain calm and composed. This last piece of advice is a tough one to implement, I know. Emotion plays a big role in the courtroom, so if you show emotion or become overwhelmed, just try to compose yourself as quickly as possible. Also remember that you're human and it's natural to show emotion during this process. Don't put too much pressure on yourself. Just do the best you can.

Rule #2: Communication with the Judge

Unless otherwise directed, you should address the judge as "Your honor." Some people also say ma'am or sir, and that's OK too. As I said a moment ago, be sure to look at the judge when she speaks to you, even if she isn't. Do not interrupt the judge! Listen to what the judge is telling you or asking you. This is very important. Nothing frustrates a judge more than when people don't listen. I realize this seems simple, but it happens all the time. Also:

- **Remember to answer the question.** You may be nervous and have trouble focusing. Or you may be dying to tell the judge something while the judge is asking you a specific question. However, if you respond with anything other than an answer to the judge's exact question, she will get frustrated. That's not a good thing. So, remind yourself to listen to the question and

186

answer it. If you don't understand, ask the judge to repeat the question. Try engaging in active listening, where you repeat the question to yourself and then answer.

- **Use words.** When answering a question, always say yes or no. Don't say, "Uh-huh" or "Hmm-hmm." Do not nod or shake your head. The judge will correct you, and if there's a court reporter present to type a written transcript of everything said, you will be reminded that the reporter can only transcribe words. If you continue to do this, the judge and the court reporter may get frustrated with you.
- **Speak slowly and clearly.** If you speak too quickly, which can happen when you get nervous, the judge will ask you to slow down and remind you that the court reporter cannot keep up with you.
- **Make sure you are heard.** Remember to speak into the microphone or loud enough so that your voice carries. Otherwise the judge and the court reporter may not be able to hear you properly.
- **Be careful with legal terms.** I have seen judges lose their patience with non-lawyers after explaining for the tenth time they are using a certain legal objection or legal term wrong. (Saying something is "hearsay" is a common one.) In my experience, judges are not going to expect you to act and talk like an attorney if you are representing yourself. Stay in your lane and only use terms with which you are comfortable. If you do use a legal objection, understand what it means and why you are saying it, as you may have to explain it to the judge or argue your position with your ex or their attorney.

Rule #3: Dress Code

Again, you want to be unremarkable here and for the judge not to remember what you were wearing. I typically tell clients to dress like they're going to a job interview at an office. Avoid anything informal or inappropriate. As a rule, if you find yourself questioning whether something is too informal or inappropriate, then assume it is and go with the safer choice. Some courtrooms enforce a dress code. I once saw a judge remove a guy for wearing cut-off denim shorts and sandals. The cutoffs, while a questionable fashion choice, weren't his only issue. The man also owed a lot of back child support. But you see what I mean.

Rule #4: Behavior in the Courtroom Audience

Even in the audience, your behavior is on display for the judge. But you want to be neither seen nor heard. A judge won't notice you if you are waiting respectfully and quietly. Here are some helpful rules: no chewing gum, keep your cell phone off and avoid whispering, talking, sleeping, drinking, or eating. If you are going to break any of these, please be discreet!

If you bring someone with you, these rules apply to her or him as well. If your companion gets in trouble, you could be perceived as guilty by association.

Now, every courtroom may have different rules about things like eating and drinking. You can ask to see if it's allowed. Always err on the side of caution and follow this rule. As a practical matter, follow these rules when you step up before the judge as well.

Rule #5: The Bailiff

The enforcer of courtroom rules, aside from the judge, is the bailiff. The bailiff is a member of the law enforcement community who is stationed in the courtroom to keep order. If you violate the rules, the bailiff will be the ones relieving you of your cell phone, telling you to be quiet, or removing someone from the courtroom. Remember, even if the judge has not come out yet, you can assume someone is always watching you.

***

Following these five simple rules will make your life easier on the day of your hearing. You will likely be nervous and focused on what you want to accomplish. The last thing you need is to be reprimanded by the judge or bailiff for something easily avoidable. It could throw you off your game plan, distract you, or annoy the judge. These mistakes are easily avoidable.

ADAM

CHAPTER 20

Organization Is Your Secret Weapon

Key moments in divorce come and go. You won't want to miss out on an opportunity to capitalize on one of these because you were not organized.

Whether it comes naturally to you or requires serious effort, being organized and well prepared during divorce is a skill that gives you a tremendous advantage. I realize this may come across as stating the obvious. Maybe it seems like a topic unworthy of its own chapter. Except that it is. Over and over, I have witnessed countless opportunities lost during *divorce* that are directly due to a failure to be properly prepared and have what is needed at hand.

The Benefits of Organization

Why is organization so important? Below are some obvious and not-so-obvious examples of how being prepared and organized can assist you. It will help you to:

- **Avoid delays.** Whether you are in court or negotiating, you don't want to waste any time. Who knows when you are going to get another chance? A court appearance is a valuable opportunity that you don't want to waste. A lack of information because you aren't organized results in missed opportunities. You may be prevented from addressing an issue because you don't have the information (a school schedule, financial records, a prior order of the court, and so on), as a result of being disorganized or ill prepared. The last thing you want to have to do is come back and do it all over again. Making frequent court visits can be emotionally taxing. Plus, every time there is a delay you are giving your ex valuable additional time to strengthen and consider his position. Bottom line: Avoid these delays when it's within your control.

- **Make it easy.** Attorneys and judges are busy people. As I mentioned before, make it easier for them to come to the conclusion that you want. For example, if the issue is visitation, show up with a detailed visitation schedule prepared explaining what you want and why you want it. Now the busy judge or busy attorney doesn't have to create something from scratch. If your ex pushes back against your proposition, you will have answers ready when the judge questions you. Not only will this make it easier for others to come to the conclusion that you want them to, it will make it easier on you too. And believe me, you want to make things easier on yourself during this process.

- **Save money and time.** Most people would like to spend as little time as possible in court, dealing with their ex. They also want to avoid paying fees to an attorney. Legal interactions cost money and time. As painful as it can be to take extra steps to get organized (probably it's the last thing you want to do after a long day at work or on the weekend), it's often worse to be stuck in court or with your attorney longer than you have to be. Court delays mean you miss more work (potentially losing income), while having to pay additional fees for things like childcare, gas and parking, or public transportation.

Remember, if you have an attorney, you want to be efficient with your time. If you don't know what you want or don't have all the information you need, this is going to cost you because the attorney will have to spend more time with you asking questions or doing that same work for you. If you have the financial resources to pay someone to do this, then great. Most of us do not.

- **Empower yourself.** When you're in a sea of chaos and uncertainty, it is empowering to be organized. And believe me, divorce can get chaotic sometimes. You don't want to be the person in the courtroom frantically looking through documents trying to locate a fragment of information or relying on others to provide you with information that you should possess. The less you can rely on yourself, the more you must rely on others (attorneys, your ex, the judge, and so on). Self-reliance through developing the habit of organization will help you to breed confidence in your abilities. During divorce, you'll need all the self-confidence you can get.

- **Hold on to an advantage.** If your opponent in court has information that you don't, you must assume he'll use it to his advantage. Do not gift that kind of leverage to your ex.

- **Earn respect.** It is important that the people you interact with during divorce respect you professionally. Put another way, if you have your act together they will know you are not someone they can take advantage of because you don't know what's going on or you are disorganized. This goes for judges, attorneys, your husband, and mediators. You don't want others to think they can walk over you.

- **Keep people honest.** Sometimes, if they don't think they will be caught, people will try to bend the truth. This is particularly true if they think it will advantage them in a divorce settlement. Organization will help you keep them honest. For example, if your ex states in an open courtroom or mediation room, "I never said that," then you can respond by producing the text message where he said it. Or if your ex states, "I can't afford that," you can show income evidence that proves otherwise. If he says, "I can handle taking the kids to their activities," you can show on paper how his work conflicts with the kids' summer schedules.

- **Benefit emotionally.** In addition to raising your confidence, being well organized reduces anxiety. I'm not saying it will eliminate anxiety or stress altogether, but reducing these levels is damn important. Imagine walking into an exam room to take a test that will decide your entire grade for that class and you aren't prepared, or you didn't prepare as much as you should. My guess is that you would be more anxious and stressed then had you walked in fully prepared and ready to go.

- **Expect the unexpected.** What happens if you get blindsided at court or the judge makes a decision you don't expect? I see this all the time. A client goes into a hearing prepared and ready to rock. Then the judge tells her that she is going to impose visitation orders the woman is opposing and wants her to disclose which days her ex can have the kids. The woman's whole plan just went out the window. Now she has to regroup and figure out what's acceptable on the fly. She is in shock and upset. But in that circumstance, the woman can react and rebound emotionally much more quickly and accurately through organization. In this situation, it can be difficult to make decisions that are measured and sound—decisions that you will stand behind later, after you have had a chance to regroup and think. This is where you rely on your earlier self, who was calm and thoughtful when she came up with a plan if this happened.

  Anticipate the possibility that the judge may throw a wrench into your plans and be prepared for it. Hope for the best, but prepare for the worst. Expect the unexpected.

Helpful Organizing Techniques

Angela didn't have time to prepare for her court hearing on custody and visitation. Then, while waiting in the hallway outside the courtroom, her ex's attorney approached her and handed her a proposed visitation schedule. After reviewing it for fifteen minutes, they were called in to go before the judge, who first wanted to know if the parties had come to any type of agreement. Angela wanted to get the process over with and felt like she had to give the judge an answer right then. So, she agreed to the proposed schedule, thinking that the agreement would work out.

What Angela had forgotten was that her work schedule was going to be changing the following month, which meant that her job conflicted with the new schedule. She also didn't realize she would be driving a farther distance and had not checked with her babysitter's schedule in advance. It would turn out that her babysitter wasn't available on some nights Angela had to work. Angela realized all this that night after she got home and was hard on herself because she knew she could have pointed out these things had she been organized.

The court still might have made some of the same orders, but at least Angela would have voiced her opposition to the proposed schedule and known she had done everything she could.

Because of being unprepared, Angela was left with some unattractive options. Her choices were to:

- Spend more time and money and go back into court, seeking to modify the order.
- Ask her husband or his attorney to agree to modify the order, but they would not be obligated to do so.
- Live with the order and try to make changes to her work schedule, accommodate her babysitter's schedule, and deal with the longer commute.

Here are some organizational principles that are helpful to adhere to in a divorce. These would have helped Angela and they can sure help you.

- **Look to the paperwork.** Divorce forms require detail and so they force you to be organized. You can use them to organize all the facts and details you need in one place. Don't gloss over these forms. You don't have to fill them out all at once, if the paperwork becomes too much, you can do them in sections. These forms require you to gather detailed income, property, debt, and expense information.
- **Establish an orderly system.** As your collection of paperwork builds, so will the challenge of keeping it organized. When you walk into court or a meeting, it is critical to have the information organized in a way that will allow you to quickly locate and retrieve what you need.
- **Make sure you keep a backup of your entries and important documents.** If something changes, make sure you update your

forms and files. Some forms even require you to list your custody and visitation schedules, which can be a great guide for you at the outset. Bring these forms with you to any hearings or meetings related to divorce and have them organized for easy access. You will never know when you'll need them.

- **Keep a journal.** This is a double-benefit activity. Writing in a journal is great for your mental health. It is a cathartic exercise to get your thoughts and feeling about events down on paper. A journal also is an amazing tool to have in your toolkit for being successful throughout the divorce process. It will naturally keep you organized.

  Very few people remember what they were doing three months ago on a Tuesday afternoon prior to a custody exchange. If neither party can recollect, then it's a moot issue. However, if you can refer to your journal and reply with confidence about what happened, it will give you an advantage. A journal puts a lot of information in your hands, which the other party may not have. *Knowledge is empowering.*

  When you keep a journal to track events, dates, and times, patterns will emerge. You might notice that the kids are usually dropped off late on certain days or that your ex seems to pick fights with you the same time every month. When these patterns develop, you can look for a cause. Maybe your ex goes to happy hour at the same time every week or once a month and then picks fights with you on those nights. Or when the new love interest is over, your ex has a pattern of dropping off the kids fifteen minutes late. Or the pattern could be that when the child support is due, the kids are dropped off late and your ex will go nuclear on you if you are even one minute late. What you do with this information is up to you. You can use it in your court case or you can use it to predict certain things and avoid them. (Like not taking his calls when you know he's been drinking.)

- **Track milestones.** If you have gone to court a few times, keep a list of when you went, why you were there, what was decided, and if you were ordered to come back to court later. If you don't keep this information straight, it's possible no one else will. You may need to refer to those milestones later.

Remember, you are your most valuable resource. In addition to court milestones, it's a good idea to keep track of milestones in your children's lives (school dates, sporting events, vacations, illnesses, and so on) and professional milestones, like when you or your ex started a new job, job promotions, or changes in salary. Track any other events specific to your life that may impact your divorce.

- **Organize your thoughts and know what you want.** Organization isn't always about notes and paperwork. You also need to organize your thoughts, intentions, and goals. Before you go to court or any kind of meeting/negotiation where decisions are going to be made, you should think about what you want. If you are going to discuss visitation schedules, you should think about what will and what won't work for you. Think about what your best case would be and what you can live with. This strategy would've been extremely beneficial for Angela.

Learning from Your Mistakes

Missing an opportunity is, of course, frustrating, but it can be turned into a positive experience if it shows you what to avoid doing in the future.

If you're prone to beating yourself up for mistakes, remember:

- **Divorce does not make it easy to be organized.** This is an understatement. Divorce can be an emotionally charged and unfamiliar process, involving multiple people with a mountain of ever-changing facts and dates. In this hectic environment, organization will keep you on course and give you an advantage in key moments. Life is complicated enough. Then the divorce process is added to your already full plate. It's a lot to handle, for anyone. You will need to apply extra effort to be and stay organized during this process, which is challenging.
- **Organization is challenging for everyone including the judge, the court staff, the attorneys, and your ex.** Don't

assume you are the only one struggling and that everyone else is super organized and prepared. This negative assumption would make it easy to get down on yourself when this process gets hard. Just remember, everyone is in the same boat. Everyone is busy and inundated with paperwork and details. Success depends on who is willing to put in the effort.

Judges are sometimes seen searching for the correct paperwork. I have seen attorneys in court who only spent a few minutes familiarizing themselves with the case file they need to litigate right before a hearing. I am constantly reminding clients of this reality. If it's hard for the other party, then you are on equal footing—meaning you can gain an advantage simply by putting in the effort.

- **Being organized in divorce requires effort, but it's not rocket science. Anyone can do it.** It doesn't matter if you are an attorney, a judge, or representing yourself. You can be well organized. You can go toe to toe with anyone when it comes to having your paperwork and facts at your fingertips, so you should not be intimidated by anyone. In fact, you may intimidate your opposition once they grasp the fact that you will come to court or meetings well organized every time.

Emotional Issues During Divorce

If you are reading Part Four, it's evident that you have decided to investigate divorce further. Even so, I can't stress enough that a huge emotional leap must take place between considering divorce and going through part of the process—even going so far as to court or mediation—and signing divorce papers. In my experience, women don't impulsively divorce. They are usually on a slow boil for quite some time. There isn't any one thing that starts the process, but a multitude of "one things." In the end, there is often one big thing that finalizes their decision. What I want you to know is that you aren't deciding to divorce on a whim. This fact will be important for you to remember as you go through this process, as your family or friends may question your reasoning.

By now, you've met with an attorney, visited a legal aid organization, or consulted websites that have advice about the laws in your state. Is there any rush to proceed with divorce? You may think that because you've begun an investigation, there is no turning back. That's not correct. You can pull back at any time. If you change your mind, that's okay. Even if your divorce becomes final, you can always remarry your husband if that's what you both want. Nothing is written in stone. There is always an escape hatch.

I'm frequently asked, "What if I change my mind?" "What if my filing for divorce is what it takes to make him know I'm serious about change and then he does change?" Those things may happen; it is not likely, however. Furthermore, you really don't want to use the threat of divorce to force your husband to see how important your marriage is. That's a risky proposition. Changes that occur following an ultimatum can be short lived. If your husband is abusive, once he has you back under his thumb, his bad behaviors not only may continue, but could increase.

Seeking divorce should be an honest plan on your part and not part of a scheme to make your husband jealous, frightened, or remorseful. That strategy will certainly backfire and you will be left as a fool. What if he tells you, "Good. I wanted to do this five years ago, but I just felt sorry for you back then. I can't wait until it's over and I can live my life"? That would hurt your feelings, not to mention that he would be calling your bluff, wouldn't he?

Please don't let anyone rush you into signing divorce papers and getting the ball rolling. This is your life and your marriage. You should take out your wedding albums or pictures with your entire family together and grieve the loss of the life you've known for so long. You are planning a big change. To do other than grieve would be disrespectful to you and your history.

No one can quite prepare us for seeing our names and our husbands' names on legal documents of marital dissolution. We look at the papers and it all seems so cut and dried, so clinical. Petitioner and respondent. Children mentioned as if they aren't the loves of our lives. It's alright to take your time. Don't let your friends tell you to just get it over with and move on with your life. They aren't living through this, you are. You may have been bullied or had your feelings disrespected for a good bit of your marriage. Now is time to respect yourself and listen to what you know is best. You don't want to regret your decision.

CHAPTER 21

What Emotions Are You Feeling?

DR. JILL

"I signed papers with a lawyer yesterday. I think I've been in a haze since then. Am I numb? I don't know. My feelings are a jumble. I want to tell you that I feel relieved; you know, the kind of relief that comes when you've thought about something hard for a long time and then it's finally done. That's how I think I feel, but I feel so guilty saying so. I mean, this is—or do I say was? —my husband for nine years." —Tricia, age thirty-five, married nine years

I'm sure you can understand how Tricia feels. I've never met a woman going through a divorce who didn't feel a wide range of emotions. Wouldn't it be great if you only felt one way: relieved that you took the correct action? Maybe you feel these emotions.

- Guilt about "doing something wrong"
- Guilt about feeling relieved
- Remorse/regret that the behavior was done
- Doubtful that you made a good decision
- Loss
- Fear
- Uncertainty

- Devastation
- Anxiety
- Giddiness
- Depression
- Settled
- Shame
- Like a failure
- Embarrassed

It's alright to feel any and all of these emotions—or others. Signing divorce papers is a big step and you haven't taken it lightly. You will have considered many factors before concluding you need to split up, but it doesn't mean that you're necessarily happy about it.

The fact that you have mixed emotions and uncertainty means that you're human and have a heart. If you only felt one way, frankly, I'd be concerned about you. I'd think that you had cut off your true emotions to get through a difficult time. I'd worry that you might begin using alcohol or drugs (prescription or otherwise) to medicate your feelings. I'd be concerned about the level of care you were able to give to your children and how present you could be for them. I'd wonder if your unwillingness to feel emotion was one of the causes of your divorce. Perhaps you were in such a painful situation for so long that you've cut off your emotions to avoid feeling hurt by your husband. I'd also worry about the time when the emotions you had kept at bay would come crashing down on you, and how well you'd be able to handle them. Trust me: All emotions come out sooner or later no matter how you try to keep them away from you.

It's alright to feel all the emotions on the list I presented above. They won't paralyze you. In fact, they will give you energy to be present for the next steps you need to take.

There are predictable stages of grief and loss everybody goes through during difficult times. Let me explain them to you, as I think they will help you recognize what you are feeling. These stages were first identified by Elisabeth Kübler-Ross, M.D., who wrote about them in her book *On Death and Dying* many years ago. Although she referred to these stages in the context of death, we all go through them during any kind of loss or difficult situation.

When you divorce, you are certainly grieving, both the loss of love, but also the loss of the hopes and dreams you had for the rest of your life. These stages will occur whether you initiated the divorce or your ex-husband did. It is often said that you will grieve one year for every ten years you were married. That's a while! This adage reinforces the message that grieving a marriage is real and necessary to move forward.

See if you can relate to these five stages.

Denial. How could this be happening? And to you? To you! It can't be real. You and your ex-husband were once so much in love. Maybe you are still holding on to a tiny sliver of hope that things can be worked out or that he'll come to his senses. Maybe you're in denial that he's found someone else or doesn't still love you. Denial is a handy coping mechanism because it allows you to see only part of what is happening without overwhelming you with all your emotions. So long as you can deny the entire reality of what is going on in your life, you can handle small bits.

Anger. Gosh darn it! It's all his fault! Why did he do X, Y, or Z? What a jerk! Maybe you can't believe you ever married your ex-husband or that you stayed with him so long. Hey, why didn't you get out sooner? Why did he make all those promises to change? He made a big fool of you. Get my drift? You couldn't be any angrier at your soon-to-be ex for putting you in this position. Maybe you take that anger out on him, sending him scathing emails or texts, or you call his voicemail and yell at him. Maybe you're short tempered with your kids, parents, or friends, because after all, how could they possibly know how you're feeling? Perhaps your lawyer gets the brunt of your anger because he's telling you facts you don't want to hear. You're just angry at the whole world these days.

Bargaining. This is the stage where you really beat yourself up and second guess your decision. This is the "If only" stage. It sounds like this: "If only I didn't believe him," "If only I saw the writing on the wall," "If only I tried harder," "If only I gave him more sex (better dinners, whiter white shirts)," "If only we went to counseling," "If only I was more fun," and so on. Essentially, you're trying to fix what has already happened in your marriage. Maybe the bargaining comes in the form of revenge on your husband: "If only he could be as miserable as I am *(because you're certain he's not)*" or "If only his car crashed into a tree."

Yes, even the last one is normal. Don't tell me you haven't thought of it.

Depression. Well, here's the big one, right? How many nights have you spent staring at the ceiling? How many days have you spent sobbing? Are you eating or are you on the "divorce diet"? Walking up a flight of stairs seems impossible. Getting the kids ready for school is an overwhelming task and if they have one more fight you will completely melt down to the ground. Work? Oh yeah, you've called in sick for the past week because you feel sick of life, sick of yourself, sick of your situation, and sick of having to deal with this all on your own. It's not fair. He's not depressed. He's out and about, having a good time and posting photos from his adventures on Facebook. You don't want to socialize because you can't look at your friends who are still married or hear one more piece of unsolicited advice. You just want to go to sleep until this whole thing is over . . . and maybe for a year after that.

Acceptance. Acceptance isn't the same as being happy. It just means that you accept that your marriage is over and believe you can begin a new life. You may still be upset that you didn't receive the settlement you thought you deserved or that your ex-husband still doesn't help with the kids' homework when he has them at his house or that he doesn't call them as often as you think he should when they're with you. It really means that, despite all this, you accept that the hopes and dreams you had for your marriage are over. It doesn't necessarily mean that you're thrilled about your situation. But eventually, when you remain in the acceptance stage for a while, you will be able to move forward into your new life and possibly a new love.

Well now, here's the most important information I can give you about the stages of grief and loss: They are not linear. That is, you don't go through them in a straight line and then you're done. The crazy-making part of these stages, especially when you are going through a divorce, is that you may be in the denial stage and then go to depression, followed by bargaining a couple of times, back to depression, and then be angry as a hornet, and then, oops here comes the depression again. But why are you so depressed when this can't really be happening? But then, yes you admit and accept that the divorce is happening.

Do you relate? Yes, I thought so.

You can go through these stages of grief and loss, up and down and in the middle in the matter of a few minutes, hours, or days. You can stay stuck in a depressed stage for a while, only to find yourself accepting where you are and wonder why you were so depressed. Then, you can get so angry you feel like your head is going to explode and don't know what to do with yourself. Don't be afraid of these stages. You will go through them and you will be alright. You're not going crazy. You're normal.

No, I don't know how long they will last. Don't be frightened, as it won't be forever. Your brain and your heart are doing their best to help you cope. Give them a break. Don't judge. Accept this saying: *Everything is alright in the end, and if it's not alright, then it's not the end.*

CHAPTER 22

Telling the Kids

DR. JILL

"I don't know what to tell my children. I don't even know when or where I should tell them. My husband told me that if I want a divorce so bad and I want to ruin our kids' lives, I need to be the person to tell them that's what I'm doing. He won't be any part of it. He's so mad at me, and wants to be the good guy in this even though he had two affairs. I know he's going to blame me and his family is going to blame me to the kids. Am I allowed to tell them that Mom is divorcing Dad because he wasn't nice to her? I don't even know what's right or wrong. I just want the kids to be okay. This is really scary."—Esme, age thirty-seven, married twelve years

I know that keeping your family together is one of the main reasons you stayed in your marriage so long. No one wants to put their children through a divorce. Yet thousands of children go through their parents' divorces each year. The better news for your children is that they aren't alone and probably know someone in a divorced family.

Telling your children about your separation from their dad is difficult. Divorce affects kids, no matter how well you prepare them. I can't tell you how your children will react. Likely, there will be shock, sadness, anger, or worry. However, there is research that shows that some kids also come out of a divorce better able to cope with stress and able to be more flexible young adults with greater tolerance for others.

Most older kids will remember exactly where they were and what was said when they were told. It will be a defining moment in their lives, so it is important to prepare as well as possible. The following items are some guidelines for that moment.

Tell your kids together with your husband. It doesn't matter if you hate each other at this point. It is important that you present a united front so that neither one of you is the bad guy who has to tell the kids alone and they won't hear different stories from each of you. Make a pledge of no guilt, blame, or anger, even if there was infidelity involved or one of you believes you did nothing wrong. Practice who is going to say what, so that neither one of you becomes upset in front of the kids.

Don't tell the kids until plans are finalized between the two of you, but do tell them before one of you moves out. It is very worrisome to tell children, "Mom and Dad are *considering* a divorce," "There is *probably* going to be a change in how we live," "We *might* get a divorce," and similar things. Sometimes, when there is a good bit of fighting, kids may ask if you're going to get a divorce. Answering that question can be a real slippery slope for parents, especially if divorce is under consideration. If no plans have been made, it's fair to say, "We aren't planning that now and if we ever did, we would tell you right away. For now, I don't want you to have to worry about anything that's going on between us. We both love you very much."

If possible, tell all the children at one time. If you have similarly aged children, addressing them as a family unit is best. Of course, you can't give a toddler the same explanation you would give a teen or even an elementary school-aged child, so use your best judgment here. What you don't want to do is give the information to the oldest child and ask this child either to hold on to the information or to talk to a younger child about the divorce on your behalf because the children have such a close relationship. Either scenario is unfair to your older child and puts this child in the position of being a parent. You are shirking your parental duties and "parentifying" your child if you do so, which you never want to do.

Do not attempt to turn over your responsibility to any of your kids. If there is a wide age gap between your children, it is alright to tell much older children before speaking to their younger siblings, but do so on the same day and never ask any of the children not to speak with the others. They need to be able to vent to each other as only siblings can.

Your talk should fit your children's ages, maturity level, and sensitivity. Very young children don't have any reference points as far as permanence goes. They understand a routine: Parents come and go in the morning and the evening, and we eat dinner together, and so on. Their home is pretty much their entire world. They don't have outside friendships or activities. By contrast, older kids have friends to lean on, as well as school and outside activities.

Very young children (ages 0–2) won't be able to understand whatever you tell them, but you do want to cuddle and kiss them as much or more than ever. Older toddlers to young school-aged children can understand something to the extent of "Mommy and Daddy are going to live in different houses so we don't argue so much, and we both love you just the same." Older kids might already have more information than you think about the strain in your marriage, as they may have overheard fights. Often, they will have been trying to piece together this information in their heads.

Include the following key points in your talk. No matter the ages of your children, you will want to say something like this (put this in your own language, of course): "Sometimes, adults change the way they feel and the way they love each other, so they disagree so much that they have to live apart. But kids and parents are always tied together, and even if they disagree a lot, they don't stop loving each other or divorce each other. Parents and kids love each other for life. What happened is between Mom and Dad and not your fault at all." These key phrases are very important, because younger kids may think that if you get mad at them you may leave them like you left Dad.

Kids of all ages take on blame and responsibility. I've had younger kids ask me if their parents are getting a divorce because they didn't pick up their toys. I've had older kids tell me that their parents are getting a divorce because they are bad kids and gave their parents so much stress that they fought and fought until they decided to divorce. Now it's their fault.

Answer your children's questions. Try to answer your children's questions as truthfully as possible without too many details. They don't need to know all the reasons for your divorce, especially if infidelity or imprudent financial responsibility was involved. They just need to know what will be changing and what won't. It is very tempting to give kids little nuggets of what their other parent did, but I implore you not to do this, even if your ex does. If they tell you, "Dad said you were a bad wife," or something to that effect, you can tell them, "I'm sorry your dad said that to you. That wasn't fair and I'm sorry if it upset you. All you need to know is that I'm the same mom I always was and I love you very much."

Kids may search for a reason that makes sense to them and ask, "Well, were you a bad wife?" I advise using the parrot response, which is to restate that what happened is between Mom and Dad, you are the same mom you always were, and that you love them.

Let your kids talk. Different kids have different responses to their parents telling them about divorce. Some kids will cry, some will shout, and some will clam up and not want to talk at all. Just like you, their reactions may change over time and they certainly go through the same stages of grief and loss that we talked about in the last chapter. However, what you can do is to let them know that whenever they want to talk to you about the divorce or anything else you will be a good listener. That last bit may be difficult for you because oftentimes it's hard to hear what they might want to tell you. It's always important to legitimize their feelings and restate that it's not their fault, it's 100 percent related to the parents' issues, and you love them.

Children of all ages are inherently narcissistic. It's not that they don't love you, but their world revolves around them, so don't be alarmed if these are their only questions after you've broken the news of your separation or divorce:

- Who will I live with?
- Will I still go to the same school?
- Can I keep my toys? Where will my toys be?
- Do I have to move too?
- Can I keep my friends?
- Can I still play baseball, gymnastics, and so on?
- Where will I spend the holidays?
- Are both of you still coming to my birthday party?

- Is this forever or just for right now?
- Am I going to have a different mommy or daddy?

It's a little daunting, isn't it?

To minimize stress to your children going forward after you break the news of your split, the most important things to remember are:

That each parent should stay involved in the children's daily lives.

To keep daily routines as normal as possible, regardless of which parent has the kids.

To keep each other informed of children's activity schedule.

Not to speak negatively about the other parent to your children, and request that other adult friend and family members do likewise.

Not to use your children as your therapists, confidantes, or lawyers.

Let Other Adults in Your Kids' Lives Know about the Impending Divorce

While you don't have to share more information than you feel comfortable with, and shouldn't give details, let adults who have continuing contact with your children—their teachers, coaches, daycare providers, and so on—know what is happening in their lives. Ask these individuals to let you know if they see any changes in your children's behavior so that you can address problems in a timely fashion. Also let them know if there is a change in routine or scheduling, such as that you and Dad will be dropping off or picking up the kids on different days.

Some of these people spend more time with your children than you do on a day-to-day basis. Keep them part of your team.

Whew! Well, that was a lot to take in, wasn't it? I hope I've helped to make a frightening situation a little less so. In later chapters, we will discuss your children further and how they change and adapt to the divorce, ways of handling differences in parenting, what to do if your ex disregards your rules, and so on. But I think I've given you enough to process for right now. I realize that what I've laid out depends upon your husband being a decent guy where the kids are concerned, and that isn't always the case. It also depends upon both of you putting your differences aside and focusing solely on what's best for the kids—and that also isn't always the case. You may need to have "the talk" alone if your ex won't behave amicably or doesn't stick to the plan. You may not do this perfectly either. The suggestions I gave you are suggestions for optimum situations and ones that I hope you can use during a very difficult time.

Next, we will deal with emotional fears and the crazy-making ups and downs you will go through on this journey. Hang in there. You're doing great.

CHAPTER 23

How Are You Doing?

DR. JILL

"I'm just so sick of this divorce. We agree on something and then he changes his mind. We decide that I'll keep the house until both kids are in high school, and then he tells me he needs money so we have to sell it now. We tell each other that neither of us will date until the divorce is final because it could be confusing and upsetting to the kids, and then I find out he's been seeing someone for a few weeks and already has introduced the kids to her. He tells me he's going to do his best to take care of the mortgage, and then tells me that's not going to work. He's late picking up the kids for visits, which messes me up. He also tries to change the dates that he has them to accommodate his social schedule and uses me as a babysitter. I pay for the kids' expenses and then must argue with him to get half of the money back. What the heck?" —Melissa, age thirty-nine, married ten years

Divorce is a fairly lengthy process. At best in many states, it takes six months. At worst, it can last several years. Circumstances shift and change during a divorce: both the conditions within you and perhaps your living situation, job, friends, finances, and so on. Just when you think you've accepted the split from your husband and the inevitable changes that will occur in your life, you may shuffle through denial, anger, bargaining, and depression for the 199th time. When will this end? You may not like my answer.

It is generally accepted that it will take one year for every ten years you were married to move past the emotional crush of your divorce. Before you slide into *are you kidding me* land, let me assure you that the entire time won't be horrific. There will be very difficult times that challenge your fortitude and even your sanity, but there also will be times of gratitude and discovery as well. You will have ups and downs.

Several years ago, my husband had a very smart boss who, when handing out criticism of items that my husband didn't accomplish well, would say, "Opportunities exist for you to . . ." He could have said, "You do this poorly" or "You need to improve in this area." Instead, he reframed the conversation in a positive light, as an opportunity. I thought that was brilliant.

Ask yourself: What opportunities exist for you in this period of massive change? Of heartbreak? Of rejiggering? Of uncertainty? Of fear? Of reexamination? Of hard work? Of anger? Of unfairness? Of guilt or shame?

Do you remember that I spoke to you about the idea that *when you can't change the situation, you must change your mind?* You are not going to be able to change your husband's mind at this point. If you could have done that you would have while you were married and you wouldn't be going through this divorce now. He cared as much as he could possibly care while you were married and that wasn't enough, was it? The truth is that he doesn't care all that much now. He doesn't truly care if you are unhappy, stressed out, or didn't get enough sleep, if your boss or your three-year-old is cranky, if you have a stress pimple in the middle of your forehead like a third eye, or if your twelve-year-old forgot her homework. He doesn't care and he really doesn't want to hear about it. He's not going to help you. Forget about that.

Is that fair? No. But the more you focus on what isn't fair, how little he is doing, how he's living his life while you are taking the brunt of the kids' anger or sadness, and—should I go on? —the less time you have for focusing on yourself and what you need to do to help yourself.

I find that women who are going through a divorce often sound like their own children with the refrain "It's not fair!" Hey, I'm not criticizing. I myself sang that phrase more often than I'd like to admit to you when I went through my divorce. But it just doesn't do any good. It doesn't change the situation one bit. Considering this, what could you be doing with your time and energy instead? That is a more productive thing to focus on.

Recently I spoke with two longtime female patients in my office. Both started therapy with me when they were in horrible marriages with narcissistic, entitled, arrogant men. During their course of therapy, they each made the decision to get a divorce after begging their husbands to join them for counseling, as well as trying the different ideas you and I talked about earlier in this book. They had run out of options, run out of time, and run out of energy and hope. Regretfully, they divorced. One woman's divorce took about a year, while the other woman fought tooth and nail over every item and changed lawyers three times. In the end, her divorce took five years and she still had an outcome that didn't please her.

The first woman wasn't a person of financial means and had to make many changes in her life that scared her, but in the end, she is grateful for how her divorce brought her closer to her daughters and opened a career to her she didn't know existed.

The second woman is a person of considerable wealth who didn't work outside the home when she was married and still doesn't have to at this point. She was able to keep her home and her stuff and entertain and financially help her adult children.

The first woman told me about the hardship of paying for her younger daughter's college education because—with counseling—she decided that it wasn't worth it to her to keep arguing with her ex-husband about paying for the education, even though he had promised to do so. In our discussions, she examined the real "cost" of having to argue with him for each payment, of listening to the false accusations that would spew from him, of following the tangents he would take her on, and so on. She eventually decided that it was less expensive to pay the tuition and cut back on other items in her life than cope with the dread she had whenever w she had to have contact about this, as well as the depression hangover she had afterward. Today, she is happy in her life and doing well in her accidental career and dating a lovely man.

The second woman continues to employ a team of lawyers to fight every single injustice—a battle I'm quite sure her ex enjoys. She has lost friends due to her constant negative attitude and carping about her ex seven years after kicking him out of the house. She has poor health, difficult relationships with her children, and has unsuccessfully dated a succession of men she is looking to take care of her. After all this time, she is generally bitter and feels she's getting a raw deal from life. She has paid a high price for fighting her ex.

You see where I'm going with this. There are many changes that take place in a divorce, just as there were many changes that took place when you married. Your life doesn't stay the same minus the husband. There is a cost to marrying and a cost to divorcing. There is a cost to having children, which is a long-term responsibility. If your ex-husband is not going to live up to his end of the responsibility, someone has to, and it looks like that someone will be you. These are just the facts. I didn't say they were fair.

If you were married to an unkind man, there are only two ways he can continue to harm you: with money and with the kids. If he was a jerk when you were married, it's unrealistic to think that he's going to be nicer now that you are divorcing. No, instead he will try to frighten and punish you financially and hurt you through the children. That's another unfair fact.

If he was a decent married man, then hopefully he'll still be decent after the divorce.

My suggestion is that you look at your divorce in the same way that I'm looking at my retirement: I hope that I will have social security payments to rely on, but I'm not counting on them and I am trying to make other financial arrangements. If I don't receive social security it won't be fair; after all, I've contributed to the system my entire working life. I'll be angry for sure. However, instead of looking to the government to keep me comfortable in my older age, I am choosing to rely on myself and make financial plans now. If social security comes through, I'll look at that as a nice surprise.

Similarly, your ex may be ordered to pay a certain amount of money in spousal support and/or child support, and certainly you should pursue legal channels if he doesn't. He may also have custody and visitation orders detailing who pays for schooling, daycare, camps, sports, and so on. Again, you are well within your rights to fight him if he doesn't live up to his obligations. He shouldn't be let off scot-free if he doesn't. But be prepared if he doesn't do it.

I suggest that you take stock of every slight, every nuance, and every objection you have and see which of these items you can take off your emotional plate to reduce your pain. You and I can agree that it's not best for your children to be introduced to a new "tootsie" so soon after you filed for divorce. It's not healthy for your kids to be involved in a cavalcade of new "honeys" either. Is it illegal for your ex-husband to date, however? No. Are you going to find some precedent that legally keeps your children away from their father because he has a girlfriend of the week (if he does)? Probably not. You're angry, sure. You're hurt because you've been so easily replaced. Certainly. You've already seen her first name with his last name as the new Mrs. and imagined your kids calling her Mommy. I get it. Can you stop him? No.

What do you do with all this injustice? You decide to focus on yourself and your emotional health. You tell the children that you are still the same mom and that this fact won't change. You tell them that they can always talk to you. If they are older, you empower them to tell their father the way they feel. Get it?

During the divorce process, emotions run high and there's a lot of hurt and unfairness to go around. Your feelings are on such a Ferris wheel that you feel nauseous a good bit of the time. No matter what kind of feelings you have during this period of uncertainty and adjustment, you can feel them, bathe in them, and cry over them. Just also have a plan for moving forward and out of them each time.

I used to tell myself that I was going to worry, cry, and fret from 7:00–7:15 AM and from 7:00–7:15 PM each day, and then would do something else. That worked. I gave myself permission to feel all the horrible things that were going on in my head and then let them go until the next time I had an appointment to fall apart.

You will continue to go through the cycles of grief and loss for quite some time and that's alright if you give yourself the grace of acceptance each time as a touchstone.

Here's what I know for sure: No matter whether you initiated your divorce or it was thrust upon you, now that you and your husband are on the path to a divorce, you are experiencing tons of fears and crazy-making emotional ups and downs that you couldn't have expected. The emotional process of divorcing is never a straight path.

So, let's look all these feelings straight in the eyes.

Irrational Fears

You are bound to experience fearful thoughts, such as:

What if I don't have enough money? Of course, this is a reasonable question. Whether you formerly lived as a two-income family or one of you worked outside the home while the other was a homemaker, the truth is that both you and your ex-husband now need to be able to live in and afford separate households. I truly don't know what that will mean for you financially, however if a professional is advising you in your divorce, this professional will be able to give you a ballpark figure of what you can expect. You may need to sell your home or move to a smaller, less expensive apartment. You may need to move in with a family member for a while. You may need to get a roommate. Life is changing for you, this is true.

Will you need to find a job or a better-paying job? Possibly. But you won't be out on the street or in a homeless shelter while your husband is living it up in a castle. That doesn't happen, even if he's threatened you that it will. He doesn't make the laws in your state and he doesn't get to decide *how much he'll give you*. The division of assets is not a "gift." It's a legal obligation. You had rights as a married woman, and your money and any property was a joint investment, not solely his to do with as he pleased while you were married, or afterward. Don't buy into his threats/promises/ultimatums. They aren't true. Once your divorce is finalized, the court will ensure he honors his legal obligation as it was set forth during your divorce decree.

What if my children hate me? Your children love you. They've always loved you and this won't change. Now, however, they may have days when they take out their grief or anger at you because you are their safe person. I know that's not fun. In those times you might be thinking, *Their father can be their safe person today. I don't need this.* I hear you. Just know that it's their sideways way of letting you know that they love you. Just stay the course and keep being the mom they've always loved. No changes, no giving in, no trying to compete with Dad. They need your security and consistency.

What if I never find love again and I'm alone the rest of my life? That could happen. It will be more likely to happen if you don't get out there when you are ready or you fail to decide to be a happy person. I know you can't see through to the other side of this drama right now, but you are a lovable person who is able to be a good partner to someone else in the future. Love will find you when you are able to be found.

What if I regret the divorce? Don't give into the dark thoughts you are currently having and believe this is the way you'll feel the rest of your life. I haven't yet talked to a woman who—a few years down the road—regretted her divorce. She may feel sad that it had to happen, but she nonetheless feels that it was the right decision.

Examining the Evidence Can Help You to Reduce Your Anxiety

Here's a little exercise I do with my patients when they experience irrational fears. Let's do it together. Pretend that I'm a judge in a courtroom and you have come to me with your case—your case being whatever fear is currently gripping you. I'd like you to make the case to me and then I'll rule impartially on it. Here's how it might sound.

Judge: I'm calling the next case. It's Ms. A. Please stand before me and state your case.

You: Your honor, I believe I'm going to be alone and unhappy for the rest of my life.

Judge: All right then, I'm ready to hear your evidence.

You: Evidence? What do you mean by that?

Judge: Ma'am, I thought you came into my courtroom fully prepared to state your case. You must have some evidence that you will be alone and unhappy for the rest of your life. Tell me what it is. We have a limited amount of time for each case today.

You: Okay, well I mean, maybe no one will find me attractive or fun and especially if I'm a Gloomy Gus all the time, like I am now. I mean, I wouldn't want to be with me. And for sure, my husband didn't want to be with me. He told me that no one would ever want me.

Judge: Where is this husband? Can I take his testimony and find out why he's made that judgment since you seem to be basing so much of your evidence on his statement?

You: No, we're getting a divorce, but what if he's right and I'm going to be a shriveled up old woman with a bunch of cats and I die alone?

Judge: Ma'am, I'm waiting for concrete evidence to all your claims.

You: I don't know, I just *feel* this way.

Judge: Ma'am, *I can't rule on feelings; I can only rule on evidence.* Hard, cold facts are what I need to rule in your favor. Do you have any of that or are your feelings the only things you're bringing me today?

You: They are my feelings, but what if they're true?

Judge: I can't find any reason to support your claim if they are based on feelings without evidence. I'm going to have to dismiss your claim and rule against you. Next case!

You see where I'm going with this? When you start spinning on the merry-go-round of fearful thoughts, I'd like you to sit still for a moment and present your case to a judge. Remember, the judge doesn't care about your feelings; she's only interested in concrete facts. If it is difficult for you to come up with evidence to give the judge then you must decide: If I don't have facts—and I only have fearful feelings—can I really bring this case into a court of law? Or the court of your own head?

Instead of trying to make a case that probably doesn't exist, take control of the things you can control: your thoughts, behavior, and reactions. You will feel better quickly.

"Help! I think I'm going completely stark raving mad!"

When I am counseling women who are going through a divorce, they experience a multitude of crazy-making thoughts, such as:

- *I want to go back to him.*
- *How can he be going out with his friends when I'm stuck taking care of his kids?*
- *Wait, he's dating already? We're not even divorced.*
- *Can he change?*
- *If I check his Facebook and Instagram I can find out what he's up to.*
- *What if he's happier with someone else?*
- *What if everything was my fault?*
- *What if the kids want to be with him full time?*
- *How can he seem so happy when I'm so miserable?*
- *What if he gets remarried before me?*
- *What if the kids start calling another woman Mommy?*

- *Wow, I didn't know I hated him this much.*

Oh, I'm sorry. Was I listening in on your private thoughts? Going through a divorce is possibly the most emotional processes you'll experience. There are tons of ups and downs every day. Eventually, it will be different, but right now you may cycle from hoping he can still change and life can be happy again, to jealousy that he's dating another woman, and then to anger, to different fears, and back again, on and on and on. This nearly constant shifting of your emotional state is normal and it will pass.

Here are a few things you can do to help yourself get through this challenging time.

Stop checking his social network timelines. I mean it. Get off his Facebook page right now and unfriend him, or block him completely from all social media you use. What exactly are you accomplishing by stalking him in this way? How are you helping yourself? What do you get from this behavior that is pleasing or makes you feel any better? I call that site *Fake-book* because everyone posts photos of their exciting, fun-filled lives, yet no one has a life the way it's presented on his page. You don't know the private agonies people face or that they drink to go to sleep or watch porn five hours a day or are spending more money than they possess to eat out at the restaurants they're posting about. Does anyone ever post "Really horrible night. Dog threw up on my comforter, baby had colic, and I went to work to find out that I was fired. But happy Tuesday everyone"?

Your ex may use social profiles with the express purpose of knowing that you're stalking him there. That way, he can make you miserable from afar. He doesn't even have to be married to you to make you miserable. He's playing you. Bonus points for him.

Why do you care what he's doing? The more you focus on him, the less you focus on you.

Tell your friends and family to stop telling you what your ex-husband is doing. That's right, your mom who tells you how much she misses him and says isn't it nice that he called her yesterday to find out if her cold was any better. Your brother who tells you that just because you're getting a divorce, it doesn't mean he still can't be friends with him, because after all, they were bros for ten years. Your friend Kate who saw him at the market and thought he looked good. Your friend Lori who heard from her friend Susan that he's dating some cute girl from his work. Your Aunt Becky who heard that he got a promotion. Tell them all to stop. You don't need to know and it's not helpful to you.

You can tell them, "I know this is interesting to you, but these are things that I don't need to know anymore and they aren't helpful to me. So, I'm going to ask you to not mention anything about him to me from now on." Well, you know what's going to happen next: They will ask you why you're so touchy about him. Which brings me to my next point . . .

Politely decline petty, unhelpful advice from people who don't know what they're talking about. "You should really stick it to him for what he's putting you through," "I'm sure if you're just nicer to him he'll be nicer to you," "I don't understand why you're getting a divorce anyway. I think it's ridiculous that you couldn't work it out with him," "Don't let him have the children on school nights," "Just go out and meet another guy and you'll feel a lot better about yourself," "You could really use a new haircut," "Just cheer up already. How long were you suffering in that marriage?" All your well-meaning family members and friends are giving you often conflicting advice and then you have to choose which thing you've heard is better.

Oh yes, and the advice could change every day.

Then what? Even if you don't think you know what's best, I'm here to tell you that you do. You know what feels best to you right now. You should listen to you, you should listen to a legal professional, and you should listen to a counseling professional. Everyone else can go suck air.

Look pal, it's hard to stick it out when the going gets tough. I understand. Divorce is not for the faint of heart. It's hard work. Wherever possible, make your life easier, not more difficult. Choose joy in any way you can get it: from watching cat YouTube vidoes, eating an ice cream cone, going for a walk, looking at flowers, making a gratitude list every night before you go to sleep, watching a funny movie, reading an inspiring book, or volunteering even an hour a week—with or without your children—for a cause you believe in. Help others, smile if you think there's nothing to smile about, repeat positive mantras, and eat healthy food that nourishes your body. Make an effort to help yourself, because ultimately, you are the only one who can.

Remember this: *If you can't change the situation, you must change your mind.*

As we wind up this portion of our time together, I'd like you to prepare yourself to sign your final divorce documents. Just when you think you have everything all handled and will be relieved to have it over, oops, you need to sign your name above or below your husband's on a document stating that he is now your ex—your wusband—and you aren't married anymore. That's a tough one. We'll chat.

CHAPTER 24

Signing the Final Divorce Documents

DR. JILL

"Okay, I just have to say this: No one prepared me for what I was going to feel when I signed those final papers that read 'Dissolution of Marriage.' I mean it was a done deal. It was real. When I signed those papers, I was a divorced woman. It's what I wanted. It's what I begged for after a year of fighting over the terms of the divorce. I should have been dancing on the ceiling. Instead, I was alone in a little room in my lawyer's office shaking and thinking, Oh my gosh, what have I just done?" —*Farrah, age thirty-four, married nine years*

Farrah is exactly right. What a mix of emotions you may feel when your final divorce documents are ready for your signature!

- Grief
- Relief
- Freedom
- Disbelief
- Happiness
- Guilt
- Numbness
- Fear

- Uncertainty
- Shame
- Anger
- Vindication
- Loss

That you may feel all those emotions within a few moments, frankly feels a little crazy.

I remember walking into my lawyer's office to sign my divorce documents. The settlement had taken a long time and I just so badly wanted it to be over and done. This was the day I had waited for. I recall walking up to the receptionist desk, expecting her to notify my lawyer that I had arrived. Instead, she produced a packet of papers with my name on it and I stood at the reception desk looking at my soon-to-be former husband's signature with mine waiting just below his. It was jarring. It was scary. It wasn't what I expected at all.

I thought my kind and caring attorney was going to invite me into his office, ask me if I wanted a cup of tea or a Xanax, pat my shoulder, and tell me, "You know, Jill, no matter how much you think you wanted this or how prepared you were up until this point, this is very difficult. Just take your time and I'm here for you."

Actually, I looked at my ex's signature—how could he have signed this before me? —and thought, *This is the same signature I've seen a thousand times. I've seen it on our marriage certificate. I've seen it on our children's birth certificates. I've seen it on his passport when we took vacations together. I've seen it when he signed checks for household expenses. I saw that first name signature when he wrote love letters to me a long time ago or signed a greeting card.*

Then I felt very, very sad.

It was such a familiar signature. Over twenty-four years of knowing each other and nearly twenty years of marriage, it was a signature that was almost as familiar to me as my own. And there it was again, except this time it didn't have *love* above the signature; it was declaring that it was almost as if we had never met. It said we didn't like each other anymore. It said that our entire time together came down to dollars and cents, who owned what, and with whom our children would spend the holidays. *Weren't we just a family?*

All sorts of thoughts ran through my head as the receptionist patiently waited for me to sign the papers. In the end, I just looked up at her helplessly, signed them while still standing at her desk, thanked her—*thanked her?* —and walked out to my car, thinking, *I am a divorced woman.*

I sat in my car and cried for a while. I don't really know how long it was. I cried for everything that was, everything that I had hoped for that would never be, and everything that would never be again. I felt crushed and relieved at the same time. I felt hopeless and hopeful. I felt frightened and expectant. I felt that my head was too small for all my feelings. My skin felt unbearably tight. I felt agitated and jumpy. I needed to get out, but *out from where?* I didn't know what to do with myself.

It was easily the most intense and unreal day of my life up until that point. As I wrote this description at a Starbucks, I must admit that I was slobbering into my chai latte even twenty years later. The intensity of that day is something I won't forget and I'm guessing you won't forget your signing date either.

How will you feel when you sign those papers? I don't know, but I wanted to share my experience with you because I was completely unprepared for the onslaught of so many different emotions. You may feel nothing other than joy and relief. I have a patient who sent out divorce announcements that looked like wedding announcements, but announcing her divorce in the happiest of terms. She was elated.

Here is what I want you to know: Whatever you feel is fine and correct for you. You can share your feelings with people you trust or with no one at all. You can cry or laugh, or do both at the same time. What I don't want you to tolerate are people who tell you things like:

- "Don't you just feel so happy? Let's go out and celebrate!"
- "I don't know why you're crying. *You* wanted the divorce."
- "You really feel upset? Should I remind you about everything he did to you?"
- "Well, it was your doing. I warned you that it would be a mistake."
- "Let's find you a guy to take your mind off it."
- "The only way to get over one man is to get under another one."
- "All men are jerks. Hopefully you won't get married again."

- "You have to knock this off and think of your children. Be strong for them."
- "By tomorrow this will all just be a bad dream."

Honestly, people don't know what to say to you. It's hard to blame them. Getting a divorce is a death: a death of dreams, of hopes, of innocence, of a certain future, of a family, of promises. Who knows what someone wants to hear when a loved one passes on? It might be different for each person, but you worry that whatever you say will be wrong.

So, remember that you are allowed to feel however you feel. You are also allowed to tell a friend or a family member that you appreciate his or her concern, but you'd rather not discuss your divorce right now. You don't have to share anything you don't want to. You don't have to ex-bash. You don't have to reveal the gory details.

You can give yourself the grace of time and reflection. You don't have to be anywhere or see anyone that you don't want to. Be kind to yourself. Yes, all these feelings will eventually pass, but not on the day you sign the papers . . . or probably the day or week or month afterward. Gradually, there will be a new normal, but not on this day.

Allow yourself to cry if you feel like crying, or to laugh if you feel like laughing. Allow yourself to dance or to curl into a ball. Just allow the feelings to come and go. They can't hurt you; they are just information about that moment. Everything you feel is just information for you to observe and take note of. That's all. No more and no less. How you feel is not a judgment of your character or your integrity. Just information.

When you feel ready, read the next section of the book where we will discuss your post-divorce life. You've gotten through the divorce if you've signed your papers, but that doesn't mean your relationship with your wusband necessarily ends—especially if you have children together or you are receiving or paying spousal support. You have a whole new life to discover and build. The prospect of your new life is exciting and it's daunting, but you can do live it well. I just know you can!

PART FIVE

After Divorce

The divorce is complete. Done and dusted. Dunzo. Whew! You can finally breathe . . . can't you? Oh wait, you thought you'd be at the end of this process, that you'd feel free as a bird and happy as puppies in a box. How could there possibly be any more feelings or any tears left?

No one ever tells you that it's not over when it's over. You and your kids still need to make a new life while navigating the leftovers of your old life. It's a little like the Olympic Rings: They intersect and overlap. So now you have this new, divorced life, but—especially if you had children with your wusband—you still have continuing contact and consideration of him on a daily or several times a week basis. And doesn't that bring up all new emotions!

There is still much to be done, my friend. In the following chapters, we will discuss:

- How to take care of yourself and your kids. Beginning life again as a new family.
- The issues of loneliness, depression, and anxiety. Perhaps you thought you'd be happier. Are you second-guessing your decision?
- How to cope emotionally and legally if you're not happy with your custody or visitation agreement. What do you mean he has them every Wednesday and every other weekend? Who agreed to that?
- Coparenting with your ex. What the heck is he doing with your kids?
- Helping your children navigate traveling between two households and having two sets of clothes, two sets of toys, sleeping in another bed, and so on.
- Contact with your ex. How much do you or should you want? Maybe you want more than you admit. Maybe it's torture to have any contact at all.
- Dealing with family and social occasions on your own. Do you really have to answer all their nosy questions?
- Are all your old friends from when you were a couple still relevant in your new life? How can you go about making new friends as a single woman?
- The fear of independence. How do you turn off the water valve and go to a movie by yourself?

- Your identity. Who are you now and who do you want to become? You get to choose!
- Starting new and healthier relationships as a new and healthier you. Stop repeating old patterns. You get a do-over!
- Dating! Sex! *Wait, what?*
- How to react when your ex-husband begins dating. Are your children going to call another woman Mommy?
- New and exciting opportunities. Life is all so overwhelming.

Discussing these matters is good . . . really. You know you're thinking about all these situations, but don't want to admit it to anyone else. That's fine. We won't tell. Let's just get everything out in the open, just us three. That way, you can move forward in a free and powerful position and claim the life you deserve. It's a little uncomfortable, but we have complete faith in you.

Let's get started!

CHAPTER 25

Taking Care of Yourself and Your Children

DR. JILL

"I've spent the last seventeen years of my life taking care of a difficult man, a man who didn't appreciate that I was trying my best and actually doing a pretty good job at it. We had three kids in eight years and life got busy. I worked full time with the first one and then part time with the second one, and then was a stay-at-home mom with the last one and ever since. Tom was doing well enough and he encouraged it. It was a good decision, but then he started holding it against me. Taking care of a house, three children's schedules, and my husband left absolutely no time for me to look after myself. That was okay, I guess, but I completely lost who I used to be in being a mommy and a wife. I know that.

"It took Tom having three affairs for me to say, 'No more.' If I'm honest, he said it for me by telling me he was in love with the last one. He left for work one morning and didn't contact me for three days. He was with her. What was I supposed to do?

"Now, when I look at myself in the mirror I don't even recognize myself. Who is this tired, old-looking, sad person? What am I supposed to do now? How am I supposed to manage my life with all this fear and sadness? How am I supposed to help my children with their father gone? We are all a mess. What comes first, second and third? I have no idea." —*Erica, age forty-four, married seventeen years*

Starting a new life, when your old life isn't available to you anymore, can seem daunting. You've had a certain routine and a kind of comfort in the discomfort. The quote "Most people prefer the certainty of misery to the misery of uncertainty" may apply to you right now. Or perhaps you feel free as a bird and happy to be done with your marriage. That's fine too. Whatever you feel and experience now is yours and it is okay. Please don't judge yourself or allow others to do so.

Perhaps, during the life of your marriage, you were a team player. Like Erica, you focused on being a wife and a mommy. As a therapist, what I often find is that men have the gift of being single-focused during the day: It's all about the job. They hope and trust that their children and wives are having a good day, but can compartmentalize and focus completely on their work.

Women, on the other hand, always have a million things on their minds. Even if they work outside their homes, if they have children they are conscious of the children's pick-up times and after-school activity schedules, how a given child feels on a given day if there was a bad morning or night before, how the children slept and the way this may impact their day, homework, or projects, who is feuding with whom, what is planned for dinner, and so on.

Married women who work outside the home and don't have children— or have grown children living away from them—may feel inequality in the workplace and confront the pressures involved with that, or they may be thinking about a discussion or disagreement they had with their husbands that morning, their plans for dinner, their laundry and housework, their social calendars, or how their parents' health is, and so on.

Stay-at-home moms usually find that most of the housework and anything involving the home or children falls to them, so a constant juggling act is involved in each day. Finances may also be strained due to their one-income homes. Such a woman may find that she is constantly anticipating what each person in her family needs.

You see what I'm trying to get across: Because women are the ultimate multitaskers and focus beyond their own needs so much with the intention of making others feel happy and secure, when faced with the reality of divorce their worlds change in ways that their ex-husbands' worlds do not.

You have many different identities: mother, wife, daughter, sister, granddaughter, niece, aunt, and friend. Perhaps you have other identities: CEO, supervisor, business owner, room mom, artist, Girl Scout leader, and grandmother. Maybe you have still more ways that you—or others—would describe you: best friend, listening ear, fundraiser, first person to call in a crisis, and person who gets things done. If we look at all these descriptions, which one has changed in your life because of your divorce? Just one: wife. You are still all the other identities. Getting a divorce hasn't taken away your title as granddaughter. You are still someone's best friend and the one who is compassionate to others. You didn't stop working either inside or outside your home.

This is not to say that a *major* piece of your life is no longer there. That part of your perception is correct. What I want you to do at this moment, however, is to stop catastrophizing, which means to stop making something so large that you feel as if you can't manage around it. You are still the same person in a different marital circumstance.

Catastrophizing and focusing on what you *don't* have keeps you stuck and doesn't allow you to move forward into what you *do* have. You can't operate from a point of loss because that doesn't serve you. There simply is no payoff in focusing on what is no longer available to you.

Now, the focus needs to be on you and your children. These are quite simply the only things upon which you can have a positive impact. If you haven't focused on yourself in a long time, now is as good a time to start as any, because now it's necessary.

Practical Considerations

Let's think about a few things that I imagine are weighing you down.

- Finances
- Job
- Living situation
- Childcare
- Time management

We will talk about taking care of yourself and your kids emotionally in a later chapter. For now, let's discuss the immediate concerns that may be stressing you out. Let's take care of those first.

Your Finances and Job

"The first thing my husband told me when I said I wanted a divorce was, 'You know you're going to have to get a better job that earns more money because I'm not going to support you anymore.' The second thing he said was, 'You know we're going to have to sell the house because I'm going to need half of the money.' I felt two things right away: complete fear and bewilderment. Didn't he have any emotion about us getting a divorce?"
—Jamie, age thirty-two, married six years

We have a couple of scenarios to work with: Either you presently work outside your home or you are a stay-at-home mom (which, it goes without saying, is a full-time job without the benefit of a paycheck).

If you have an outside job, you are already producing income. You will need to decide if your current job pays you enough so that along with any child support and spousal support you may be receiving your expenses are covered. Is it necessary to think about another job or source of income? Because your salary was used in the calculation of your support, your usable income may have gone down.

If you haven't worked outside your home before the divorce, do you need to do that now? Sometimes, in divorce proceedings, a husband will "demand" that his wife earns a salary going forward. This, of course, lessens his support obligation. Or he may stipulate it just to be cruel. If he has children, he knows that childcare arrangements will need to be made and that their lives will change because Mom now has a job.

Sometimes, the man doesn't really care that much. This causes a huge amount of emotional stress to the woman. If this is your situation, I can only tell you that I'm sorry. But if there is nothing to be done legally about it, it will benefit you to recognize that staying resentful and bitter will not help your situation. You will need to look for a job. Whether that is a full-time job or a part-time job depends upon the support you are receiving and your expenses.

Perhaps you haven't worked in several years and have lost skills necessary to be competitive in the technological world. I would suggest looking into your local junior college, career center, YWCA, Apple store, or Microsoft store for help in getting up to speed. I have also found my nieces and nephews to be an invaluable source of tutoring! If you don't know what kind of work you'd like to do, I find that starting small and gaining confidence is the way to go. Working in a retail environment for a while can help you get your feet wet again in a nonthreatening atmosphere. You have responsibilities—but not overwhelming ones—and in these settings, you can practice interacting with adults (as opposed to children) in different types of situations.

Don't feel that you need to be a workplace rock star straight out of the gate. That would put undue pressure on you and could leave you feeling paralyzed. You don't need to know what you want to do forever right this moment. Give yourself some grace, if only for a short period.

If you already work outside the home, do you have a job or a career? If you have a job that you aren't passionate about, something you've done to help make ends meet, or a job that doesn't have an opportunity for advancement, you may need to think now about employment that meets different criteria. It may be time to have a conversation with your supervisor about the opportunities available to you. If you need to make more money than you're currently earning—and your current job will never offer you what you need financially—be unemotional about the issue of changing your job. It's time to look for one that fits your new requirements. I know that may sound harsh, but this is now your reality.

Your divorce may be a wonderful opportunity to make a career change or a location change that you've been avoiding. We often stay stuck in unfulfilling roles because there isn't a compelling reason to change what we are doing. Crisis may mean opportunity. Keep your mind open to that idea and force yourself not to live in a fear-based state of mind.

Your Living Situation

"I have no idea where the kids and I are going to live. We have to sell the condo and my ex has already moved into a swanky new apartment complex with a gym and a pool. The kids think it's great. I can't afford something like that, so I'm sure they will want

to spend more time with him. The condo is in escrow and there wasn't a lot to split up financially. I'm in total panic. I'm afraid we're going to be homeless." —Sandra, age thirty-nine, married ten years

Divorce most often causes chaos in a woman's living situation. The common stereotype is the man moving out of the home and the woman remaining with the children. That worked in the 1960s, but is not true today. Now, very commonly, the family home will be sold to split proceeds or pay outstanding debts. A woman and her children will often downsize in either their home or apartment for financial reasons.

Because women tend to have emotional attachments to their residences, the thought of uprooting yourself and your kids may seem more devastating than losing your husband. I understand. If this is what you are facing, you are permitted to feel crushed. You are permitted to be angry and resentful. But if you need to move, you'll need to think of viable alternatives because that day is going to come whether you have a lot of feelings about it. *Kapeesh?*

Because moving into another home is such a daunting and emotional experience, I advise you to ask someone you trust who is smart about his finances to help you think about your budget and what you can afford in a monthly payment, including utilities, homeowner's or renter's insurance, property taxes, maintenance, repairs, and so on. Then, start looking around for what you need—and look with new eyes, not eyes that are bitter at having to look at all.

Do you need to move in with a relative or friend for a short amount of time until you land on your feet? This may feel humiliating to you, certainly. Try to understand that you also give this person a great gift by allowing this person to help you temporarily. You would do the same for this person. You can "earn your keep" by doing chores, making meals, gardening, running errands, taking care of children, and the like, even if you can't pay rent. Remember: This is a temporary situation. Everyone needs help at different points in her life and this may be one of those times for you.

Stubbornness and pride are not attributes you need to entertain right now. Don't be too stubborn to do what is right for you and your children, and don't have so much pride that you make ill-advised and unnecessary decisions. If you are lucky enough to have people in your life who care about you and want to help, don't be too prideful to give them the opportunity to do so.

Your Childcare

"I had a job where I had some flexibility to my hours. If my little girl was sick or there was some sort of event at her preschool, I could work at home. I just got a job that pays more with less flexibility and I have no idea what I'm going to do with my daughter. And you know what? Her father could care less. He doesn't care that she's going to be in daycare longer than before or that it's all going to be up to me to get her there and back. He doesn't have a care in the world where that's concerned." —Maryann, age thirty-four, married six years

If you are going to work outside your home and you have children, you will need to make childcare arrangements. There are many sources to look at, with the one that's right depending upon your financial situation, the hours you need to work, and your children's ages. Ideas to think about: after-school programs at your children's school or a program bus that picks them up from school, in-home care (in your home or in the home of a daycare worker, a relative, or a friend), or co-op childcare, if you are able to participate. In any of those situations, you will need to know how many days and hours your children will be attending, what opportunities they have while there (such as help with homework, sports, craft activities, socialization), how many children are in attendance per each provider (this is especially important if you have infants or toddlers), the price per week or month, any additional charges if you are late in picking the kids up, and the childcare workers' qualifications and certifications. In calculating the cost of the childcare, you will want to understand your ex's financial participation and if he is going to pay his portion directly to the provider. That would be my recommendation along with making a written agreement that you are responsible only for your portion of the bill and that your provider takes up any financial difficulty she has with your ex directly with him.

If you haven't worked outside your home before and you have always taken care of your children yourself, putting your kids in daycare is an especially big step and a difficult one. Most children do very well in a childcare situation. Studies have found that children develop more independence and social skills and have a lot of fun when they're around other kids. Do your due diligence on any childcare situation you are thinking about and observe the other children in attendance. Do whatever is necessary to allay your concerns.

Time Management

"This is going to sound ridiculous, but it's the little things I miss: He used to take out the trash and empty the dishwasher. When the smoke alarm went off, he found which one it was and changed the battery. He called the guy who cleaned the gutters. Now I do everything. I can do it, of course, but I also have to do everything else. I still must shop for food and make meals and do laundry. I don't know how much longer I can do all this. It's just too much." —Nola, age thirty-eight, married thirteen years

No matter how much or how little your wusband participated in the daily running of your household and children, that contribution is now gone. If he read one child a book at bedtime while you took care of the other one, you are now tucking in both children. If he did home maintenance, you are either doing it or finding others who can. If he dropped off the kids at school or daycare and you picked them up, it's now your turn to be the two-way carpool. There probably don't seem to be enough hours in the day, which can leave you feeling depleted and like a failure.

I remember when my children were very young and I was trying to do absolutely everything: meals, housework, playtime, laundry, baths, story time, and a part-time job. I nearly lost my mind every single day. I was just one person and I felt like I was failing on every front. I was exhausted and irritable. Then I read a book entitled *The Good Enough Mother.* What a revelation! I was trying to be the perfect mother whereas I found out that good enough really was good enough. It was impossible to be anything other than good enough. It was liberating and I ended up being a far better mom in ways that truly counted to my children because of it.

Here is my advice: Prioritize what is important. Will your squirming daughter lose friends if she doesn't have a French braid in her hair tomorrow? Will your son be kicked off the team if he shows up to baseball practice with dirty baseball pants? If the house isn't spotless, are you going to lose it? If you read a shorter story tonight, will the world end? If you pick up a pizza two times this week, will your children's health suffer?

Guess what? Their teeth don't need to be brushed scrupulously tonight. Give it a break. Give yourself a break. Take a breath. Watch a mindless reality show when the kids go to sleep instead of doing the laundry and cleaning the house. These things can wait tonight. Not every night, but tonight they can—and for more nights than you think.

Invite a girlfriend over with her kids, have a glass of wine, and let the kids make a mess. Who cares? You can all pick it up at the end of the evening.

Again, the key to time management is prioritizing what is important, and you are important. Put yourself on your to-do list. Not everything can get done in a day or in a week. You are in a different position than you were before. Understand that your life has changed and give yourself some grace for small things. They add up to bigger things. You will be happier doing less rather than more. You don't have anything to prove to anyone else. Be kinder. Be simpler. Invite joy rather than stress into your life.

CHAPTER 26

Helping Your Children Navigate Two One-Person Homes

DR. JILL

"Grace and Bobby hate having to go back and forth between their dad's house and mine. They say it's not fair and we're the ones who got the divorce, so why do they have to move around? I don't know how to even answer that question, but I feel guilty all the time. They're right: We did this to them." —Sandra, age thirty-nine, married thirteen years

"My ex lets the kids do whatever they want at whatever time they want when they are with him. He's the fun guy and they don't get enough sleep or eat well when they are with him. Then they get home to me and are complete basket cases for two days and I'm the bad guy because they must go to sleep at a reasonable time on a school night and do their homework and eat vegetables. They get to eat fast food and frozen pizzas with him. It's just not fair that I'm always put in this position." —Vicki, age thirty-seven, married eight years

"My little boy doesn't want to go with his dad. He wants to stay with me. It breaks my heart. He cries and screams and hangs on me when his dad comes to pick him up. He thinks that I'm creating this, but I'm not. Honestly, time with his dad gives me time to do errands and have a little me time and I also know it's what's best for my son. I really don't know how to help him." —Tamara, age twenty-nine, married four years

"My kids have gotten very secretive about what goes on at my ex's house when they are there. They don't want to talk to me about it. They tell me to stop asking them about it. It worries me. What if something bad is happening there?" —Lizzie, age forty-one, married sixteen years

You may relate to some of those stories. Helping your children transition from your home to their father's home can be challenging at best and gut-wrenching at worst. Unless your ex has done something illegal, he most likely has some custody and/or visitation. You may feel proprietary, that they are *your* children, but in fact they are his as well and he is entitled to time with them.

The research has shown that a 50/50 split in time sharing is what is optimal for children, if they aren't infants or toddlers. That same research cites that children have higher self-esteem and fewer trust issues when visitation is shared in this way. Children show the highest levels of stress in divorce situations when parents continue to battle, especially over the children.

Something to keep in the front of your mind as you read this chapter is this: *You and your husband chose to divorce, whereas your children did not. Your children weren't given the choice. You made the choice for them. You divorced their father, but they didn't divorce their father. He still is, and always will be, their father. They are just innocent bystanders.* I think those are important concepts to remember because although you undoubtedly had very good reasons for the divorce, your children just go along with whatever you and your wusband decide.

Given the ideas in the previous paragraph, what are the best steps to help your children transition from one home to another? Well, if I had my way, I would agree with Sandra's kids that it would be fairer to let them stay in one home and have the parents go back and forth to other homes. That seems fair, doesn't it? Why do you get to keep all your clothes and "toys" in your house when the kids need to pack and unpack their things every week? Why do they have to adjust and readjust constantly when you and their father get to enjoy the comfort and stability of the same home all the time? How would you like what is being expected of them? Makes you think, doesn't it?

Let's take look at some practices that will best help children adjust and create success in a divorce situation.

Make a Parenting Plan that Reflects Your Children's Ages

An infant cannot go back and forth successfully several times per week. Very young children need consistency to establish a daily routine and experience optimal emotional health. A teen's schedule often includes sports or club events, lengthy homework sessions, and leisure time for friends. While time with a parent is also important, these other commitments and events should be considered as well. A grade-school or middle-school child may have birthday parties to attend on weekends or sports practices, which are important as well. Each parent should understand these limitations and be flexible enough to allow for them.

Let Your Kids Have a Say in Their New Surroundings

If you are moving, help your children adjust to the transition by allowing them to choose something simple, such as the paint colors for their rooms or some new decor. If they are staying in your home and transitioning to their father's home, you can suggest that he do the same. This suggestion may or may not be mutually embraced. But it would give your children a small feeling of control over their environment when everything else is changing.

Be Consistent

Even though the world around them is changing in major ways, consistency in your household gives kids something they can expect. Setting boundaries and limits, as well as establishing routines is important. While they may protest, this measure of consistency gives them a feeling of security and sameness.

Don't Compete with Your Ex-Husband

If your ex has moved to a new place and bought new furnishings, your children may be excited about this. That's good. You want your children to feel comfortable and happy in their alternate home. If your ex takes them out to dinner every Wednesday while you cook meatloaf every Thursday, that's fine. Believe it or not, your children look forward to Meatloaf Thursdays. If he takes them to the movies every weekend while you are trying to scrape up enough money for your half of school pictures, that's OK too. Your children understand that things may be different in each household and doesn't feel slighted by you. Only you feel slighted.

Limit Packing and Unpacking

You don't love packing and unpacking for a vacation, do you? Imagine doing that every week or every other week like your kids may have to do. It's not fun or fair. Talk to your ex about keeping duplicate items that are frequently used at both homes, such as toiletries, books, games, basic clothing items, school and team uniforms, and favorite "lovey" objects. If your child will be transitioning directly after school, pack the night before instead of in the morning to relieve stress. You and your ex should have a plan for delivering your children and their packed items to the other home. I generally suggest that the parent who currently has the children take responsibility for delivering them to the other parent.

Maintain a Consistent Schedule

Yes, unexpected plans come up occasionally, but not every week. If they come up on your time, it's your responsibility to talk to your ex and vice versa. It isn't your children's obligation to change plans. It is important to your children's well-being that they know what their schedule is each week, and that, by and large, this schedule doesn't change. I suggest keeping a big calendar of each month hung up at each parent's home with your days highlighted in one color and your ex's time highlighted in another color.

That way, you and your children can easily see when they're at your house and when they're at their father's house and can plan accordingly.

This practice is especially valuable for anxious children, but also for teens and pre-teens that generally have active schedules of their own.

Show Enthusiasm for Your Children Spending Time with Their Father

Many children feel conflicted loyalties and are made to believe that they must choose a side. The most important thing you can do for your children is to help them understand that they are the children and you and your ex are the parents, tell them that you both love them very much, and explain how they aren't responsible for your happiness. To reinforce this intent, it goes without saying that children should *never* be privy to financial disagreements, learn the reasons for the divorce, hear any name calling, or be asked to act as messengers of information between you and their father.

Non-Negotiable Rules to Teach Your Children to Live By

Most experts agree that a few ideas are non-negotiable for children.

- Don't ask one parent for permission to do something if the other parent said no.
- When in Dad's house you obey his rules.
- When in Mom's house you obey her rules.
- Start your homework within an hour of arriving home so there can be some family time in the evening. This rule applies to the homes of both Dad and Mom.
- If a child doesn't want to go with a given parent at an appointed time or wants to come home, reassure the child that the child is fine and you will see the child when the child comes home.
- Establish a homecoming ritual for your child, whether it includes a bath, music, eating a snack or meal together, reading, or another way to help the child unwind and settle back into your home.

Always be aware of how you want your child to remember you in the future and how you want to be remembered during this transition. Again, I can't stress enough, you cannot control what happens in your ex's home. Fortunately, children are remarkably resilient and will adjust to the differences in your two homes so long as they feel secure. Try not to pass judgment on what goes on in your ex's home just because it's different than yours. It may not be optimal, but it may be good enough.

Oftentimes, dads need an opportunity to learn how to be a part-time father full time. As moms, we usually have it down pat. Whereas your ex may not have learned yet about your children's nutrition, how to give baths, reading books before bed, how to make pigtails, and who their friends are because you did all that for the both of you while you were married. He does deserve a chance to learn. He won't be as competent as you are. That may be a given, but if your children are reasonably happy, his parenting may be good enough for them and that's what's important.

It is crucial that you don't make your children feel that their dad is incompetent or laugh at his attempts to be a good parent. He is their dad, after all, and very important to them. Laughing at or criticizing him is like laughing at or criticizing your child.

This is a challenging time. Try not to get too far ahead of yourself and give both you and your ex some grace and kindness, knowing that everyone has a trial period of change and new knowledge. Your kids will be the beneficiaries.

How Are the Kids Doing?

Children go through the same grieving process adults do. They are in shock and disbelief about their parents splitting up. They are angry. They may try to bargain with both their parents and feel sad and depressed. Eventually, they will accept that their lives have changed and that having parents in two separate homes is the new normal. That doesn't mean that they won't let you have it as often as they feel it. But it will be tolerable.

Kids may ask time and again if you and Dad can get back together. They may tell you that the entire divorce is your fault. They may come back from spending time with Dad and tell you that he's sad or can't eat or sleep. They might tell you that they wanted to go to a movie, but Dad said he didn't have enough money because he was giving all of it to lawyers and to you. He may be indiscreet and give them details of the divorce they shouldn't have. He may press them for information about you or use them as couriers to tell you things. All this is wrong to do, of course, because it creates stress with children.

Your children have a right to feel sad and angry. After all, you feel that way, don't you? Except the divorce was an adult decision that they weren't consulted about. They also don't know—nor should they—the real reasons for the divorce, so they have a right to feel very confused and therefore even angrier than their parents.

The best way to help your children during this confusing transition period and beyond is to be the same mom you've always been, or maybe a better one. What you want them to know is that even though the situation is changing, the mom remains the same. Everything else around them might be in flux, but the center of their lives—you—will remain stable. They may not be able to rely on everything they did before, but they can rely on that one fact.

Invite your children to talk to you. Don't be defensive. Hear what they say, even if it's painful or brings up guilt. You don't need to allow them to be disrespectful or rude. Teach them that there are other ways of expressing themselves that you can hear better than this. If their father was disrespectful to you, they may have learned poor ways of communicating, but they possibly also saw that disrespect was effective in getting your attention or in their father getting his way. They will need to unlearn those habits and you will need to be firm and patient to encourage them to do so.

The only person your kids may be able to be angry with is you, because you are their safe parent—the one to whom they can reveal their genuine feelings. That's not fun I know. They may seem to give their father a lot of grace and to give you none. That's really no fun. They may say "Daddy's the greatest" and "You're the worst." That's absolutely no fun at all to hear.

Remember, for every feeling you have, young children will have it multiplied times ten because they don't have a context, perspective, or words for their feelings. Be gentle, but firm, with them. Be consistent and fair. Open a space for them to express themselves and let them know that all of you won't always feel this way and things will get better but that you are always and forever their safe place to land.

CHAPTER 27

How to Cope When Your Ex Begins Dating

DR. JILL

"*My ex-husband starting dating exactly three days after he left our home. Who does that?*" —*Marcia, age thirty-four, married five years*

"*So, my two little kids come home from visiting their dad the other day and tell me about the nice lady with the baby. I ask more about that because I'm a little confused, and it seems that Daddy is not only dating a woman with a six-month-old infant, he's doing it on his custodial time with our children. Here's the kicker—he wouldn't help me when his own kids were six months old.*" —*Audra, age thirty-seven, married nine years*

"*My ex has 'seriously' dated four women—all of whom have children—since our separation less than a year ago. Apparently, he began his adventures in dating less than a month after he tearfully moved out of our house. What a crock. My three children become attached to each of these women and especially their kids, because their father tells them that he might marry this woman and then they will all be family. I can't stand it and don't know how to make it stop.*" —*Guinevere, age thirty-nine, married fourteen years*

"*We agreed that we wouldn't date anyone else until our divorce was final. He didn't keep his promise, but he insisted that the women he had dinner or drinks with were only friends and not dates. Okay. The divorce has been final now for more than a year and I still don't feel like dating. I still want what we had. He obviously doesn't feel the same way because he's Mr. Man-about-town and dating up a storm. I know from my friends that he's gone on vacations with a few of them, which means vacation sex—and I don't think I can stand to think about that. How can he just forget about me after twenty-two years? How can he be so heartless?" —Rebecca, age forty-nine, married twenty-two years*

Here's the ugly truth: Men newly out of a marriage usually begin dating very quickly. I mean, *very* quickly. Within days or weeks. That seems unbelievable, doesn't it? I asked several men I know who are divorced about this conundrum and their thoughts about why men begin dating so quickly. Here are some of their replies.

- "It's fun."
- "I couldn't date while I was married, but now that I'm not with her, why wouldn't I?"
- "Nobody can stop me."
- "It's nice to have companionship."
- "I'm lonely without a woman."
- "To make myself feel better about myself."
- "Sex and lots of it."
- "I was married for sixteen years and never strayed. Do you know how hard that is?"
- "I like having a woman in my life."
- "To give myself something to look forward to."
- "Am I supposed to stay home by myself every night?"
- "New experiences."
- "It's a challenge."
- "My buddies introduce me to women all the time."
- "It's like I'm back in college, except this time I have money."
- "It's exciting, especially dating the younger ones. You have no idea."
- "Women come on to me. I'd be stupid to say no."

There you have it. It's not pretty, but it's true. It appears that men— unlike most women—can jump out of a marriage and into the dating world without skipping a beat. I know that can make you feel very unimportant and feel like total reject. I hear this all the time in my office: "We were married for fifteen years and the second he lands himself an apartment, he's off dating anything that moves. Isn't he even a little bit sad? Am I that easily replaced?"

I realize it appears that he's trying to quickly replace you and that he doesn't have a second's thought about the end of your marriage, but what I hear from men is that it couldn't be further from the truth. The fact is, many men are dating partially because they don't want to think about losing you or about missing you and their home or family. Perhaps, given the circumstances of your divorce, you had to initiate the separation because of an affair, addiction, abuse, or a whole host of other reasons. You would be correct to think that if he cared so much about your marriage, your family, or his home, he would have changed what he was doing that initiated the divorce. That's true. It is also a moot subject at this point.

If you can realize that he will be the same in every new relationship he entertains as he was with you. Perhaps not in the beginning, when he wasn't with you either, but over the long haul. You can rest assured that he wasn't a weasel with you, and now, suddenly, he's going to turn into a prince for "her." He may have many relationships and date like crazy. He may seem like a bird let out of its cage, and that may be accurate.

There are a few things for you to consider.

- Are you ready to be done with your marriage?
- Are you ready to be done with him?
- Are you jealous of his willingness to try new things?
- Are you focusing enough of your attention on yourself?
- Do you like where you are in your life?
- Do you feel stressed and overwhelmed?
- Do you feel resentful that you have the kids more than he does?
- Do you feel stuck?

These are all important considerations that add fuel to the anxiety or hurt feelings you have regarding his dating—ones that I'd like you to think about now. I see many women who obsess over whether their exes are dating and everything that entails. They may say things like, "Oh sure, if I didn't have to work full time and then get the kids to baseball practice and yell about homework and make all the meals, I'd have time to date too. It's so easy for him." That may be true and it may also be an excuse for you not to date.

When you will begin to date is for you to decide and act on when you're ready. Meanwhile, what are *you* doing while the kids are with their father? Cleaning house and doing laundry, or doing something good and nurturing for yourself?

Men are experts at doing things for themselves. We know that.

One thing I know for sure is that if you spend a good deal of your time focusing on your ex-husband, it takes away time that you could be focusing on yourself. He may be moving his life forward because he is obviously focusing on himself, right? What about you? What are you doing to move yourself forward?

"Are my children getting a new mommy?"

"My ex is dating a woman with kids and hers and mine get along like best friends. They prefer to be with him now because they are all together like a family already and when they are with me it's just us. I have a lot of good friends who have kids and they always loved being with them, but now she and her kids are the big prize. It hurts me. They are going to have a new family so what are they going to call her? Mom? Mommy? Mama? It feels like a knife in my stomach all the time. I can hardly breathe. I feel so hurt and rejected, but I always try to act enthusiastic in front of them." —Sami, age forty-two, married thirteen years

"My twelve-year-old came home the other day and proudly showed me her newly shaved legs. When I told her that we hadn't discussed doing that yet, she told me that her dad's girlfriend taught her how to shave them. I went crazy, I'll admit it. That's something a mother is supposed to teach her daughter, not some girl her ex-husband is dating. When I told my daughter that, she said, 'Mom, she isn't just some girl. They're probably going to get married. Dad is looking at rings, but she doesn't know because he wants it to be a surprise. He's actually asking my advice and everything.' I didn't know what to say. I felt like the earth had dropped out from under my feet." —Hallie, age forty-one, married fifteen years

If you have children, the idea of them gaining a new mother figure in their lives can feel threatening. After all, how do you compete with the shiny, new object? You don't.

What do you want for your children? Love? Happiness? Heath? Positive influences? Good relationships? What if this woman offers those to your child? Would you deny them that opportunity because you are personally hurt? Because you feel replaced?

Don't get me wrong; I understand your feelings 100 percent and they are valid. I'm not denying that. The reality is that you aren't going to stop your ex from getting remarried, if that's what he wants to do. Whether you like his future new wife is completely unimportant to him. If she treats your children well, that now needs to be your main concern, because she will be an influence in their lives, in either important or incidental ways. Your focus must now shift to—try not to scream here—fostering that relationship, because it benefits your children to do so.

If you don't like this woman, I'd like you to really take stock of the reasons and decide if they are valid. If it is because your ex spends so much time and attention on her, you now feel your children are being neglected, that's his fault not hers. If you think he's showering money and gifts on her—when in your mind these should go to your children—that again is his choice, even if she got them by whining for a new purse or a fancy vacation. He's the one who makes the decision to make that happen. Perhaps sadness or jealousy is at play here.

Female patients of mine routinely tell me things like, "Oh sure, he says he doesn't have enough money to pay for the kids' camps, but he can take her away on vacation," "I'm working full time to try and make ends meet with the small amount of support he gives me, but she can work some little part-time job," or "He spends money on her kids like it's going out of style, but tells me he can't afford new shoes for our kids." All bad situations, I grant you, but again, it's his decision to go along with this.

You can try talking to a lawyer to see if you have grounds to request an increase to your support payments, since he has the funds to do so, but that must come with the warning that it may be very costly, time consuming, and emotionally draining to fight him for them in court, and it would be a situation your children would certainly know about.

Again, I ask you: What would happen if you spent less time focusing on him/her/them and spent that time focusing on you? How is paying attention to his dating life serving you?

Let me also reassure you that no one—and I mean *no one*—is going to take your place. This woman is not going to be your children's flesh and blood mom, and over time—once the newness and excitement wear off—your children will come back to appreciating all that you offer them. They don't see Dad's new wife as a replacement mom; only you see it that way.

Be patient, be kind, be loving, be consistent, be gracious, be generous. You may even want to seek her out and become as friendly as possible with her. Trust me, any serious girlfriend or new wife is going to be intimidated by you. After all, you are the children's mom and she knows it. She can't hold a candle to you. She can only approximate a mother role.

Forming a good working relationship with their stepmother is a wise plan of action. She can make your children's lives a lot easier and happier if she believes you are working together. This is especially important if you don't have the best post-divorce relationship with their father.

You are going to have many occasions to interact with this woman: birthdays, sporting and school events, recitals, graduations, weddings, and on and on. It is a wise woman who makes her life and her children's lives better by embracing the stepmom. Some families even spend holidays or vacations together. Imagine that!

Of course, all of this is a lot easier if you are involved with someone you are serious about or married to. It's no fun when your ex moves forward quicker than you, so the matter of finding a new partner of your own may be an issue for you to consider.

What I'm really asking you to do is look past your hurt and rejection and all the other complicated feelings you have about this situation and do what will ultimately be best for your children, not only now, but in the long run.

I know that I may be asking something very difficult of you at this moment, but you're a good woman and a good mom. I know that with some soul-searching you can do it.

CHAPTER 28

Coparenting
with Your Ex

DR. JILL

"I truly thought that Thomas and I wouldn't have any problem parenting our son together. While I wouldn't say that he did fifty percent of the parenting when we were married, he was a decent enough dad. Tommy always had a lot of fun with him. Thomas was a big, outdoorsy guy and the two of them did a lot of sports together. Thomas taught him to surf and fish, and they even went skateboarding together. Tommy's friends thought his dad was cool. I was the enforcer: the toothbrush enforcer, the homework enforcer, the manners enforcer, the going to sleep on time enforcer. I wasn't so much fun. Tommy got pretty good grades in school and teachers always said he was a pleasure to have in class. That's because I kept his home life structured. He came home from school, had a snack, and did his homework. Then, he could play.

"I thought that when we divorced, Thomas would see the success of the way I did things and keep it the same way. But that didn't happen in the least. When Tommy visited his dad during the week, he never did his homework. Thomas brought him home well after the 8 PM end time when his bedtime was 8:30 PM on a school night. He picked him up from school and was supposed to supervise homework before they went out for dinner. But they usually did a sports activity and then went straight to dinner. When he came home, his homework hadn't been touched and he had to get ready for bed. That meant he either had to stay up until 10 PM or wake up at least an hour early so he could do his work. Then, on the weekends when he stayed with Thomas from Friday

after school until Monday going to school, he had homework or projects that had to be completed to turn in Monday that were never done.

"I spoke to Thomas about this because our son's teacher was sending me emails saying she was concerned about the change in discipline. His answer was that he only had him a certain number of days with his son and he wasn't going to spend them being a taskmaster. He told me, 'Look, he's in fifth grade. None of this counts anyway. He needs to have fun with one parent and it's not you. The kid needs a dad to pal around with and take it easy. You're the hard-ass parent, so you just keep that up. He loves coming over here. If he misses a little homework, well, he shouldn't have homework in fifth grade anyway.'

"Our son would come home on Monday cranky because he didn't get enough sleep over the weekend. I was fighting a losing battle." —Shauna, age thirty-six, married ten years

"The judge awarded my children's father forty percent custody. I was livid and very scared. I had been a stay-at-home mom and he worked a lot. He knew nothing about their schedules, their friends, or their activities, not to mention he hadn't cooked a meal since we got married. He had to travel for business sometimes. The custody schedule was ridiculous. I asked the judge how he was going to feed our kids and he said, 'He'll learn to cook just like everyone does when they have to.' I asked how he was going to manage their schedules, especially when he goes out of town and the judge said he could hire a nanny or have his mother help. I questioned the sense in hiring someone or asking his mother when the kids already had a mother who could do it. The judge said to me, 'Ma'am, we need to let this man have the opportunity to be a father. It's good for him.' Great, it's good for him. Isn't it supposed to be good for my kids?

"I was a wreck. He has undermined my authority ever since. If I took our older daughter's phone away because she was on her phone instead of doing homework, he had another phone for her when she was with him. If I said no computer games until grades are improved, he had games at his house. Now it's been five years and their grades have fallen, they are disrespectful to me, and they no longer think they must do chores at my house. I tried to have the custody modified, but my ex's lawyer accused me of doing it so that I could get more child support."—Emma, age forty-five, married seventeen years

Do you identify with Shauna or Emma's story? I see a lot of women in the same boat. They have a great deal of difficulty coparenting with their exes.

First, please understand that I fully believe your concern and don't diminish your worry. What I'd like you to focus on are the things you can change rather than on trying to control your ex's actions, because that will certainly be a losing battle, if only to spite you. Remember: You have control of *your own* thoughts, actions, and reactions. You can't change his. If you could, you wouldn't be divorced.

As difficult as this suggestion is, I'd like you to concentrate on this question: Are my children in danger or is my ex just not parenting as effectively as I am? What I mean is, could they fall in a pool, go out into traffic, or otherwise hurt themselves? Is he acting in a negligent manner or is he just not as careful as you are? Those are big differences. I see moms who have called the police or Child Protective Services because their level of concern for their children's safety was high. Sometimes such worries are warranted, but most often, the authorities come to the house, do a check, and find nothing alarming to the extent of taking action. Therefore, it's beneficial for you to consider what rises to the level of concern to the police and what rises to the level of concern as a mom who loves her children. The standards are very different.

You've taken care of your children in a certain way that has been beneficial to them. You'd like their father to continue their routines and level of care, and he may not be doing that. This doesn't mean that they may not thrive with the difference and learn how to adjust. If he is not negligent or harmful, but you still have concerns, you can let your kids know that they can always call you while with Daddy. You can give them a voice to express their concerns with Dad. A three-year-old can learn to say, "I don't like that" or "I'm scared" when she feels that way. An older child can help a younger child. What you don't want to do is grill your kids when they return to your home and ask for details. You also don't want to put an older child in charge of parenting or of acting as your mouthpiece to her father.

It's very difficult to accept that life will be different for your children in the divorce. You ex isn't you and he's not going to do things exactly—or even minimally—as you do. Children grow through change and learn to adapt. They will develop a new normal. They will likely accept that rules or structure are different at each of your homes. The nanny may, in fact, be better than your ex at keeping them in line. Your former mother-in-law loves your children even if she doesn't like you.

The worst thing your ex-mom-in-law may do—and it truly is bad—is talk poorly about you. That's not right and she shouldn't do it. Are you going to talk to her son and tell him that her badmouthing you is harmful to the children? Sure, you can try that and it may work. On the other hand, he may deny it or tell you to get over it. In that case, you can tell your children that their grandmother has her own opinions and you're sorry she's saying those bad things to them. You can tell them that it's unkind to speak poorly of other people and use this as an opportunity to build compassion and grace in your children.

No matter what happens in their father's home, or what he may say about you, I tell my patients that the best offense is to be consistent and keep being the mother that they've always known. That is tremendously comforting for a child who is going through a major life transition. It's not always easy and it's not always fun. When your children know what to expect from you—and know it's not going to change—they develop a sense of security. If they are rude or mouthy with you, you do what you've always done and tell them it's not acceptable and tell them what the consequences are for their behavior. Then, you follow through, even during the I-hate-you-and I-want-to-live-with-dad moments that crush your heart.

You are the parent—perhaps the only one with maturity and guts—and it's your job to teach them what is acceptable and learn the consequences of unacceptable behavior because you aren't just going through a custody disagreement, you are training your children for life beyond your home. You must be the bigger person, the adult, and the teacher.

You also need to have your own life outside of your children. You want to have activities, hobbies, and friends to call upon when your children aren't with you while being accessible if they need you. It's alright to have fun when they are with their dad. You're still a mom and a good one. So many of my patients sit at home and cry when their kids aren't with them. They worry constantly. They feel guilty if they have a manicure. They deny themselves any happiness without their children. This is not only bad for you; it's bad for your children. Being a martyr and creating a life only about your children isn't healthy for any of you.

Children need to understand that their mom is an entire person without them. Raising children who think the sun rises and sets with them sets the stage for entitlement and a feeling of superiority in the household. This is very confusing to kids who know that you are the alpha dog in the home. You can therefore expect rude behavior because you have put yourself and your needs far below theirs, even when they aren't with you. I hope that makes sense to you.

How Much Contact Do You (or Should You) Want with Your Ex?

"When the kids come home from their dad's house, they're cranky and rude to me. They haven't slept in two days, they've eaten a bunch of sugar, and they're running wild. They don't have any rules at his house. Then, they come to my house and they have discipline, so I'm the mean mommy. I've told their father every week that they need to go to bed on time and eat proper meals, but he doesn't care. He tells me that I'm an uptight bitch, which is why we're divorced. Um, no! We're divorced because you were an uncaring father. I keep telling him the same thing: This isn't good for the kids and why can't you just be unselfish for once and take care of them? I'm tired of texting him and his replying with crude remarks. How can I get through to him?" —Sally, age thirty-seven, married six years

"My ex-husband is crazy. I don't know if there's any other word for it. He calls or texts the kids non-stop, to the point where they don't want to answer him, and then he sends me a nasty-gram telling me that I'm alienating them from him. He sends me at least five long emails each day telling me how horrible I am as a person or what a bad mother I am. He accuses me of things I've never done and I feel like I must defend myself so I get into a back-and-forth email rant with him. He tells the kids lies about me and I have to correct them. I know I must have contact with him because of the kids, but I wish he would just go away. This constant contact is so exhausting." —Terri, age forty-three, married seventeen years

"I wait for my ex's texts. I keep hoping he'll tell me that he's ready to give our marriage another try. I feel like I always want to be available for that and when I hear something positive about him from a family member or mutual friend, I make sure I text him to congratulate him or say something nice. We're still friends on Facebook and I find myself 'liking' his photos. Even though we're divorced, I hope he'll come to his senses eventually and reconnect with me. I want him to see that I still care and that I'm a nice person." —Ellie, age thirty-one, married four years

Communicating with your ex can be a tricky matter. You may be torn between how much contact you would like with him and how much contact you need to have with him, especially if there are children involved. Discussing children's schedules, activities, homework, illnesses, vacations, and so on is vital to coparenting. If these communications can be conducted in a fair and friendly way, that's absolutely the optimal way of doing business with your ex. It's best for you and it's certainly best for your children. Kids want to see their parents get along with each other and don't want to be involved in animosity.

But let's be realistic. You divorced your ex for a reason. Maybe you grew apart. Maybe you married too quickly or too young and didn't know any better. Maybe one of you was unfaithful. Maybe he lied to you. Maybe you felt stifled in the relationship or couldn't be yourself. Maybe he was abusive. Maybe he had addictions he wasn't willing to address. Maybe he was negligent and uncaring. Maybe you felt you were disappearing and lost your identity or joy.

For whatever the reasons, you are divorced. I'm guessing there was some discussion and lots of unhappiness that you tried to help him understand. So, let's say that you were unsuccessful in helping him understand your point of view or in persuading him to make changes you felt were important to you. You've already talked and talked. I think it's fair to say that he may have been more invested in hearing you talk when you were married than he is now that you're divorced, right?

I'm making these points to you because in my clinical experience, nearly every divorced woman I speak to tells me the same things. "My ex-husband . . ."

- "Is doing X number of things that are upsetting to me and no matter what I do I can't make him understand."
- "Is messing up with the kids in X number of ways and I can't make him understand."
- "Still tries to keep tabs on me and I can't make him understand."
- "Needs explanations for everything the kids do and I can't make him understand."
- "Sends me texts several times a day saying mean or nasty things to me, and I can't make him understand how upsetting it is to me."

Do you see a pattern here? *"I can't make him understand."* That's right because if you could make him understand, you'd still be married. So, the question really is: How much time and energy do you want to invest in something that no longer exists that you don't have any ability to change? My very strong advice is for you to stop spinning your wheels in trying to convince him to understand your point of view—even as it involves your children.

Note: If you believe that your ex is truly conducting himself in a harmful way as it applies to the kids, that's a subject about which you may need to seek legal counsel.

I do understand that it's enormously frustrating if your wusband refuses to coparent in a beneficial manner. When he doesn't have the same rules as you, of course it's tempting to blast him a text and tell him how irresponsible he is and point out that he doesn't care now and couldn't pull it together when you were married (again, I've heard it all). To what end? Will it change his behavior or will you just become more frustrated? Will you feel better?

Maybe you want to answer every unfair accusation he levels at you, you want to defend your position, or you want to lob your own bomb over to him.

Just stop. Please. Just stop. This isn't helping you move forward in your life in a healthy way. You stay involved in an unhealthy relationship without the benefits of marriage. You engage your children in a combative environment. You aren't present for your life or theirs. It robs you of your own happiness.

You can't and won't change his mind. He won't see you as a nice person. He won't have regrets. Going back and forth with him, addressing false claims, answering all his questions, berating him for his behavior, reading long emails or texts, justifying your position, *none of it will change his position or make your life better.*

Why not concentrate on your own life instead, and use that energy you're spending engaging with him to make a difference where you can: with yourself and your children? There are many ways you can use your voice and your passion to make positive changes in the world. Communicating with him isn't one of them.

Are you able to have a constructive conversation with your ex-husband and tell him, "I'm sorry we didn't work out, as that wasn't what either of us hoped when we married. We still have a life that is connected (because of children or mutual friends or family) and I'd really like it to be a positive experience for both of us. Let's think about what each one of us can do to make this happen"? Sometimes, even after the most contentious of divorces, when one person waves a white flag and tries to be reasonable after a protracted period of arguing, it's a relief for the other person, who is exhausted as well. It's worth a try. If you are met with hostility or blame, at least you know you were the bigger person (again) and gave it your last and best effort to be reasonable post-divorce. Such an attitude can only benefit you and your children, no matter how old they are.

Being divorced changes with your age and your children's ages. When they are school age, by necessity there is a lot of communication about their schedules, schoolwork, visitation, doctor appointments, activities, and holidays. Calls, texts, or emails may occur daily. You may see your ex often. There are sports activities, school visits, teacher conferences, and recitals. Picking up or dropping off usually involves at least a passing glance or mumbled hello. You may have decided to share holidays, birthdays, or family meals together. When you have adult children, you may see your ex or communicate with him less frequently, but there are still graduations, holidays, weddings, birthdays, and grandchildren.

It behooves you to decide as to how you want to conduct yourself around your ex no matter how he is conducting himself around you. Remember that you have control of your actions and reactions to him. That gives you much more personal power than your attempts to change him when it's too late to do so.

Take a moment to think about that last paragraph. You have more personal power when you take control of yourself rather than spending that energy to control the uncontrollable. The only option you have—and it's a good one—is to change your own behavior as it relates to him. Stop wasting your happiness trying to get him to understand your point of view, even if it's the right one. That doesn't matter. You know it's the right one and that's all that matters.

If the kids' homework isn't done when they are with him, you can help them understand that their homework is ultimately their responsibility not his. They can tell him that they will have a problem the next day at school if it isn't done. They can tell their teacher that they were with their dad and he didn't help (at least the teacher will understand the situation). They can see if they can make up the homework while they are with you. If they come home cranky or rude, you can let them know that you're sorry they didn't get enough sleep, but it's unacceptable for them to treat you this way and let them know the consequences.

If they tell you that when they are at dad's house, they don't have to brush their teeth, go to bed at 8 PM, make their bed, take their dishes to the kitchen sink, or whatever rule you are enforcing, you have the right to tell them that there are different rules at Mom and Dad's house and when they have the opportunity to be at your house these are the nonnegotiable rules. They may not like it, but it will also give them a sense of stability and constancy. You don't need to send your ex a text telling him what joke of a father he is and start a new and unpleasant conversation that you can't win. Communication, even in this scenario, isn't necessary.

I hope you'll think about these ideas and be honest with yourself about the possible payoffs you're getting from your communication with your ex. Yes, you're getting a payoff and a big one if you continue to engage. Decide if a better payoff would be peace of mind, happier surroundings, more energy, or more joy in your life. I hope you will, as you deserve that.

ADAM

CHAPTER 29
Post-Divorce Legal Issues

I only have a few things to cover in this section. Not surprisingly, the same concepts (realistic expectations, control, informed decisions, and so on) that I've been discussing throughout the book are just as important in the aftermath of a divorce. Rather than rehashing these seminal concepts, I will focus on two common questions and some perspectives to keep in mind when these issues come up.

"Can my ex pull me back into court?"

A look of panic will come across my client's faces as this question forms in their minds. Even after obtaining a great result in court or after a woman's divorce has concluded, this idea tends to creep into the picture, and it can quickly snowball into panic or anxiety.

The reality is that, yes, people can file post-judgment requests with the court. Some of these requests are common and normal, and could realistically happen. But some are way out there and less likely for a court to be willing to consider granting. Understanding the difference between the realistic and unlikely things you might have to readdress in a courtroom will help you navigate your life after divorce. Luckily, you can do this by utilizing the same concepts we relied upon elsewhere in this book.

- **Get informed.** Before you spend time and energy worrying about the possibility of being taken back to court, take some time to educate yourself on what is realistic and what is less likely. Utilize the different research opportunities available to you, such as online research, legal clinics, pro bono attorneys (reread Chapter 10 for more details).

  In California, for example, either parent can typically go back into court to modify custody, visitation, and child support if circumstances have changed. Maybe one parent lost her or his job and needs to reduce/increase the child support payment. Or maybe a parent's work schedule has changed and that parent now wants to modify the visitation schedule. These examples would fall in the realistic category.

  On the other hand, the possibility of your ex filing a request years down the road to change the terms of your divorce judgment because he wants more of the household furniture is less likely. My point is this: Get informed so 1) you don't drive yourself crazy worrying about possibilities that will likely never happen, and 2) you are aware of the realistic possibilities so you can.

- **Set realistic expectations.** Informing yourself will do wonders for setting realistic legal expectations for life after your divorce is completed. You don't want to live in a state of perpetual anxiety over waiting to be pulled back into court. The truth is that everyone is in the same boat, so you are not alone. Now, how you deal with the possibility of a return to court in the future is up to you. I mean, it's possible that you could get hit by lightning, but it's unlikely and you don't want to stay indoors 100 percent of the time or be filled with anxiety. Set your expectations and move forward with your life.

- **Focus on what you can control.** Remember, your ex's decision to pull you back into court is ultimately outside your control. Of course, that doesn't mean all hope is lost. You can still influence this outcome by focusing on what *you* can control. This could include opening a dialogue, being reasonable, and making a good faith effort to be collaborative and resolve different issues. This may not be enough, but remember: *Energy spent on issues within your sphere of control is not wasted energy.* Trying to control your ex's decisions on the other hand, now that is a waste of energy!

- **Identify and verify legal threats.** Unfortunately, you ex's threats won't necessarily go away just because your divorce is over. As long as a return to court is possible (no matter how unlikely), potential legal threats can live on. After your divorce, you should still deal with legal threats in the same way: Identify the threat, verify the threatened consequences, and then make an informed decision. Remember, making a threat takes almost no effort. Following through on it is another story. Going back into court can be a costly endeavor of time, energy, and money—and that may be sufficient to deter your ex from acting on his threats.

- **Remember that your actions are evidence.** If you can be pulled back into court, then your actions are still evidence even now, after your divorce is finalized. Do not let your guard down. Be mindful of the decisions you make and the texts/emails/social media posts you put out into the world. It's all potential evidence that can be used against you in a court of law should things ever go that far. Your ex's actions are evidence, too!

"Can I pull my ex back into court?"

If your ex can do it, so can you. This decision is within your control. So, let's flip the perspective on what we discussed above.

- **Get informed.** At this point, this should go without saying. I have seen plenty of self-represented parties in court on a post-divorce motion make this mistake. They show up to court only to find out that their request is procedurally improper (for example, because too much time has passed or they aren't allowed to make this type of request) or they learn their request never had a chance (for example, because of insufficient facts or the law is not in their favor). Although you may not prevail in court, your decision to return to court should always be an informed one.

- **Set realistic expectations.** Once informed of your legal rights, you can set realistic expectations about what your decision to go back into court will look like and whether you should go back to court at all.

- **Focus on what you can control.** From this perspective, you have the control to make the decision to return to court. But it's a decision you may be trying to avoid. In fact, you may want to try and work it out. When you have a problem, you may want your ex to be amenable to opening a dialogue, being reasonable, and making a good faith effort to be collaborative and resolve the issue. This is outside your control. It isn't a waste to invest time and energy to pursue these options with your ex, but you can't force him to be reasonable. You can't make him collaborate with you. No one can.

- **Use legal threats judiciously.** Yes, you can make legal threats too. Legal threats aren't always nasty or intentional. Sometimes it's a simple statement of the reality of a situation: "Look, I've tried to work with you on this, but you're not leaving me with a lot of options. If we can't figure this out, I'm going to have to file a motion with the court." When it comes to legal threats, I'm not saying do it or don't do it. That is an informed decision that is up to you. I just want to encourage you to think through the process before you make the decision.

  Also, be careful of overuse. For example, regularly making legal threats can create an environment that is not collaborative. It also devalues the utility of a legal threat. If you use threats all the time, without following through, your ex is going to be less likely to take them seriously.

- **Your ex's actions are evidence.** While you remain mindful that your actions are evidence, your ex may not. Remaining aware of this will help you keep track of and retain records of any actions, communications, or events that could be useful evidence to support your case in a court of law. Do your best. No one expects you to keep a comprehensive log and catalog every detail

270

of your ex's life. And remember, emotions can get in the way. In the moment, you may have the urge to delete an aggravating or upsetting Facebook post or text from your ex. Try to resist the impulse to delete anything until you've had a chance to think about it. You can trust your instincts! If you're not sure you should keep it, err on the side of caution and save it.

CHAPTER 30

Dealing with Nosy, Disapproving Family and Nosier Friends

DR. JILL

"I didn't tell a lot of people what was going on in my marriage. I was taught that you keep your family business private. That's what my mother did when I was growing up and my father came home drunk. Half the town probably knew that he was a drinker and the other half of the town probably knew of the women he had on the side. I feel bad for my mom because she really tried hard, you know? But he made a fool of her and she refused to give up. So, I think I developed a lot of her behaviors. My friends could see what was happening in my marriage, but not because I told them. I made a lot of excuses for his bad moods or his indifference or why he didn't come to the kids' events. But they knew the real reasons; how could they not?

"My mom thought I should try harder, that marriage isn't easy. But I didn't think my marriage had to be so hard. When I couldn't deny his second affair, I got so depressed I could barely get out of bed to take care of our three-year-old, I knew then it was either get a divorce or die. When I told my mother my decision, she was furious with me. She called me a 'stupid little girl' and told me I was spoiled. She told me that marriages have 'seasons' and 'men are men' and thought I was making a selfish decision. After a year of therapy, I now understand that she was really projecting her feelings about her marriage and her mistakes on me.

"When I'd go to family events during and after the divorce, my aunts and cousins wanted all the details. I didn't want to talk about it and they were so insistent. They asked rude questions about things that were private to me and I felt pressured to answer. They'd crowd around me until I felt like I was a prisoner. Sometimes they'd give me disapproving looks or tell me that divorce would change my daughter forever. One of my aunts told me, 'When you take a vow in front of God it's forever, not until you get sick of it or bored.'"

—Patricia, age thirty-seven, married nine years

Maybe the family and friends in your life are being unintentionally hurtful. Perhaps they just want the best for you and so offer unsolicited advice, thinking they are being helpful. Maybe they ask so many questions in order that they can understand your situation better. Maybe . . . Let's choose to think that's their rationale.

Whatever, the reason for their prying—well-intended or malicious— if it's hurtful to you, that's enough reason for you to tell them that you don't want to share any details right now. Just because they want to hear it doesn't mean that you're obligated to tell it. Nor does it mean that you must listen to advice you didn't ask for. You are in charge of your life and know what is best in your situation. No one except you and your husband had to live in your marriage. No one else knows what really took place. And in fact, only you truly understand your perspective.

People are going to say things to you that they may think are helpful. Or maybe they will say things that they know are lousy just because they think you are at a weak point in your life and they want to feel superior and smug. Maybe they are having difficulty in their own life or marriage and your divorce takes their mind off it. Whatever the reason, just because someone asks you a question regarding your divorce doesn't mean you need to provide the answer.

Here are some suggestions of responses that worked for me when I was asked nosy questions shortly after I separated from my first husband.

- "Thank you for your interest. I prefer not to answer."
- "Out of respect for everyone involved, I'm not going to answer that right now."
- "This is a difficult time and I just need some breathing room."

- "I'm not sure why you're asking me that."
- "I'm sure you would never want to say anything hurtful to me, so I'm certain that wasn't intentional."
- "You are making me feel uncomfortable."
- "I'm going to have to end our conversation now."
- "Thank you for your concern."

You can be as polite or as rude as you'd like; it doesn't matter. What you need to remember is that no one is entitled to your information or decisions. You are not obligated to answer questions you're uncomfortable with, nor are you obligated to sit there and take it while your disapproving aunt tells you that young women are a different breed now because in her day "women stuck it out and made it work." There were plenty of times that I got up in the middle of a "conversation" and walked away. Why would I care if someone thought I was being rude or crazy? If they could think that way about me or if they were so inconsiderate to make upsetting remarks, why would I care how they felt about me? Do you see what I mean?

This is an important topic, because I guarantee you that these same scenarios will appear over and over. Decide how you want to address it when people are nosy, and stick with whatever you say the first time since many of these people will swap stories and gossip.

Here is where the rubber meets the road, friend. Here is where you find out who your true friends are and which family members truly care. As I tell my patients: All this is just more information in your education about who you want to become. It's data, that's all. It's all part of the journey to a better destination. Hold your head up. You've done nothing to be ashamed of. You're a brave woman who finally—and with a great deal of thought—decided she was better than the marriage she was in. If your family or friends don't understand that, it's time to make new family and friendships with women you decide are your new sisters, women you admire for their similar strength and courage, with men who respect you, and with new mentors and guides.

That doesn't mean that you must give up the people who are currently in your life. I'm not suggesting you eighty-six your entire family. On the contrary, this is your opportunity to develop new and clearer boundaries with them, and show resilience. They may not understand or agree with you, but if you come from a place of strength and goodness, in the end they will get used to your divorce and move on to something else.

CHAPTER 31

What Happened to All Those Friends You Used to Have?

DR. JILL

"I had a very active social life before my divorce. You know, other moms and couples' friends. I met a lot of my best friends when my oldest was in preschool and together we went through all the ups and downs of toddlers, and having another child, and all the angst that happens when you have young children. We told each other secrets and kept them. We switched houses for play dates and took each other's kids when a mom was sick or just needed a break. I felt closer to these women than my own sister, who lives across the country and never had children. My husband liked their husbands and it was so nice when we'd get together as families and have a barbecue or go to the lake.

"Then, the divorce happened. We had all shared frustrations with our husbands. I knew a few of them were going through very rough times at several points. One of them had a husband who drank too much. One had a husband who didn't help with the kids for a moment. One had a husband who partied with younger male and female coworkers, and she suspected that he'd had more than one affair. But I was the one who got the divorce. They stuck with the misery for lots of reasons. I didn't judge them; I understood that women stay in marriages for reasons that seem logical to them. I wasn't given a choice. I came home from a visit at my mother's a day early and thought I'd surprise him, but I was the one who was surprised when I walked into my home and found my

husband and a woman cooking pork chops naked in my kitchen. I had my kids with me and they saw the whole thing. I didn't react well. They didn't either. It was horrifying.

"Apparently this affair had been going on for four years, which means that it started when I was pregnant with our youngest child. The first people I called—when I composed myself and got my husband and his lover out of the house—were my girlfriends. They acted shocked. Eventually, though, it came out that one of them knew about it and didn't tell me. She said she didn't want to hurt me. Another had suspected he was having an affair because of something her husband told her. What I found out was that this was a big topic of conversation within the group, and they had pitied my stupidity. As I went through my divorce, they started falling away slowly and then completely. I was like the plague. No calls, no texts, no invitations. They avoided me at school. My children weren't invited to their homes. They declined invitations to have their kids come to my home. They kept their contact with my husband through their husbands. He was invited to birthday parties and other social occasions.

"I couldn't believe it. I was never so devastated in my life. Their betrayal was even worse, in some ways, than my husband's. I thought that I could somehow get over his choices because, when I really thought about it, he was the same guy all along, but I had chosen not to pay attention. But my female friends? I thought this was the real deal, that we were sisters. It's been three years now and I'm still upset over this. I don't allow myself to trust any other women since then." —Raylene, age forty-one, married twelve years

When you divorce your husband, you naturally think that your "good" female friends will commiserate with you, hold up boxes of tissues when you go on crying jags, and bring you endless cartons of Chunky Monkey and bottles of cheap wine. They will tell you that ditching your husband was the smartest thing you've done because you were too good for him anyway and *everyone* knows he married *way* above his station. They will eventually introduce you to their cute cousin who recently divorced also and is so clever and smart. You will have girl's nights and girl's weekends and it will all be fine because you have your besties holding you up.

Then, you find out that they switched teams. They may be on Team Ex or maybe they are just staying with the Home Team. Whichever team they choose, they are still girlfriends together and you are on the outs. How is that even possible? I'll fill you in: They are scared. Not just a little scared. They are shaking in their boots.

Your former pals are afraid of you for several reasons.

- **You had the courage to leave**. The courage they don't have.
- **You know their secrets.** You must be kept far away because you could expose them.
- **You hold up a mirror to their relationships.** And it's not one they want to look at.
- **They envy you.** You have freedom and choices now that they wish they had.
- **They see you as a threat.** You're a single woman on the loose: Lock up all the men! You're coming after their husbands and every other man!

It is a well-known observation that when women get a divorce, they often lose many of their female friends. The common belief is that the married women suddenly see a divorced woman as a threat to their marriages since she's now a single woman, and of course, would want to play the hokey-pokey with all their husbands. I know it sounds ludicrous— and it is. You didn't know that, along with signing your divorce papers, you apparently also developed an alter-ego who steals husbands and will try to destroy your friends' homes and families. You are suddenly an object of desire for every married man out there. Cool, huh?

Okay, what I think really happens is that you used to be one of them. A married gal with a home, family, and husband. Your life looked just like theirs. You had a lot in common. Maybe your kids played together. Maybe you went out as couples. Now, these same gal pals feel foolish and afraid. If this could happen to you, what does it mean for them? Should they look at their marriages more closely? No, no, a thousand times no!

What you are seeing when your female friends forget your phone number or don't meet your eyes is fear—fear of what your divorce means for them.

Alright, now that you get it, maybe it's a touch less hurtful, or maybe it's even more hurtful, because whatever the reason, it would be great to have your squad surround you now. On the other hand, it may be another great opportunity to rid your life of any toxicity. Now that you know who your friends are and aren't, you can stop pretending.

What you shared was real, at the time, because you weren't happy and they were all you had to sustain you. But if they can't roll with your new status, it's time to move on from them. They served their purpose at the time, but don't serve a purpose in your new life. Now that you honor yourself and your decisions, you will meet new people who feel likewise about you. You can be angry and you can sulk and hit pillows. It's unfair to be rejected and you'd like to think that you'd be a bigger person if the situation were reversed. I understand how hurtful rejection by other women can be. I went through the same thing during my divorce. I couldn't comprehend how this could happen.

Do you remember a concept we discussed earlier: Every crisis is an opportunity? In one of my previous books, *Destructive Relationships*, I led my readers through the idea that if you know you're in one unhealthy relationship—such as your marriage with your husband—you are probably in many others and just have never realized it until now.

When I look back at the relationships I had with my girlfriends, I can see how gossipy they were and how envious of others. I can see how I chose to look past small slights because I loved them.

Is this crisis in your life, in fact, an opportunity to rid yourself of every unhealthy relationship and start over with shiny, new, mutually respectful, and trusting relationships in every area of your life, including friendships? Is this your chance to decide exactly what you are looking for in a friend instead of just allowing friendships to come to you accidentally or through happenstance?

Here is an idea: Why don't you write out a list of every quality you'd like in a true friend. Remember, you need to be (or to become) everything on that list as well. As a matter of fact, you need to become your own true friend. You need to be kind to yourself. You need to be accepting of yourself. You need to give yourself encouragement and respect.

Once you have done this exercise, hang out where other women you would like to meet (or where the woman you'd like to become) would hang out. She will be there.

A short while ago, I was spending some quality time in the shoe department of my favorite department store. A woman was looking at a pair of shoes in the mirror. She was giving them the walking test. They were beautiful on her and just perfect for her feet, and I told her so. "Those shoes are fabulous on you. You should really get them. You're going to get a lot of well-deserved compliments." She was shocked and started giggling. "Do you really think so?" she asked. I told her I was certain. She thanked me and then I didn't see her for a while. I had gone off to another department where she caught up with me and showed me her bag with the shoes inside, and then asked me if I'd like to join her for a cup of tea and pastry. I sure did. She was a delightful woman and we still keep in touch. She was so appreciative of my comments to her, especially since she was having a difficult day with a child and contemplating a little retail therapy.

Lovely women—women who won't betray you—will be there as soon as you are over your heartache and decide you want better for your life. Yes, that includes being done with a marriage that no longer serves you and depletes you and "friendships" that do the same.

When you evaluate all your relationships, you may see a pattern of unhealthy behaviors. Maybe you have many people in your life who aren't that kind to you or people to whom you give and give without much—if anything—in return, friends who give you little digs or offer unsolicited advice.

You may decide that you need to give away all your unhealthy relationships or may see that most of your relationships are unhealthy now that your husband is gone.

Use this heartbreak and crisis as an opportunity to assess all those in your life and decide that you deserve a fresh start. Think about what that fresh start and that life would look like and make small steps toward it. You can do it and when you do, you will wonder how you ever allowed these "friends" in your life before.

CHAPTER 32

Going to a Movie by Yourself and Other Weird New Activities

DR. JILL

"Three days after Mark moved out the smoke detectors went off in the middle of the night. Seriously? Did he plan that? I didn't know if there was an actual fire or if the battery was low. My three- and five-year-old started screaming and crying. My dog began howling and shaking. I ran out of my bedroom to comfort my kids, but didn't know if I really should have been getting them out of the house in case there was a fire. What do you do when the smoke detector goes off at two AM? I'd never dealt with that before. I thought, Okay, Sabina put on your big girl panties and figure this out, *because Mark isn't here. Then I went around the house and started sniffing for smoke or gas and then feeling the walls because I saw to do that on some TV show.*

"Everything seemed alright, but the noise was deafening and I didn't know which smoke detector was going off because it was just so loud. I thought my neighbors were going to call the police. The kids were still crying and I thought the dog was going to drop dead of a heart attack. I finally figured out which alarm it was and stood on a chair and disconnected it, but I didn't have new batteries to put back in so was praying we didn't have a real fire before I got them.

"How come no one ever tells you that this stuff is part of the learning curve in a divorce? Someone should write a divorce manual that says, 'Here's all the stupid junk

283

you need to know about when you decide to divorce.'" —Sabina, age thirty-six, married nine years

Sabina makes a great point. There may be many things your ex took care of that you never gave a second thought to. Now they belong to you. There are household chores he may have done that are now staring you in the face. How do you turn off the gas or the water? What's the contact info for the plumber and electrician, or if you live in an apartment, who is the best person to talk to in the management office who does the best favors?

Then, there are all the semi-social items that are strange to navigate, like going out to a meal by yourself or maybe a movie. You know, all the places where you see families with a mom and a dad or couples holding hands, places you've never been to by yourself.

How about the etiquette of how you go about dining alone: Do you bring a book or your laptop, or do you have the guts to just pleasantly people-watch? What do you do if a man approaches you, for heaven's sake?

There are so many questions you never thought you'd have to ask. But this is real life now. Sure, sometimes you'll bring a girlfriend or a parent or sibling. Sometimes, you'll bring your children. But the day will come when you feel like going to a movie on a Saturday night and feel out of place or wonder if others are looking at you and thinking you're a loser. You know, the people you used to judge for going to the gym on Saturday at 7 PM.

The real question is: Are you uncomfortable in your own skin? The secondary question is: Do you have a fear of independence? Can you be a *me* when you used to be part of a *we?* Do you judge yourself? Do you consider yourself damaged or a failure?

There is a learning curve to being divorced and single. I remember the first time I went to a movie by myself. My kids were with their father and I didn't know what to do with myself at noon on Sunday. They were gone all weekend and I had managed to fill Saturday at the mall with a girlfriend. There was a good movie I wanted to see and I thought, *Okay, Jill, just go to the movie. Why do you need to go with someone else?* I put a little mascara and blush on—not knowing why really, as I was going someplace dark—and bought myself a ticket and sat where I wanted to in the theater. That was a big deal because my wusband had never wanted to sit on the left side, which is my favorite side, and I always gave in and sat where he wanted. That felt pretty good.

Before I went in, I also bought myself a box of Milk Duds, which my ex had always complained about, so we always got popcorn instead. I had the whole box of Milk Duds to myself! I was already sort of liking the solo movie experience.

Slowly, other singles trickled in along with the inevitable couples. Apparently going to a movie on your own was a real thing, I discovered. I had never noticed this when I was part of a couple.

I admit, it seemed like a very long time until the coming attractions started, and I didn't know what to do with myself without having someone else to talk to. I also thought it was going to be strange not to discuss the movie with anyone afterward, but all in all, it really was fine.

Just when I thought I was going to slink out of the theater, another single woman walked up next to me and asked, "Could Brad Pitt have been any cuter?" I agreed and we started laughing, then we ended up going to a Starbucks across the street and discussing the relative hotness of Brad Pitt compared to George Clooney. That's how I made a new friend who was also a divorced gal.

I have found that if you are open to new experiences and don't attach a value system to them, interesting things can happen that never would have happened if you were on a date with your ex. I also decided to write a long list of everything I didn't know—like how to reset the DVD player when it goes out—and bring that list to the nice husband of a friend of mine for tutorials. In the beginning, he said things like, "You know, you just flip the thing on the back of the TV and hold it there for a few seconds," but that wasn't helpful, so I enlisted his patience several times until all my questions were answered. Then I felt so empowered! I didn't know what to do if the toilet still ran after you jiggled the handle, but he taught me. Wow, what a revelation!

After a few tries, you may find that you enjoy going to a restaurant by yourself, with or without pretending to be occupied with your phone or reading a book. How nice is solitude when you eat, especially if most of your meals are full of wiping kids' faces or hustling them off to the next activity? You can enjoy a leisurely glass of wine like an adult.

What I'm trying to tell you is that instead of fearing your new independence you can make a choice to switch to perceiving the upside of experiencing a new life. Accept your new status willingly and embrace its many dimensions. You are on a journey whose destination is yet to be revealed, but I can assure you that it's a far better place than where you've been. There is a world out there that you haven't been a part of and it's waiting for you!

CHAPTER 33

Managing Feelings Like Loneliness, Depression, and Anxiety

DR. JILL

"It's been three months since the divorce was final. The whole process took a long time and I just couldn't wait for it to be over. When it was, I breathed a sigh of relief. No more fighting over stuff. No more negotiations. No more lawyers. I thought I'd feel free and happy. That was the plan anyway. But now I'm sad a lot of the time. Not the same kind of sad I was when I was married, but an empty kind of sad. I feel scared a lot, too. I'm not exactly sure what I'm scared of. Mainly, I feel lonely at night, especially after my son is asleep. I have a bunch of activity during the day with work and getting my son to and from school and daycare, and then doing dinner and a bath and the whole nighttime routine. But after he goes to sleep, I find myself staring at the TV, sometimes with a glass of wine in my hand, and just feeling alone. On the weekends, when my son is with his father, I'm at loose ends. I thought I'd be happier. I thought a whole new life would open for me. Did I make a mistake by getting a divorce?" —April, age thirty-five, married six years

April describes such common feelings after the intensity of a divorce and the decisions leading up to the whole process. Just coming to understand the finality that you are going to get a divorce is intense. Then going through a divorce is extraordinarily difficult, even in the best of circumstances. When it's completed, there may be immediate relief or sadness, or a combination of these two emotions. But when you have settled into "singledom" and your new and different life is your regular reality, feelings of sadness, anxiety, and loneliness can set in. Not for every woman, but if this is the way you're feeling I don't want you to feel embarrassed or wrong, or that you're failing at divorce.

Your married life wasn't a piece of cake, but it was your life and you knew what to expect. You knew how to deal with it. If you were married for many years, there was a routine to your life. You may not have liked everything about that routine, but there was a definite rhythm and cadence to it: There was grocery shopping on Saturday, laundry on Tuesday evening, takeout on Thursday, watching *Homeland* on Sunday. Knowing what time dinner was most nights. Knowing there was another adult in the house.

There also may have been an unexpected insult made for no discernable reason. There may have been unexpected scolding or intimidating or disappointed looks. There may have been an unexpected affair.

But now, there's just you—and maybe your children. You trying to keep everything together all by yourself. You trying to look brave for your kids and assure them that everything will be alright when you're not 100 percent sure of that yourself. You trying to be smart and efficient at work so maybe you can ask for a raise. You're trying to figure out what you're going to do if a child is sick or if you can afford a new washing machine if yours breaks. You're trying to scrape together enough money for your son's baseball uniform because his father tells you that he pays child support for those sorts of things. You're wondering what you will do if your daycare provider takes a vacation.

You have good reason to feel overwhelmed by the enormity of it all, my friend. There are days or weeks when it's too much and you may question your decision to divorce. What I want you to know in this moment is that it *will* get better. You will develop new routines and a new normal. You will begin a new life that will feel like yours. That may be difficult to believe right now, but I promise you it *will* happen. But it will take time.

If you are feeling scared and uncertain that you made the right decision, what I'd like you to do is to go get a pad of paper and a pen. Go ahead, do it now. I'll wait. Good.

Now I'd like you to think about everything that happened in your marriage over the last year with your husband that made you so sad, demeaned, humiliated, and uncared for. It may be a long list. Try to think of every little look and every small behavior, as well as the larger ones. Write each of these down on your pad of paper.

Now, think about the three years before that and do the same. Things that you've buried will start to come up and you'll find yourself saying, "Gosh, I had forgotten he did that."

Now, think about when you were dating, about all the things you overlooked that you can see clearly now as a pattern he continued into your marriage.

Think about your first couple of years of marriage. When did you feel uncertain or not good enough? When did you apologize when it wasn't your fault? When were there awkward silences or excuses for his behavior or times when you said it was your fault? Write all these incidents and occasions down as well.

When you finish this exercise, you may feel worse. You might feel foolish for sticking it out for so long or taking what you took. You may recognize that you felt very sad, anxious, and lonely throughout your marriage. But it was a different type of sadness, anxiety, and loneliness than you feel now. Why? Because, when you're married, even though occasional conflict is considered normal, there is an expectation that you're going through life together as partners so it's unusual to feel how you felt. It is expected to feel lots of feelings when you make a big change, such as divorce. It was worse then, wasn't it?

Now you may be thinking, *Um, thanks, Dr. Jill, for making me go through the drama all over again.* I'm truly sorry. But I think it's important for you to understand the reasons for your divorce and the similar feelings you had when you were married. You've taken a brave step and I'm here to tell you that almost anything is better than what you've already experienced. You went through that and you can go through this now. Just hang on.

Sometimes Painful Feelings Persist or Get Worse

"Maybe I made a mistake, but it's too late to go back now. He told me he wanted out of the marriage and that he hadn't been happy for a very long time. Neither was I—to tell you the truth—but I had made a vow, we had kids and a life together, so I wasn't going to divorce him because I was bored, you know? I mean, what kind of person does that? Well, he does obviously. He wanted a divorce because he was bored with me, bored with our non-sex life, and so on. I guess he never heard of menopause, but whatever. He wanted his 'freedom' and what was I supposed to do? I begged and pleaded for him to talk to me, go to couples counseling, work it out, but he said he was done a long time ago. That was humiliating news to me since we had just come back from a nice vacation. Apparently, he had been plotting his exit for a long time. I, however, was not.

"Well, it's been two years since it was final and my friends tell me I haven't moved on. Apparently, moving on *means dating sketchy men and buying lingerie at Fredericks of Hollywood—neither of which is cute for a fifty-six-year-old woman. They made me a ridiculous profile on an online dating site, which didn't make me happy. I don't know how to date; I haven't dated in almost thirty years. Now, you must swipe right or put winking faces on your computer when a strange man contacts you. It's ridiculous, not to mention a part-time job. My friends tell me I am pathetic and need to get on with life because my ex-husband is getting on with his. He is dating every night.*

"Most of the time I'm just blue and don't want to face the day. I feel lonely for my husband, which is embarrassing to me, and I'm worried a lot of the time. I really thought I'd be feeling better by now." —Ellen, age fifty-six, married twenty-six years

I don't know if you're feeling like Ellen, but if you are, I hope her story made you feel better rather than worse. I counsel so many women who are having difficulty coping with their divorces. Whether the divorce was at their instigation or their husband's makes little difference, because divorce is divorce. At the end of the day, you're divorced and while it may make you initially feel a bit better if it was your idea, once the reality sets in there is inevitably a feeling of loss, which may lead to depression and anxiety, which in turns leads to loneliness. Sometimes, the loneliness leads to depression and anxiety. It is certainly more difficult the longer you were married, but this is an enormous change and to expect yourself to be thrilled and have no negative feelings would mean that you never treasured the marriage to begin with.

Perhaps your ex has "moved on" and is dating . . . a lot. Maybe, he's found someone with whom he's spending a lot of time. If you haven't done likewise, it's a horrible feeling. You may feel tossed away and that you were never important. He's having such a great time. He's so active. He looks better than ever and trying new things that he wouldn't do for you. Maybe he's lost weight, gotten a new wardrobe and a new hairstyle, or a car. He's furnished his new place and, according to your kids, it's super fun! That's not your life.

At some point, your friends or family don't want to hear about you feeling out of sorts. There's a quick fix for that: Get a new man! Go out with your friends more! You can get a new wardrobe and hairstyle too! Cheer up! Get a life! You can't be all about your kids; they grow up and leave and then where will you be?! Go on a shopping spree at Victoria's Secret so you feel pretty and not so frumpy! Get to the gym. Your aunt's friend found a nice man there and she's seventy years old!

Yes, yes, maybe that's all good advice. But you may not be feeling it at all. As one of my clients told me: "If one more person tells me to get out and get some exercise I'm going to slug them. I wish it were that easy. Obviously, they don't get it."

Your life has changed drastically. Give yourself some time. However, if you're still feeling lonely, depressed, and anxious after several months, it's important to look at your situation more closely.

If you've been feeling unhappy more often than not for more than two weeks, you may be depressed. If you have usually been an upbeat person, you may have what is known as *situational depression,* which is your mind trying to manage a stressful event . . . like divorce. Depression can be mild (feeling like staying home and watching TV instead of going out with friends) to severe (which may involve thoughts of suicide or self-harm). You may also be perfectly happy sometimes and then become totally depressed in a matter of days.

There is no absolute course of depression and it varies from person to person. As we discussed in a previous chapter, if you're depressed you may have trouble going to sleep or staying asleep, or you may sleep for long periods at a time. You may lose interest in activities or hobbies you once enjoyed. You may have lost your appetite, either because you aren't hungry at all or because you aren't concerned about your well-being. On the other hand, you may be eating everything in sight even though you know you aren't hungry for real. You may have disregarded your personal hygiene. Maybe you are very touchy, irritable, impatient, or feel criticized much of the time. If any of these things is true, please reach out to your medical doctor or a therapist.

Then there's anxiety. Everyone worries. Whether it's concerning children, friends, a work project, a parent's health, speaking in public, and so on, it's perfectly normal to be apprehensive at times. Anxiety is different. Anxiety is excessive worry, meaning feeling persistently anxious and having anxious thoughts on most days for at least six months. These thoughts interfere with your daily life and cause great suffering and dysfunction.

As with depression, anxiety may cause sleep problems. You may lay awake at night worried, mind racing, going through possible scenarios in your head, and can't calm down. If you can fall asleep, you may wake up exhausted or feeling wired. You may have physical symptoms, such as cramping, bloating, and diarrhea, which are essentially signs of anxiety in your digestive tract. You may have headaches or feel lethargic, like you can't move one more step.

As you can see, depression and anxiety look a lot alike, and oftentimes, a depressed person is anxious and an anxious person is depressed. The great news is that this malady, like depression, is very treatable.

Avoiding Your Feelings Is Not the Answer

Oftentimes, women in an anxious or depressive state use unhealthy ways to avoid feelings. Drinking, overusing prescription medications, shopping, and sex can temporarily dull the pain of facing what you don't want to think or feel, however, it is not the real answer.

In their own words, women say:

"After Patrick left, I really couldn't stand being alone at night. I was okay during the day because I worked full time and I could use work to keep my mind off the loneliness. But when I got home, the first thing I did was look for a bottle of wine. I would stock up at the market; there was fifteen percent off a case so I'd buy a case every week when I did my regular food shopping, and I'd go through the entire case every week. Drinking helped me forget and it helped me fall asleep by myself. But I became

dependent on the wine and stopped accepting invitations to go out with friends so that I could drink. If I went out once-in-a-while, I'd make a fool of myself by drinking too much alcohol at dinner. Then, I didn't have to worry about not accepting invitations because my friends stopped inviting me." —Tammy, age forty-nine, married twenty-two years

"My doctor prescribed me a medication for anxiety and sleep. It was a miracle. I felt a lot better in the beginning, but then it stopped working as well so I decided to take two pills instead of one. That worked great also—until it didn't. So, pretty soon, I was taking two pills in the morning and two in the afternoon, and another two to go to sleep. My prescription was written for one in the morning and one at night. I went through them too quickly for a refill, so I had to tell my doctor that I accidentally spilled the bottle on my kitchen floor and it was dirty so I had to throw them away. I knew that was wrong, but I wanted the refill, which he gave me.

"Then, when I was taking three pills three times a day I told him that I had travelled and put the bottle in my luggage, which was lost. He didn't believe that one and told me I needed to come in. I didn't want a lecture so I just found a new doctor to prescribe the medication. I went through them too quickly also and finally—long story short—I checked myself into a rehab for thirty days. There I learned new skills for dealing with anxiety which work. It's really easy to get hooked on those pills." —Jesse, age thirty-two, married six years

"Shopping was the only thing that made me happy. I'd see something pretty at the mall and charge it. It didn't matter that I had a limited budget. I told myself that I deserved it after a long, horrible divorce. My ex started living with the woman he was having an affair with as soon as he moved out. It destroyed me. He was buying her vacations and clothes and hardly paid me any alimony. If he could buy her nice things, then surely, I deserved some too. The problem was that I didn't have the money for it. I was working a low-paying job. After being out of the work force raising our kids, I had to take whatever I could find.

"Whenever the kids were visiting their dad and his girlfriend, I made myself feel better by going to the mall. I was so sad and I was so worried about my future that I couldn't sleep. When my credit card companies came after me for payment, I finally saw how deep in debt I was and had to declare bankruptcy." —Tara, age forty-four, married eighteen years

"My ex-husband had multiple affairs while we were married. Finally, I confronted him and he said he wasn't attracted to me. When he left, I couldn't eat or sleep. I stayed on the couch all day and watched TV. After about four months of this daily routine, I was persuaded by a girlfriend to put on some makeup and a dress and go to dinner

with her. All my clothes were too big since I'd lost a lot of weight. I didn't want to go, but she wasn't taking no for an answer. There was a bar at the restaurant that I had to walk through to meet her. She watched me walk toward her and told me that several men were checking me out. I thought she was lying to make me feel better, but then two men approached our table and asked if they could buy us a drink. She answered yes for both of us. She had been divorced for two years and knew the ropes. At the end of our meal, they approached again and began talking to us.

"My friend ended up leaving with one of the men and I stayed talking to the other one. It was unsettling and I just wanted to go home. He walked me out to my car and asked if he could see me again. I was shocked, but said he could and I gave him my number. He texted me fifteen minutes later and asked if he could see me right then. It was flattering that he was so insistent so I said yes and he came to my house. We had sex, which was both very uncomfortable and very gratifying. Someone was interested in me. I saw him a few times, which really meant we had sex several times. Then I started repeating this process over and over. It felt so good that men thought I was pretty and desirable. It took away my awful feelings about myself. I wasn't being rejected; I was being pursued. A man wanted me just like my husband wanted other women.

"Eventually I wanted a relationship. So, I began therapy and started feeling my feelings, and while that was difficult and upsetting, it also didn't kill me; and my therapist gave me ways to feel and express myself in a healthier way, which ultimately led me to start a real relationship two years later." —Aimee, age forty-eight, married eighteen years

Helpful Interventions and Coping Strategies

Being a psychotherapist, I'm going to advise you as I would advise patients of mine in your situation. By the time a woman comes to me, she has decided that therapy is worth a try, and that's a great idea because talking through problems and worries often helps shine a light on them and gives you a different perspective or a plan of attack you may not have thought of. A therapist can help you air fears and other thoughts you don't feel comfortable telling anyone else. A good therapist can help you develop strategies for feeling better. If you are depressed and anxious, it seems like there is no way out of it and no way for it to end.

When you are lonely—especially when your ex seems to be having the time of his life—the world is a dark place. Your kids are having fun with him, your friends are enjoying their lives, your coworkers have significant others, and everyone seems to be occupied except you. The lonelier you are, the lonelier you get, because you may end up isolating yourself from others. How do you recover from loneliness? You get busy with others, not something you may want to hear. When you are anxious and depressed, you tend to isolate yourself and don't have the energy or patience for being around others.

Aside from therapy, exercise of any sort is another good idea. You don't have to start running or kickboxing. Doing yoga or tai chi is a wonderful way to reconnect with your body and spirit. Yogis are usually a generous and supportive group of people. You also could join a walking group. You can certainly exercise to fitness videos in your home, but I prefer my patients to get out in the air, since vitamin D is good for our moods, and to be in nature or with other people to reestablish socialization. It may seem forced in the beginning and perhaps be a terrible strain. But keep at it and I do promise you that you will begin to feel better.

Volunteering for a cause you connect with is another good way to become involved and interested in your life. In helping others, we always end up being of more help to ourselves. This is also a great way to meet new people with whom you don't have a previous history and don't know your ex or your ex-life. This can be wonderfully freeing. Volunteering takes you outside yourself and your suffering and allows you to help others. It gives you more perspective on your life as well.

Picking up a new hobby is also a great way to relieve depression and anxiety, especially when that hobby involves other people. Joining a book club, a crochet group, a quilting circle, a walking club, the Junior League, or a cooking class are all enjoyable ways to get out and meet other like-minded people. Maybe you've always wanted to learn a new language. Why not now?

Lastly, there are wonderful new medications for depression and anxiety. I know what you're thinking: I'm afraid to take drugs or I should be able to handle this and taking medication is a sign of weakness. Actually, it's not. And many times, a short course of mild medication solves your issue if you are also going to therapy. This is a subject to discuss with your therapist and then your physician. I just don't want you to close your mind to something that may be helpful because you have preconceived, inaccurate information. I have seen new, modern medications make a world of difference to many of my patients. A cloud lifts that enables them to see their lives more clearly and therefore make better decisions.

If you had diabetes, you wouldn't refuse to take insulin because you should be able to "pull yourself up by your bootstraps" or think that it was a sign of weakness. The same is true of taking medications for depression and anxiety. Just think about it and obtain consultation in order to make a good decision.

I promise you that the way you are feeling will not last forever. But I also promise you that nothing will change until you put yourself out in the world and try new things. Try not to be resistant to change or to trying some of these techniques. You know how you feel now. Nothing can change unless you make a solid attempt to change it.

If you would like more information about depression and anxiety, I encourage you to look up the following resources online.

- The National Institute of Mental Health: www.nimh.nih.gov
- The National Alliance on Mental Health: www.nami.org
- American Psychological Association: www.apa.org

CHAPTER 34

Men and Dating and Sex . . . Oh My!

DR. JILL

"I can't imagine another man kissing me. And touching me? Sex? Are you kidding me?" —Loris, *age fifty-four, married twenty-two years*

"I've had sex with one man in my life and I married him. I can't imagine having sex with another one." —Glynnis, *age sixty-one, married twenty-seven years*

"I haven't dated anyone in seventeen years. I wouldn't even know how to do that. The whole thing frightens me and just sounds horrible." —Pam, *age forty-six, married seventeen years*

"All my friends are trying to fix me up with 'great guys' they know. They are so disappointed that I don't want to date. I just don't want to get involved with all that again. They tell me I have to jump back into the dating world, but honestly, I don't know why I do." —Jaclyn, *age forty-two, married eleven years*

"How does a nice woman meet a man with any maturity these days? I'm not going to a bar. No way. And I keep hearing that men my age want young, skinny girls. I'm not young, I'm not skinny, and I'm not a girl. So, do I just forget the whole thing?" —Rosamund, *age forty-eight, married twenty-one years*

"All the divorced women around here look so desperate and silly. They are ridiculously cosmetically enhanced, wear those awful tight, short dresses with stilettos, and basically look like they're charging for services. Do I have to look like that to attract

a man? Because I'm not willing to look like that. I feel pretty hopeless." —*Sophia, age forty-five, married fourteen years*

"How do people meet these days? My teenaged daughter told me she's going to write something called a profile for me so that I can meet men online on those dating sites. Is that correct? I'm supposed to meet a man of substance online and after exchanging a couple of emails, I meet a total stranger somewhere? She tells me that's how people date now and it's fun. That doesn't sound fun at all to me." —*Grace, age forty-nine, married twenty years*

"I thought I was over my ex until I went out on a couple of dates. To be honest, none of those men hold a candle to him. They aren't interesting, they don't have goals, and they're cheap. They all want to meet for coffee and when I arrive, they already have their coffee, so I'm buying my own. Is this what dating is now? Then, after I have a latte, they want to talk about going over to a hotel. Is this a joke?" —*Barb, age fifty-one, married twenty-six years*

When it comes to getting back on your feet and investigating dating again, everyone has a theory and a plan for you. Before you upset yourself from the dread of it, first, know this: There is no hurry to start dating.

You may feel pressured by friends or your parents. You may hear "wisdom," such as "The only way to get over a man is to get under another one" (a particular *non*-favorite of mine). You might be told that your ex has started dating again and feel the need to compete. You may think that it's pathetic that you don't want to date yet or ever. *That's fine!* There really is no hurry.

If you've been married for a long time, the thought of baring your soul—not mention your body—to another man may seem unthinkable. I understand and have been in your shoes. Think of it this way: If you have more than one child, could you have thought of having another one right after having the first? Even one year later? The pregnancy. The delivery. The grueling lack of sleep. The constant diaper changing, feeding, planning your life around naps. Not being able to take a shower for days on end. But . . . you did and now can't imagine not having the other child or children.

Dating is a little like that. The awkwardness and difficulty is real, but you go through it anyway, and like having children, you learn something each time you do it. Each date is its own separate experience. Some—like days with children—are frustrating or aggravating, and you wish they would end, or they are just plain exhausting. Others—like days with children—are fun and exciting and you wish they would never end. Just like being a mom, you may feel uncertain, not good enough, or rejected. Dating is all a process of getting to know yourself better. If you meet someone you like a lot, it's really a bonus.

Do You Swipe Right or Left?

"This online dating thing is a full-time job. I'm on three sites because my friends told me they all offer different things. But each night after work, I have to go on the sites and see if anyone has messaged me, and if they have, I have to get back to them. I guess I'm supposed to send little winking or smiling emojis. It seems so silly and juvenile. We can't exchange phone numbers until we exchange a certain number of emails through the site. But I'm forty-six years old and I've haven't been told what to do about a date since I was a teenager. The whole thing seems so ridiculous, and yet I'm told this is how I have to meet men now. 'It's a new world,' my son keeps telling me. I'm pretty comfortable in the old world, if you want to know." —Janice, age forty-six, married eighteen years

How are you supposed to meet a man? Yes, there is online dating and a lot of women are very successful in meeting a nice man that way. There are the large well-known sites that you may have heard of, and smaller sites that specialize in women and men over the age of forty or fifty. I won't list them because by the time I do, there will be twenty others. Just Google "dating websites" and put in your personal criteria. All this can seem overwhelming and impersonal, however. Janice's assessment of using online dating sites being a job is correct. If you want to go the online route, you need to make a commitment to stay with it and respond to men who have viewed your profile and find you interesting. You also have to commit to meeting with any man you find even remotely interesting. If you're on a dating website, you have to commit to actually dating. For every fifty dates—yes, fifty! —you may find five interesting men. You never know which date he will be.

It may seem obvious that if you join a site, you need to meet some of the men, but so many women I know sign up as a lark or experiment, and when there is interest at the other end, none of the men is magically good enough. It's a risk, certainly, and uncomfortable and unnatural, but give it a shot. Drive your own car to the first and second meetings, and don't give out your home address. Avoid talking too much about your ex and invite your date to talk so you can find out as much as possible. This is what informs you if you want to see him again. Don't be too quick to judge—he's as uncomfortable as you are—but also listen to your gut.

Introductions by Friends and Family

"My best friend told me her cousin was a great guy and a great catch so she arranged a meeting for us. I have never been so disgusted with a man in my entire life. I couldn't believe he was her cousin. He was so arrogant and never asked me one thing about myself. He kept going on and on about his cars and his business, and how many women he had dated. Not to mention that his breath was atrocious. I excused myself and went into the bathroom to text my friend. I told her to get down to the restaurant right away and get me out of this mess that she had created. How can I trust an introduction from someone I know again?" —Cecily, age thirty-five, married nine years

Yes, that can happen too. Your friend may think the recently divorced best friend of her husband would be great for you. Then, it would be so fun to double date! Or your coworker knows a man in her apartment complex who seems lovely. Your daughter's friend's dad has been widowed for a few years and seems like a great guy. Your mom met a nice man at the supermarket the other day and he wasn't wearing a wedding ring.

Those could all be great connections for you. Your family and friends should know you better than anyone else and you may be able to trust their opinions. It's certainly worth a shot. Ask more about the man they want you to meet and if he seems interesting, you can let them give him your email address. I don't recommend a strange man having your work, cell, or landline numbers. Again, take it slowly and take your own car to the first few meetings. A woman should neither be at the mercy of a man to take her home, nor should he know where she lives too soon. Give him a chance and try to find the connection your friend or family member thought you would have.

Groups, Clubs, and Organizations

"I thought I'd meet a nice man through church. Then, I found out how nonreligious some of those men really are!" —Cassie, age thirty-two, married six years

Well, sure that can absolutely happen, but in my opinion meeting a man through an organization for which you have a passion is the best way to make a connection. You already have something in common. Your house of worship is a good place to start. A sport or hobby is another one. Taking a class in photography, painting, yoga, or anything else that strikes your fancy is a great way to meet nice men who share your interests. Volunteering for a political or other cause you feel passionate about is fantastic. When you meet a man in this way, you've already done a good deal of the legwork and it's very natural to get a cup of tea or a sandwich after you finish whatever endeavor you're involved with. It makes a possible connection much easier. Plus, it puts you out in the world in a way that speaks to you.

When Do You Become Sexually Intimate?

"I've gone out with men who are too handsy on the first date. I don't know who they think I am, but I'm not that woman. I've been on three dates with some men and somehow the number three is well-known to be the date on which you're supposed to have sex. I was shocked. I didn't know any of those men well enough even to think about sex with them. Then, I've been out with men a few times and I thought that maybe I'd like to have sex with them and wondered if that was sending them the wrong message." —April, age forty-nine, married twenty-three years

"Are there new tricks now? I know that sounds stupid, but I haven't been with a man other than my husband in more than twenty years. I knew how to have sex with him, but wonder if there are there different things that men want now—because I don't think I'd be comfortable doing a bunch of crazy things. I'm not a prude, but I hear that other women do all sorts of things that I don't want to do." —Sarah, age fifty-one, married twenty-two years

"What do women do now? Ask for a blood test? Find out if he has STDs? Oh my God!" —Farah, age forty, married sixteen years

"Look, my body isn't like a supermodel. I'm flabby and I'm perimenopausal. I don't look great naked and my libido is almost nonexistent. Now, I'm supposed to get my hair done every week and buy new clothes and shoes, and go to the gym. All so a man will want to take me to bed? Is it really worth it?" —Agatha, age forty-seven, married eighteen years

The idea of being sexually intimate with a new man may be exciting or it may make you cringe. If your marriage ended because of an unfaithful spouse, you may feel very insecure about your appearance and your sexuality. It's okay not to have sex right now. There's no rush. It may be hard to believe that someday you could be interested in romance, but if it doesn't appeal to you now, you don't need to force the issue.

There is no rule as to when it's best to have sex with a man. But usually you want to wait until you know as much about the man as you feel you need to to tell him something special about yourself. There is no "right" number of dates or "right" amount of time. You will know when you're ready and when you trust him and yourself in the relationship.

Some women wait until they're engaged or married. Some women wait until they've introduced their children to the men they're dating. Some women don't want to introduce their children to a man they haven't had sex with in case it doesn't work out. There is no right or wrong way to decide, except by determining what is right or wrong for you.

Sex with a new man can be a wonderful experience or it can leave you empty and devastated, if you have more invested in the relationship than the man does. You may want to spread your wings and have sex with several men right after your divorce. Maybe you want to feel attractive to men and this is how you're doing it. Maybe you want to see what everyone's talking about, after having been married for a long time. Or maybe you can't think about having sex ever again and you're fine with that, too. Whatever is good for you is good.

When you decide to have sex, if you decide to have sex, just make sure to take care of your body. You are in charge of birth control and/or prevention of disease. And take care of your heart. You always have a right to say no, and just as your mother told you when you were much younger, if a man doesn't accept your decision not to have sex, he's not the man for you.

When Should You Introduce Your Children to a Man You're Dating?

"My single friends invite the man they're seeing over to the house to meet their kids and get their opinions of him before they go further. Then, when the relationship doesn't work out the kids are confused or sad. I keep getting different opinions about what's right, but I don't want to make a mistake." —*Abby, age thirty-six, married eight years*

This is an important topic because, if you have children, you aren't the only person dating a man; your kids are as well. There are several schools of thought about when is the right time to introduce children to a suitor, and here's mine.

Wait until you've gone out on enough dates that you feel certain that your relationship is going forward in an exclusive manner. By that, I mean that you are only dating each other and you've seen him through enough personal situations that you can reliably gauge whether he would be a 100 percent positive influence on your children. Why would you introduce them to anyone who isn't a potentially positive person?

If he has been married, he should be divorced, not merely separated, before he meets the kids. Yes, even if it's a lengthy divorce. The reason why I say this is that I've seen many, many situations in which a couple is separated and going through a nasty divorce. There is no way they are getting back together and so a nice woman begins dating the man. Then, out of the blue, he announces that he and his soon-to-be ex are giving it another shot. Maybe a child became ill or splitting up finances became too grueling, but for some reason they called off the divorce and the nice woman is devastated. So are her children, who became very fond of the man.

Do you need your children's approval to date a man? That's a sticky wicket. They may feel threatened by your attention being elsewhere and decide they don't like the man simply because of this, or they may be trying to tell you that they are still having difficulty adjusting to the divorce and need more of your time. They might think that if you date it means Daddy is never coming back, as many children continue to hope for reconciliation long after the divorce is finished. They may also feel that a new man is going to replace their dad. Tweens and teens might think it's just plain weird.

Whatever your kids feel about you beginning to date, take time to talk to them and really listen. Don't laugh and say, "Oh, that's silly," because their feelings are not at all silly and are very real to them. You and your ex have changed their lives. They didn't ask for it and now they must live it, so try to put yourself in their shoes and take their feelings seriously.

Once you do start dating, it's wise to do so when they are on their dad's time. It goes without saying that any man should not be spending the night at your home with your children present. You may date many men before you introduce your kids to one of them. Certainly, don't make your home a revolving-door dating service. Many women do that and I see the results in their children in my therapy practice. Inviting your "friend" for dinner is a good way to introduce your kids. That way, they are on their own home turf and if they are uncomfortable or bored, they have an escape hatch.

Do not merely have your new companion "surprise" all of you by showing up at a sporting event or a restaurant. Kids aren't dumb and you've already begun the relationship on an untrustworthy note. Additionally, if the man has children, you don't need to rush to make this a Brady Bunch event, as hopeful as that may be. Let your children become well acquainted with the man you're dating before you decide to bring his children into the mix.

What Are Your Criteria for a New Partner?

"It's been so long since I dated, I don't even know what I'm looking for? There were things about my husband that I really liked, but others that I don't want to repeat. I guess I don't know what I want. Will I just know it when I see it?" —Lindy, age forty-two, married seven years

No, you won't just know it when you see it. I think that every woman should be very clear about what she wants in a date or future mate, because in the absence of that we settle for whatever the man says he wants. Here's my bulletproof plan for finding the right man.

1. **Write a list of nonnegotiable traits.** Get a legal pad of paper and write down every single character and behavioral trait you want in a man. Take your time and make it a very long list. Another trait may come to you when you're not thinking about it, so don't rush this process. Don't judge yourself. No one is going to look at this list but you. After you've finished your list, go over it several times and put a check mark next to every item that is more important than others. This will narrow your list dramatically. Now, look at the check marked items and put a star next to the ten traits that you absolutely will not compromise on. This is your list of *nonnegotiables.* Your man must have every single item on that list of ten to be the man of your dreams.

2. **Look at your list of nonnegotiables and ask yourself if you yourself embody every one of those traits.** Aha! A catch! Yes, this is an important one. You cannot ask a man to be something that you are not. You cannot ask for a man who is honest when you yourself are a little sketchy. You can't ask for a man who makes a six-figure salary when you make very little, because this would put you in a precarious financial and control position. You can't ask for a reliable man when you sometimes don't keep your word.

3. **Do the work to become your own perfect partner first.** You must become everything on your list of nonnegotiables. That may mean seeking therapy or reading self-help books or aligning yourself with a woman you admire to mentor you. When we ask a man to be the things we are not, we look to him to fill in holes in our consciousness. We ask him to "complete" us, rather than going into a relationship as a whole and healthy person ourselves. There is a big difference. When you go into a relationship confident that you have done the necessary work on yourself, you will attract someone as mentally and emotionally healthy as you are. It's the law of attraction.

Now that you've done all this important work, let's finish up.

Conclusion

DR. JILL AND ADAM

Dear sister, we are coming to the end of our time together. You have explored your emotions, shortcomings, and relationships, and you have learned to look at your life realistically and stand up for your needs and legal rights, and the legal rights and needs of your children. Now you are divorced and your life belongs to you. What do you want to do with that new life?

Please remember that you never must settle in any part of your life. You *always* have choices. While you may not have a choice as to how others see you or treat you, you do have complete and total choice regarding the decisions you make about your degree of contact with those people and how you allow them to affect your view of yourself and your world.

When you feel anxious, helpless, powerless, or depressed, the very best plan is for you is to push through those feelings, knowing that they are temporary and that you've already survived perhaps the greatest pain you'll ever face in your life. Take positive action on your own behalf and make decisions based upon what you want your life and the lives of your children (if you have them) to look like, not on what others tell you your life should look like.

There are so many new and exciting opportunities waiting around the bend ahead of you. Don't just dream about what you want, plan for it. Write out a step-by-step plan detailing the small and positive steps you can take that don't seem overwhelming to make those dreams come true. Then follow the plan and modify it as necessary once you build up some momentum. Of course, you can do this. Why couldn't you? There are numerous resources available to you if you will only reach for them.

If you ever feel defeated, depleted, or down, afraid, unsure, or wrung out, put your hands over your heart and breathe in and out slowly until you feel calmer and gain clarity. You are not alone in starting over. Some of the world's most successful and happy women have divorced and moved on. You have been tested and endured. If you remain steadfast in pursuing the good in life, you can accomplish anything you desire. I love this quote from Carl Jung: "I am not what happened to me, I am what I choose to become." Please take it to heart.

Take care of yourself. Listen to what you tell yourself. Be as kind to yourself as you would to your best friend. Above all, remember: *Love is a behavior.*

We believe in you and in your strength and wisdom. Take good care . . . and now go take on your life!

About the Authors

JILL A. MURRAY, PSY.D.

Dr. Jill A. Murray is one of the nation's leading experts on unhealthy relationships. In addition to *The Empowered Woman's Guide to Divorce*, she is the author of three full-length books on the subject, among them *But I Love Him*, *But He Never Hit Me*, and *Destructive Relationships*, as well as seven short ebooks.

Dr. Murray has appeared on more than 450 television shows, including *Oprah*, *20/20*, *Montel*, *Anderson Cooper 360°* and several other shows on CNN, *Dr. Phil*, *The Today Show*, and *Good Morning America*. She has also lent her expertise to more than 300 radio programs. Her work has been featured in hundreds of print and online magazines and newspapers.

Dr. Murray has spoken before Congress on behalf of a teen dating violence bill, which passed unanimously, and has also spoken twice at the National Press Club in Washington, D.C. She is a charter member of the governing council of MTV's A Thin Line campaign, as well as participating in several other campaigns that involve creating healthy relationships.

Dr. Murray is a highly sought-after presenter at national and international conferences on relationships and has taught courses on relationships at the graduate level. She is frequently called upon as an expert witness in court proceedings revolving around destructive relationships and their effect on children.

Dr. Murray maintains a waiting list private therapy practice in Laguna Niguel, California, where she sees women, men, couples, and children experiencing relationship difficulties.

Visit her website www.drjillmurray.com.

ADAM R. DODGE, J.D.

Adam R. Dodge is a former divorce attorney who now devotes his career to empowering women to represent themselves in family law proceedings. Adam is frequently featured in or contributes to print and online news articles for media outlets, including *The New York Times*, *The Wall Street Journal*, *SELF Magazine*, *The Orange County Register*, and others. He also writes for *Huffington Post*. Adam's television and radio appearances include *Dr. Phil* and he is a frequent speaker and guest lecturer at law schools, universities, and national conferences. He is Legal Director of Laura's House, where he works to advocate for the legal rights of domestic violence survivors and their children. *The Empowered Woman's Guide to Divorce* is his first book.

Visit his website www.adamrdodge.com.